Information or Market Power: What is Governing Dealers' Pricing Behaviour in FX Markets?

STUDIEN ZU
INTERNATIONALEN
WIRTSCHAFTSBEZIEHUNGEN

Herausgegeben von Prof. Dr. Michael Frenkel

Band 13

PETER LANG
Frankfurt am Main · Berlin · Bern · Bruxelles · New York · Oxford · Wien

Markus A. Schmidt

Information or Market Power: What is Governing Dealers' Pricing Behaviour in FX Markets?

An Investigation in the Spirit of the Microstructure Approach to Exchange Rates

PETER LANG
Internationaler Verlag der Wissenschaften

Bibliographic Information published by the Deutsche Nationalbibliothek
The Deutsche Nationalbibliothek lists this publication in the Deutsche Nationalbibliografie; detailed bibliographic data is available in the internet at <http://www.d-nb.de>.

Zugl.: Gießen, Univ., Diss., 2008

D 26
ISSN 1618-503X
ISBN 978-3-631-57928-2

www.peterlang.de

Preface

This work was submitted as external doctoral thesis entiteled *Information or Market Power: What is Governing Dealers' Pricing Behaviour in FX Markets? An Investigation in the Spirit of the Microstructure Approach to Exchange Rates* at Justus-Liebig-University of Giessen, Germany. I am deeply indebted to my supervisors Dr Stefan Reitz and Professor Dr Jürgen Meckl for supporting me in every imaginable way in both academic and organisational issues.

In addition, I am very grateful to the bankers who provided the data investigated herein as well as to my former employer who enabled me to prepare this thesis concomitantly to my job. Besides them, I owe thanks to my current superiors for their encouragement while I was finishing last details of my thesis.

Of course, this work would not have been realised that way without inexhaustible support by my family, especially by my parents Karin and Rainer. I am deeply indebted to you. Furthermore, I am thankful to my girlfriend Kerstin for giving me encouragement.

Besides them, I am grateful to Professor Steve McCorriston who was the first to make me thinking about doing a Phd. In addition, I owe thanks to Professor Richard K. Lyons, Professor Martin D.D. Evans, and Assistant Professor Norman Schürhoff for answering all of my questions concerning their respective models.

Though many people provided their help and support to this work, all errors are mine, of course.

Albeit the data used in this study originated from trading activity of an entire team of currency dealers working with a German bank and a number of transactions might hence be dealt by female traders, I treat the market maker(s) investigated here as male for reasons of convenience. To ensure that females are not disrespected, I am using female form for the customers, regardless of their actual gender.

Markus A. Schmidt

Table of content

List of figures

List of tables

Introduction

With an average trading volume of USD 1.9 trillion per day (Bank for International Settlements, 2005), foreign exchange is the world's largest market. On weekdays, FX trading happens almost 24 hours a day, starting in Asia (Tokyo and Singapore), continuing in Europe (Frankfurt, Zurich and London), and ending in New York. During the worldwide trading day, the market-wide trading-rate is extremely high. Transactions happen that frequently that they cannot be explained by the arrival of fundamental news only, as proposed by standard macro models of exchange rate determination. In the introductory chapter of his book, Lyons (2001) narrates very colourful about the "cultural shock" he experienced when he spent a few days at a foreign exchange trading desk – even though he considered himself an expert in the field to this time. Indeed, standard macroeconomic models suffer from serious empirical trouble, especially at higher frequencies.

Short-run dynamics in exchange rates are a longstanding puzzle for economists to explain. Despite of many years of intensive research, standard macro models of nominal exchange rate determination perform poorly on frequencies higher than one year. In their seminal contribution to the field, Meese and Rogoff (1983a) conclude that monetary and portfolio balance models can generally not outperform a random walk at short horizons. Cheung et al. (2005) confirm this conclusion for more recent models such as, among others, interest rate parity and productivity based models. Bacchetta and van Wincoop (2003), too, find that fundamentals are the main driving forces of the exchange rate in the long-run, but their influence on short and medium horizons is marginal. Indeed, Johnston and Scott (1997) are able to improve fundamental variables' explanatory power for exchange rate movements by adding distributional aspects of the latter, but jumps in the time series remain to be an unresolved problem.

Up to now, there are primarily three central questions that remain to be unanswered within standard macroeconomic frameworks. The first one, termed *forward bias puzzle*, is stated in Lyons (2001, p. 14). It describes the phenomenon that excess returns to speculating in foreign exchange are possible, though not explicable yet. This puzzle refers to one of the best-known international parity conditions, namely the so-called *uncovered interest parity* (UIP), which is going to be discussed below.[1] Additionally, Lyons (2001, p. 14, 2002a, p. 52) highlights the so-called *determination puzzle*, i.e. virtual independence of the exchange rate from its macro-fundamentals, and the *excess volatility puzzle*, meaning that exchange rates' volatility exceeds volatility of assumed driving macro-fundamentals.

In practice, these puzzles make a variety of different appearances. For example, Bacchetta and van Wincoop (2003), Evans and Lyons (2005a), and Engel and West (2004, 2005) find at least slight evidence for spot exchange rate's predictive power for future fundamentals – a result absolutely contrary to standard propositions of the macro approach. In addition, standard macro models assume that exchange rates are driven by information publicly available to all market participants. A change in these fundamentals changes the relative value of the currencies to one another and thus their exchange rate. However, as shown in Evans and Lyons (2007a), news are not instantaneously transmitted into exchange rates. Macro news are evidenced to have persistent effects on a currency's price over days.

Furthermore, macro models are not able to explain the existence of FX trading, since a change in publicly known fundamentals does not necessitate trading in foreign exchange to move the exchange rate to the appropriate new level. Nevertheless, foreign exchange trading happens with an enormous volume every day. All those empirical contradictions indicate that the macro approach is likely to miss some key features of FX markets.

Ascribing the aforementioned puzzles to omitted variables seems not very plausible, since Meese (1990) stressed the considerable imagination of empirical researches in their specification search. Thus, all those years of research did not yield any significant improvements in exchange rate economics since Frankel and Rose (1995, p. 1709) concluded that *there is remarkably little evidence that macroeconomic variables have consistent strong effects on floating exchange rates, except extraordinary circumstances such as*

[1] Because of the forward bias puzzle, so-called *currency carry trades* become potentially profitable, since future exchange rate movements over a given time period do not systematically equal international interest rate differentials at respective maturities. This fact results in an empirical rejection of the uncovered interest rate parity hypothesis.

hyperinflations. Such negative findings have led the profession to a certain degree of pessimism vis-à-vis exchange rate research.[2]

Up to now, there is a growing literature seeking for rationale for the reported lack of explanatory and forecasting power. Behavioural finance, for example, is mainly trying to explain asset price dynamics by market participants' behaviour. For instance, De Grauwe and Rovira Kaltwasser (2007) show that divergence of beliefs about a currency's fundamental value might cause "waves of optimism and pessimism", which are alternating in an unpredictable way, since these "waves" are entirely detached from the currency's objective fundamental value. According to their model, even small changes in market participants' beliefs are sufficient to alter the time path of the exchange rate.

As overviewed in LeBaron (2006), some literature on computational economics is closely related to insights known from behavioural finance, especially when it comes to agent-based modelling. LeBaron and Yamamoto (2007), for example, investigate investors' learning and adaption by using simulation techniques. In doing so, they show how these aspects contribute to long-memory effects in trading volume, stock return volatility, and the signs of market orders.

Mathematical finance provides another school of thought, which is mainly arguing with respective time series' martingale properties to explain impossibility of predicting asset prices in general and exchange rates in particular. DeMeyer and Moussa-Saley (2003), for example, argue that information asymmetries among market participants raise an unpredictable Brownian term in the price dynamics of stock prices. This is because informed traders are assumed to try to exploit their informational advantages while instantaneously seeking to camouflage their information. DeMeyer (2007) revisits this study and shows that stocks' price processes will be a continuous martingale of maximal variation under these circumstances.

Further contributions to this literature, providing potential rationale for forecasters' poor performance especially in FX markets, are works by Engel and West (2004, 2005). As they show, unpredictability of short-run exchange rate

[2] Further surveys by, among others, Isard (1995) and Taylor (1995) qualitatively confirm this conclusion.

movements might be caused by some unobservable fundamentals that are following an I(1) process. If this was the case, the exchange rate shows time series properties arbitrarily close to a random walk, since the discount factor in the present value equation approaches one.

Nine years before Engel and West, Flood and Rose (1995, p. 5) already came to the conviction that *the most critical determinants of exchange rate volatility are not macroeconomic*. In the run-up to this work, empiricists and theoreticians primarily discussed two alternatives to overcome this scientific "exchange rate crisis", being *rational speculative bubbles* and *irrationality*. Speculative bubbles are basically used to model extraneous variables in standard macro frameworks as done, among others, in Dornbusch (1982), Evans (1986) and Meese (1986). Blanchard (1979), for example, shows that speculative bubbles are indeed consistent with rational expectations. However, in their investigation, Flood and Hodrick (1990) conclude that rational speculative bubbles appear unconvincing. The second alternative, irrationality, seems not plausible to many economists, too. In particular, Evans and Lyons (2002a) argue that the view, exchange rates might be affected by avoidable expectational errors, as described, among others, by Dominguez (1986), Frankel and Froot (1987), and Hau (1998), is up to now suffering a lack of empirical account.

Inspired by Flood and Taylor's (1996, p. 286) conclusion *that our understanding of the short-run behaviour of exchange rates is unlikely to be further enhanced by further examination of the macro fundamentals*, short-run exchange rate economics took a turn when many authors began to apply microstructure tools to the foreign exchange market during the 1990's. Until then, microstructure theory was already well established in other fields of financial markets research. In fact, von Hayek's (1945) conviction that information are dispersed across the economy and that markets aggregate those information, already paved the way for market microstructure theory. Early theoretic contributions on different aspects of asset pricing go back to a work by Garman (1976). During the 1980's, micro-tools were heavily conducted in analysing pricing processes at stock markets.[3] However, stock markets differ substan-

[3] For instance, Grossman (1988), Genotte and Leland (1990), Jacklin et al. (1992), and Romer (1993) used microstructure tools to investigate the 1987 stock market crash.

tially from foreign exchange markets, because they are centralised, so-called *specialist markets*, while foreign exchange markets are decentralised, so-called *market maker markets*.

Maureen O'Hara (1995) was the first to channel the rather fragmented theoretic works on market microstructure into a unified new approach. Nevertheless, it took until the seminal work by Lyons (2001) to establish a unique microstructure approach to exchange rates. Up to now, this theory seems to be particularly promising for understanding the long-lasting exchange rate puzzles at higher frequencies. For example, Evans and Lyons (2002a) are able to explain over 60 percent of daily deutsche mark / U.S. dollar log changes by using a "hybrid" model that consists of both interdealer order flow data and interest rate differentials. Interestingly, the bulk of their model's explanatory power is due to the order flow data used therein and thus caused by a central microstructure variable. Lechner and Nolte (2006), Osler et al. (2006), as well as chapter 3 of this work provide further empirical evidence for order flow's explanatory power for high-frequent exchange rate movements.

One major advantage of microstructure models, compared to their macro counterparts, is their ability to account for asymmetric information. Hence, Lyons (2002a, p. 51) terms those models in microstructure theory that deal with information aggregation via trading *the dispersed information approach.* In fact, microstructure models relax many critical assumption of the macro approach; one of the most important ones among them is the proposition of homogenously informed market participants. As shown in Evans and Lyons (2005b), heterogeneity among end-users is the natural cause of some of the FX market's most specific features like different price impacts of different end-user segments. Consequently, private information and identity of the counterparts involved in FX-trading, as well as trading mechanisms used during transactions, become important features of these models.[4]

To avoid any misunderstanding, micro models do not compete with the macro approach. As Lyons (2001) points out, microstructure models are about pur-

[4] The existence of private information in foreign exchange markets is repeatedly empirically evidenced. See, among others, Payne (1999), Rime (2000), Marsh and O'Rourke (2005a, 2005b), Osler et al. (2006) and chapter 3 of the study at hand.

chasing and selling assets, too, just like the asset market approach. Micro models are rather complementary to macro theory, since they are adding aspects like strategic behaviour in the presence of potential asymmetric information. As highlighted by Sager and Taylor (2006), the relatively opaque and heavily decentralised structure of the foreign exchange market makes information asymmetries both very likely to exist and to influence pricing behaviour of market makers. Hence, microstructure theory interprets trading as the main mechanism to aggregate dispersed (private) information among market participants.[5] Trading, in turn, results in two basic variables of microstructure finance, being order flow and bid-ask spreads. In this way, as mentioned by Evans and Lyons (2005c), order flow may explain the surprise part of the exchange rate equation, which is by definition orthogonal to public information.[6] Thus, order flow and bid-ask spreads might be "omitted variables" not yet recognised by standard macro-frameworks.

Its informational focus, its ability to allow for heterogeneity of market participants, as well as its feature to account for the role of different institutions in FX trading, makes the microstructure approach actually relevant for macroeconomic analyses. Chen (1997), Calvo (1999), Carrera (1999), and Corsetti et al. (2004), among others, conduct microstructure tools to exchange rate collapses during the 1990's and their macro-economic consequences. In addition, Lyons and Moore (2005) show how information aggregation among market participants is affected by direct and indirect ways of trading. As they argue, information revelation of a direct transaction, say EUR against JPY, is not equal to an indirect trade, i.e. trading euro against U.S. dollars first and then trade USD against Yen. Their model hence provides a rationale for the finding that some currency pairs never trade directly and how trading in one currency pair might affect other currencies, which are not directly involved in the respective transaction.

The close link between micro- and macro theory is well documented. For example, Andersen et al. (2003) find that announcement surprises cause jumps

[5] Albeit there is information aggregation among market participants during the trading process, Evans and Lyons (2004b) find that much of order flow's information was not compounded, even after three months of trading.

[6] Even more, Evans and Lyons (2004b) find that currency order flow bear superior predictive power for future fundamentals than spot exchange rates.

in spot exchange rates' conditional mean. Hence they conclude that fundamentals are indeed linked to high-frequent exchange rate dynamics. In addition, Evans and Lyons (2001) estimates reveal that approximately one third of order flow variation in EUR / USD is due to macroeconomic announcements. Compatibly to this, Evans and Lyons (2002a) find that almost two thirds of USD / DEM exchange rate volatility are caused by order flow originated from portfolio shifts unrelated to macro information, i.e. changes in agents' risk preferences and hedging demand. In their (2007b) contribution, Evans and Lyons once more confirm the considerable correlation between FX order flow and macroeconomic news flow on both daily and intra-day frequency. According to them, at least half of macro news' effects on exchange rates are transmitted via FX order flow induced by these news. These findings are basically in line with Dominguez and Panthaki (2006). Evans and Lyons (2005a) argue that effects of macro announcements on order flow and hence on exchange rates may be due to different interpretations of macro information among market participants. Phylaktis and Chen (2005) find that macroeconomic news indeed influence dealers' currency pricing behaviour and increase information asymmetry among different market makers.

Additionally, the microstructure approach is important for macroeconomic policy issues. Hanousek and Podpiera (2003), for example, show the need for financial market regulation via their micro based analysis of stock markets in newly industrialising countries. Another macroeconomic field of application for microstructure analysis is monetary policy. Evans and Lyons (2002c, 2005d), Dominguez (2003), and Reitz and Taylor (2006), among others, specifically focus on central bank interventions, while Guembel and Sussmann (2001) analyse optimal exchange rates. All these studies highlight a rather close link between macro- and micro models and make clear that these approaches are not competing with each other.[7]

[7] Further studies investigate microstructure consequences of macro-announcements on various financial markets. For example, Christiansen and Ranaldo (2005) analyse bond-stock correlation after macro-announcements, Andersson et al. (2006) focus on news effects on the euro area bond market, Rangel (2005), Wongswan (2005), and Entorf and Steiner (2006) investigate macro- and monetary policy announcements and stock markets, and Menkveld et al. (2007) analyse treasury futures markets.

In microstructure theory, it is important to differentiate between interdealer and customer order flow. The interdealer-, i.e. interbank market is used for information aggregation and is thus, in theory, responsible for the actual determination of the exchange rate. Evans and Lyons (2002a) develop a theoretical model that specifies how interdealer order flow maps information to exchange rates. In contrast, customer order flow is seen as the ultimate source of private information. This is because dealers maintain business connexions with a variety of different customers such as corporations, asset managers, hedge funds, and central banks. Lyons (1995), Ito et al. (1998), and Bjønnes and Rime (2001) indeed confirm that customer order flow is the primary source of private information for currency dealers. Consequently, Sager and Taylor (2005) argue that customer order flow will be consistently more informative during the exchange rate determination process than interdealer flow.

The work at hand is in the spirit of the microstructure approach to exchange rates. Thereby, it is not about the institutional setting of the foreign exchange market and influence of different trading mechanisms.[8] As mentioned in Madhavan (2000), this is only one of four areas of application in microstructure finance. This study is primarily about (private) information and the role of different types of market participants during the process of exchange rate determination. To analyse this, we are using a data set containing the entirety of transactions in euro against U.S. dollars of an average-sized bank in Germany. In contrast to standard models of market making under asymmetric information, we find that bid-ask spreads are tightest for transactions with presumably well informed customers, while potentially worse informed counterparts get higher spreads. These findings support the view of Osler et al. (2006), stressing the potential role of strategic behaviour and market power during the pricing process. This is because Osler et al. (2006) argue that dealers might have an incentive to subsidise well informed order flow by lowering bid-ask spreads if order flow conveys information about short-run exchange rate movements that are easily exploitable for the dealer. Alternatively, a relatively weak bargaining position of the market maker vis-à-vis specific

[8] Readers who are interested in market design and issues related to the institutional setting of markets are refered to, among others, Hartmann et al. (2001), Lyons (2002b), Rime (2003), Lo and Sapp (2005), Lyons and Moore (2005), Beltran-Lopez and Frey (2006), and Gil-Bazo et al. (2007).

customer groups might force the dealer to quote narrower spreads in order to transact any trade with them. Which one of these two "new channels" is particularly true for the bank examined here is in the focus of subsequent chapters. Results of the numerous tests point to the conclusion that it is market power rather than strategic dealing that makes the dealer behaving the way described above.

The remainder of this work is as follows. Chapter 1 overviews the microstructure approach to exchange rates and clarifies the most important terms, notions and assumptions. Its aim is to introduce the main ideas and most important literature in the field of microstructure finance and high frequency economics. Chapter 2 describes the data set used herein for empirical investigation in greater detail.

Chapter 3 focuses on investigating the dealer's pricing behaviour. As Lyons (2002b, p. 13) points out, in floating exchange rate regimes *there is no price other than the price these people* (the currency traders) *set*. Thus, understanding currency dealer's pricing behaviour is key issue to understand short term exchange rate dynamics. In order to familiarise the reader to the main literature, chapter 3.1 gives an overview. Afterwards, the bid-ask spread, being a key variable in microstructure theory, is analysed in greater detail by investigating two well-known microstructure models. First, chapter 3.2 illustrates theoretical background on the Madhavan and Smidt (1991) model, before chapter 3.3 moves on to the theory behind the Huang and Stoll (1997) model. Empirical results of these approaches, which are augmented to account for different types of counterparts, are shown in chapter 3.4.1 and 3.4.2, respectively. Additionally, results of a rather intuitive approach are presented in chapter 3.4.3, describing the properties of directly observed (half) spreads.

Empirical results presented in chapter 3 indicate that asymmetric information indeed plays an important role for bid-ask spreads. However, results are contrary to predictions of standard models of pricing in presence of information asymmetry, supporting the argumentation of Osler et al. (2006) and their hypotheses on strategic dealing and market power considerations. Whether or not information content of order flow and thus strategic dealing is responsible for the observed dealer behaviour is in focus of chapter 4. In 4.1, a cointegration analysis is employed to identify a potential stable long-run equilibrium between order flow and exchange rates. To do so, the Engle and Granger (1987) methodology is used for a first assessment (4.1.1). Results are then reviewed by running the Johansen (1988, 1991) procedure to test for cointegration (4.1.2). Chapter 4.2 investigates short-run dynamics of the interaction between order flow and exchange rates by calculating the related vector error-correction model and tests for weak and strong exogeneity of the respective variables.

Findings presented in chapter 4.1 and 4.2 do not support the widespread optimism in market microstructure literature that (customer) order flow is the high-powered source of information easily exploitable for short-run speculation. Thus, the strategic dealing hypothesis is generally not support in the data. Order flow seems to convey rather mid-term information on exchange rate movements. Hence, chapter 4.3 analyses whether medium-run exchange rate changes could be predicted by using Evans and Lyons' (2005c) model of micro-based exchange rate forecasting. Chapters 4.3.1 and 4.3.2 provide theoretical background on that, while section 4.3.3 presents empirical results.

In contrast to Evans and Lyons (2005c), there is hardly any empirical evidence that information conveyed in order flow are actually exploitable on a rather medium-term horizon. However, to investigate whether or not the few indications for order flow's useful forecasting power support the strategic dealing hypothesis, one has to clarify if dealers themselves are aware of their potential source of private information. If they were, speculation should be profitable for these dealers. Section 4 of chapter 4 analyses revenues and profits due to speculative positions of the dealer in question. Summarising the results of all tests conducted in chapter 4, we conclude that it is very unlikely that strategic dealing is the driving force for our dealer's pricing behaviour.

As a consequence of the rejection of the strategic dealing hypothesis, market power should be responsible for results shown in chapter 3. Thus, this issue is in focus of chapter 5. By using a stochastic frontier model, it is possible to identify the degree of market power the dealer exhibits vis-à-vis different types of counterparts. Findings are truly promising. Actually, the dealer has virtually no market power in transactions with presumably well-informed, say financial customers. As a result of this, bid-ask spreads are minimal for financial counterparts, because they can easily transact with another market maker. Hence, the market maker considered here has to quote very tight bid-ask spreads in order to compete with other market makers and to maximise probability that financial customers transact any order with him. In contrast, while trading with commercial customers, the dealer is able to exert a small proportion of market power. Not surprisingly, the dealer's bargaining position is best while transacting with internal customers, so he can implement widest spreads.

Lastly, chapter 6 summarizes all of the empirical findings, concludes and identifies tasks for further research.

The book at hand is both theoretical and empirical. While the theories underlying the specific models used here are described within the text, econometric instruments are not explained in greater detail. Readers who are not familiar with econometric analysis will find a comprehension of the most important econometric techniques used herein in the annex of this book.

1. Becoming acquainted with microstructure finance

According to O'Hara (1995, p. 1), market microstructure is *the process and outcomes of exchanging assets under explicit trading rules.* Alternatively, Madhavan (2000, p. 205) defines market microstructure to be *the area of finance that studies the process by which investors' latent demands are ultimately translated into prices and volumes.* Both of these interpretations are, indeed, rather broad definitions. In this work, a more centred interpretation is used. Following Evans and Lyons (2004a, p. 1), the essence of the micro approach *is dispersed information and how information of this type is aggregated in the marketplace.* In their understanding, bits of information about changing variables like money demand, risk preferences, future inflation, as well as different trading responses to publicly observed data are dispersed across market participants. Exchange rates have to impound all of these information. Thus, Evans and Lyons (2004a) interpret this information problem and its solution as the basis of the microstructure approach. This is exactly the interpretation that is used in subsequent chapters.

By this definition, the work at hand covers three out of four areas of application of microstructure finance mentioned in Madhavan (2000, p. 205). The primary focus of this work is on *price formation and price discovery*, including information aggregation during the trading process, and the determinants of trading costs. However, some parts of this study deal with further two fields of application, namely *information and disclosure*, which is closely linked to the aforementioned price formation process, and *interface of market microstructure with other areas of finance*, especially asset pricing. The fourth area of application of market microstructure mentioned by Madhavan (2000, p. 205), being *market structure and design*, is not of this work's interest.[9]

Literature on market microstructure is vast and covers almost all kinds of financial markets. While early works mainly were purely theoretical or experimental, a growing availability of datasets, first based on quotes, later comprising actual transaction prices, too, has led to an increasing number of empirical studies during recent years. Readers who are seeking for an overview

---

[9] See footnote 8 for references on this issue.

to key theoretical works on market microstructure are refered to O'Hara (1995). Keim and Madhavan (1998), and Coughenour and Shastri (1999), in contrast, are focusing on experimental and empirical contributions. An useful comprehension of the market microstructure approach in general is provided by Madhavan (2000).

While deliberating about microstructure models, one should not think that these approaches are solely relevant for analysing and optimising a single market participant's behaviour. Microstructure models actually provide important insights to macroeconomic problems. For example, as Lyons (2001) emphasises, microstructure theory can, inter alia, help to understand trading volume in foreign exchange markets. While trading volume is often misunderstood and associated with excessive speculation, it is rather a result of risk management, as it is going to be explained in chapter 1.1. Microstructure theory thus is important to address macro-economic questions and it can help to avoid faultily political decisions that result from a misunderstanding of key features of the foreign exchange market.

Under the aforementioned definition of the micro approach, two variables get into the centre of interest, namely order flow and bid-ask spreads (spreads henceforth). To understand the essence of the microstructure approach to exchange rates, it is vital to understand the behaviour of these two variables. Sine qua non for that is an appropriate dataset. Availability of transaction data, often alternatively termed as *ultra high-frequency data*, possesses new perspectives for econometric analysis of financial markets in general and the foreign exchange market in particular. However, as mentioned in Hautsch and Pohlmeier (2002, p. 5), transaction data is still the *informational limiting case* for high-frequency economics.[10]

In addition, working on microstructure models and analysing transaction data requires to get acquainted with the trading usance at over-the-counter markets. While interpreting order flow, one has to be aware of the fact that this variable is not just a proxy for quantity. Neither are spreads just proxies for

[10] For a detailed discussion of econometric issues specific to high-frequency data, see, among others, Campbell et al. (1997), Dacorogna et al. (2001), and Gourieroux and Jasiak (2001).

prices. Therefore, it seems to be necessary to clarify their interpretation. However, before proceeding with order flow and spreads, the following section describes trading usance in over-the-counter (OTC) markets and the role market makers play in there.

1.1 Over-the-counter (OTC) markets and the role of market makers

OTC markets are defined by a lack of a centralised and organised market place. An investor thus has to call various market participants until she finds one who is willing to trade with her.[11] While she is looking for an appropriate counterpart to trade with, the investor is suffering various costs, usually summarised by *search costs*. Search costs comprise explicit costs, such as telephone bills, as well as implicit costs, like the value of time needed until the search ends, or opportunity costs.

Search costs are not marginal. Hence, some market participants provide market making services, i.e. they are willing to buy or sell a certain asset without having a primary interest in investing in this asset. These market participants are called *market makers*. Whenever an investor is willing to trade an asset, she can call a market maker to reduce search costs.[12] Clearly, market makers do not provide this service for free. They get compensated by the difference between the price they are willing to buy at (bid price), and the price, they would agree to sell (ask price) the asset for. This difference is termed *bid-ask spread* and it is going to be explained in greater detail later in this chapter.

---

[11] In recent years, electronic trading gained in importance. While talking about electronic trading, it is necessary to differentiate between trading systems of certain market makers, which enable their customers to communicate with the market maker *directly* via the internet instead of calling them by phone, and brokerage systems, which will only match demand and supply and will not take positions in the respective asset. The latter are more usual in foreign exchange markets than the former. Two of the best-known FX brokerage systems are EBS (Electronic Brokerage System), founded by a partnership of the world's largest FX market makers and now owned by ICAP, and Reuters Dealing 3000 Spot Matching. Nevertheless, for didactical reasons, we assume telephone trading here. For detailed information on electronic trading systems, see Rime (2003).

[12] Note that as soon as there are multiple market makers competing with each other, search costs may arise from searching for the one offering the "best price".

But what exactly is a market maker's service? Obviously, market makers provide liquidity. In fact, as stressed by Grossman and Miller (1988), market makers provide *immediacy*, since they do not only guarantee liquidity, but are willing to bear risks during the time period of the arrival of sellers and buyers. Of course, they, too, will manage their risk by using various instruments like quote shading or self-initiated, i.e. outgoing trades. These techniques are to be explained in subsequent sections, too.

When a market maker is approached by an investor, he does not know whether the investor is willing to buy or sell the asset. In foreign exchange markets, the investor does only reveal the currency pair she is willing to trade and the amount of one of the respective currencies. It is then up to the market maker to quote her a bid- and an ask-price that holds good for this amount. The investor, in turn, decides whether or not she is willing to transact under these conditions and hence can end the telephone call (and not transact at all) or she can reveal the direction of the trade by saying "to you" (selling) or "from you" (purchasing). The telephone call then ends after the market maker has confirmed the transaction by answering "from you" (investor sold) or "to you" (investor bought), respectively.

1.2 Order flow

Though spreads take a prominent part in microstructure finance, many theoretical models abstract from their existence. Order flow, by contrast, is a vital element of every model in microstructure theory. Lyons (2001, p. 7) argues that the fact *that microstructure models of all kinds tell us this variable is important expands microstructure from the narrow concept of "institutional structures with price effects" to the broader concept of "a new lens for viewing markets".*

Order flow is *signed* transaction volume. While working with order flow, it is important to be aware of the data frequency used during the analysis. On a tick-by-tick basis, order flow is signed transaction volume of every single trade. Due to the sign, it is theoretically and empirically different to standard trading volume – a fact that becomes obvious in the following example: If a customer approaches a dealer to sell him EUR 5 millions against USD, transaction volume is EUR 5 millions, whereas order flow is minus EUR 5 millions. The sign of order flow always refers to the trade-initiator's side of the transaction. Hence, if the dealer's customer, acting as the trade-initiator, sells (purchases) euro, euro order flow for the dealer gets a negative (positive) sign. The fact that order flow refers to transactions initiated by the dealer's counterparts, i.e. the *non-quoting* or so-called *active participants* in the transactions, is of great importance. This is because only customer-initiated order flow can, if at all, convey information for market makers. Customer order flow originates in shocks to customers' hedging or liquidity demand, diversity in interpretation of public news, or conclusions they draw from their own research. To analyse whether a market maker is able to participate on these information necessitates focusing on customer order flow rather than on so-called *outgoing trades* of our dealer.

Over a longer time period, order flow is *cumulative* signed transaction volume. Thus, as mentioned in Reitz et al. (2007), order flow is the net of buyer-initiated and seller-initiated currency orders. The fact that the focus is on incoming trades only, is again of great importance – this time in order to distinguish between order flow and inventory. In analysing high-frequency data, it is a common assumption that FX-dealers desire a net zero position in their inventory between two trading days. Amihud and Mendelson (1980) back the assumption of a preferred inventory position of market makers empirically. According to the dealers we have spoken to, the proposition of a desired net-zero inventory position is, in general, realistic, though it is not unusual to keep "small" inventory positions over night. However, because of this assumption, high-frequency datasets are usually manipulated in a way that inventory positions at the start of each trading day are set to zero.[13] To understand the point here, it is necessary to be aware of the difference between order flow and inventory positions. Order flow is initiated by customers only. Current inventory position, in contrast, is the net of both incoming and outgoing transactions. From an econometric point of view, order flow usually follows an I(1) process, while inventory positions are, at least because of the above-mentioned assumption with respect to inventory management, following an I(0) process.[14]

[13] This procedure was suggested first by Lyons (1995).

[14] A time series is said to be *integrated of order d*, written I(*d*), if it is necessary to take a minimum of *d* differences to obtain a stationary series.

After distinguishing order flow from transaction volume and inventory, it is important to see that it is different to excess demand, too. In equilibrium, excess demand always equals zero, but order flow usually does not. As stated above, order flow is defined as cumulative signed transaction volume on frequencies lower than tick-by-tick. Due to the specific market structure, foreign exchange orders are usually initiated against market makers. Market makers buy and sell foreign exchange even though they have no primary interest in trading the specific currency. If one abstracts from speculative trading, market makers' only motivation is to get a proper compensation for their service, that is absorbing imbalances between buyers and sellers. As hightlighted in Evans and Lyons (2004a), order flow equals zero only if the volume of buyer-initiated trades coincides exactly to the volume of seller-initiated transactions. Whenever this is the case, it is purely incidental and is not defining an equilibrium.

Additionally, a second feature distincts order flow from excess demand. As Evans and Lyons (2004a) point out, order flow is not even equal to demand, as it measures actual transactions only. As mentioned in the introductory chapter of this work, in standard textbook models demand might change without triggering any transaction. If, as argued by these models, changes in demand are fully driven by commonly known information, the demand curve shifts immediately[15] and no order flow occurs at all.

Besides its technical definition of signed transaction volume, order flow can be interpreted as buying or selling pressure and is hence quite similar to standard views that prices increase as there are more buyers than sellers. However, Evans and Lyons (2004a) emphasise that the order flow concept goes beyond that simple argumentation. As mentioned by Grossman (1976), Kyle (1985), Glosten and Milgrom (1985), and Madhavan (2000), among others, order flow conveys information. This conviction is the essence of the microstructure approach. As many surveys of foreign exchange dealers, e.g. works done by Goodhart (1988), Cheung and Wong (1999, 2000), Heere (1999), Cheung and Chinn (2001), and Cheung et al. (2004) show, FX-dealers themselves are aware of the informational content of order flow. Thus, order flow

[15] Furthermore, standard textbook models assume that all market participants interpret the new information exactly in the same way.

indeed is likely to affect dealers' expectations about future prices and the development of fundamentals. From an empirical point of view, order flow thus can be seen as a proxy variable for market participants' expectations. This is, not least in the work at hand,[16] empirically evidenced, since transactions of different customer types have different effects on price, implying that information content of order flow differs by counterparts.

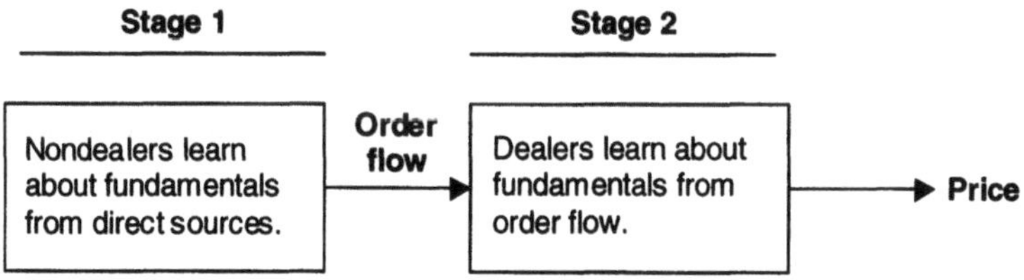

Figure 1.1
Two stages of information processing, Source: Lyons (2001, p. 8)

The way order flow is embedded in information processing is illustrated in figure 1.1. As it depicts, there are two stages of information processing in microstructure theory. On a first stage, non-dealers, i.e. mutual and hedge funds as well as corporate clients, jointly termed as *end-users*, learn about fundamentals by direct observation, by their business activities, or by conducting their own research. As stated in Fan and Lyons (2002), end-user order flow represents underlying currency demand in the real economy. It is assumed that market makers are not able to observe these information about fundamentals directly at the same time. Thus, non-dealers have private information that they can use to adjust their expectations about a currency's future value. Consequently, non-dealers will trade in accordance to their private information with market makers, resulting in end-user order flow.

In stage 2, market makers use their observed customer order flow to learn indirectly about fundamentals. In this way, market makers revise their expectations about future price of the currency and trade on their part via the interdealer market. While market makers set off undesired inventory from customer trading via interbank dealing, a process begins that Burnham (1991, p. 135) terms *a game of 'hot potato'*. Whenever a market maker purchases USD

[16] See Chapter 4 for empirical results on this.

against EUR in a customer-initiated transaction and resulting flows move his USD inventory away from his desired level, he will try to set off this amount of USD immediately. Hot potato trading thus is most likely when the initiating customer is a presumably well informed counterpart.[17] Changes of the exchange rate will then take place in the interdealer market (where the hot potato trading process continues), when the initial information is aggregated with other market makers' observed order flow.[18] Understanding the causes of hot potato trading hence is crucial for understanding the tremendous trading volume in foreign exchange markets. Flood (1994, p. 151) emphasises that the *large volume of interbank trading is not speculative in nature, but rather represents the tedious task of passing undesired positions along until they happen upon a marketmaker whose inventory discrepancy they neutralize.*[19]

Many empirical results support the process of information aggregation in the foreign exchange market as it is depicted in figure 1.1. For example, Evans and Lyons (2005b) find that customer order flows forecast exchange rate returns since they are correlated with future market-wide information flow. Moreover, according to Engel and West (2005), exchange rates help predicting future fundamentals. This finding can be directly explained by using the aforementioned argumentation. As highlighted in Lyons (1997), market makers' observed end-user order flow conveys information regarding recent developments in fundamentals. Because fundamental news are usually published with a significant time lag that is due to data collection, fundamentals, at last, confirm these information that market participants already extracted from order flow during the inquiry period of the specific fundamental variable.[20]

The focus of figure 1.2 is slightly different to figure 1.1. It depicts the basic difference between macro- and micro-based models by stressing the role of or-

---

[17] To start a process of hot potato trading, a market maker's actual inventory necessarily has to differ from desired inventory.

[18] More theoretical background on information processing and interdealer trading is to be found in section 1.5.

[19] In this way, hot potato trading is an important feature of market makers' risk management. Hence, any policy that aims to control or reduce trading volume in foreign exchange, e.g. the so-called *Tobin-tax* (Tobin, 1978), bears a potential risk to interfere this risk management process and thus to destabilise the global financial system as a whole.

[20] For corporate clients, this view is not supported by the data investigated in this study. See Chapter 3 for details.

der flow. As mentioned above, macro models suggest that news about fundamentals directly result in changes of the exchange rate. Because of its lack of empirical evidence, this view is obviously missing a key feature. Hence, microstructure theory argues that fundamentals that are not common knowledge at the respective point in time and thus are private information to non-dealers, trigger order flow. This order flow, in turn, influences the exchange rate via the transmission mechanism shown in figure 1.1. Few approaches, so-called *hybrid models*, combine the macro- and the micro-view.[21] Consequently, exchange rates are driven by both fundamental news and order flow in these approaches.

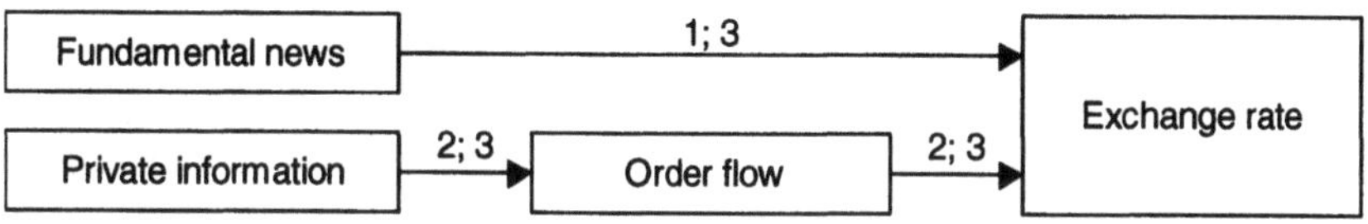

Figure 1.2
The macro view (1), the microstructure view (2), and the hybrid view (3), Source: Lyons (2001, p. 175), slightly modified.

In reality, not every single trade really conveys useful information. Indeed, traders often transact for liquidity reasons. Order flow resulting from these kind of transactions does not convey information exploitable for a market maker's own speculative trading. The presence of possible liquidity trading thus complicates the learning process of market makers.

A standard working proposition in microstructure literature, first of all used in Hasbrouck (1991a, 1991b), is that public information does not cause order flow. Even though it is a standard assumption, it was often mistrusted and believed to be wrong. According to Evans and Lyons (2004a), doubts against this proposition are usually due to a misunderstanding of the difference between order flow and trading volume. Of course, public news will cause trades in assets. As mentioned in Evans and Lyons (2004a), if there are two kinds of rational agents, one being risk-averse while the second is risk-neutral, public news about an increasing riskiness of foreign assets will induce

[21] See, for example, Evans and Lyons (2002a, 2002b).

foreign asset selling by the risk-averse and purchases of that assets by risk-neutral agents, so (net) order flow is zero in this case. Trading volume, in contrast, increases due to public information and the exchange rate will adjust immediately in accordance to the news. Foreign currency's external value is thus going to depreciate. Hence, it is trading volume instead of order flow that increases due to public information, so public news are not likely to be causal for order flow.[22]

A further facet of order flow is its relationship to price changes. One might have the opinion that price changes induce order flow and thus reverse the microstructure view to causality. These arguments bear in mind a behaviour that is often termed *feedback trading*, specifically *liquidity provision*. Agents might be willing to sell (buy) foreign exchange even though the exchange rate is following an increasing (decreasing) trend. Their motivation to do this is their conviction that observed price changes are not entirely justified by fundamentals. This behaviour is fully rational and refers to *stabilizing speculation* as described by Friedman (1953, p. 162 et seq.). First of all, microstructure theory does not disagree to rational feedback trading of this kind. It is indeed realistic that causality runs in both ways. However, as mentioned in Evans and Lyons (2004a), there is a consensus among the majority of researchers that causality runs *predominantly* from order flow to exchange rates and only *partly* the other way around. This is because the alternative to flow driven exchange rates – namely price changes due to the arrival of public information – is not at all empirically supported. Hence, the basic question is not whether causality is running from exchange rates to order flow, but to which extend this is the case.

Answering this question gets complicated by the fact that order flow should only convey information if it is due to shifts of the demand curve and is not representing movements along the demand curve. In empirical studies, this

[22] In standard microstructure models, market makers' only source of information about fundamentals is order flow. In reality, this assumption seems to be too strong. The Madhavan and Smidt (1991) model described in Chapter 3.2 offers an opportunity to estimate to which extend market makers revise their expectations with respect to public information and order flow, respectively. However, even in that model, order flow is not driven by commonly known information about fundamentals, but the exchange rate impounds those information as well.

issue is, once again, addressed by focusing on incoming end-user order flow only. Nevertheless, as Evans and Lyons (2004a) point out, even when order flow is measured in a theoretically correct way that accounts only for actual demand curve shifts, it will still react to price changes. Coefficients resulting from OLS analysis will thus be biased according to the direction of the reverse causality, i.e. positive or negative feedback trading.

However, the argumentation that positive feedback trading is responsible for strong positive correlation between order flow and exchange rates found in aggregate data has a major shortcoming. Evans and Lyons (2004a) stress that those arguments imply that the *majority* of market participants is trading in accordance to momentum- or chart-technical trend strategies. There is no doubt about the fact that *some* traders are following these strategies. However, to explain the above-mentioned correlation phenomenon, the market has to conduct feedback trading *on average*. This, actually, is quite unlikely. In contrast, Evans and Lyons (2002e) find slight evidence that the direction of feedback trading in aggregate interbank data is negative. Causality running from price to order flow thus seems to be unconvincing in explaining positive correlation between these two variables.

One should always bear in mind that order flow is just a proximate cause of exchange rate changes, not the driving force itself. Order flow, in fact, is used by market makers to adjust their expectations. Thus, the primitive cause of exchange rate changes is dispersed information. In this way, order flow is not an exogenous variable in microstructure theory. It provides an instrument to understand how information are aggregated in the market place and hence move exchange rates.

The last criticism, or misunderstanding, refers to the duration of order flow's effects on price. Microstructure effects are often believed to be temporary because of their high-frequency focus. Indeed, some effects (e.g. intra-day seasonalities, bid-ask bounce[23]) of order flow on prices are temporary.[24] Never-

---

[23] The term *bid-ask bounce* describes the effect that transaction prices bounce back and forth between the bid side and the ask side of the market maker's price schedule as alternating buy and sell orders arrive. See Evans and Lyons (2004a).

[24] Because of those temporary effects, many empirical studies analyse order flow data that is aggregated on a daily basis.

theless, Evans and Lyons (2004a) argue that as long as order flow conveys information, its effects *should* be persistent. As they point out, exchange rate changes in major currencies are arbitrarily close to a random walk. Since innovations in a random walk are persistent and order flow is an appropriate variable to explain these innovations, order flow effects to exchange rates are permanent, too. Furthermore, both the level of exchange rates and aggregated order flow are following an I(1) process and are possibly cointegrated.[25] If this was really the case, order flow effects to exchange rates were indeed persistent. Backed by many empirical studies like Evans (1997), Rime (2000), Evans and Lyons (2002b), and Payne (2003), it is now commonly accepted that order flow has significant permanent effects on exchange rates. In empirical studies, persistent effects are assumed to result from information, whereas temporary effects are believed to be due to pricing errors (French and Roll, 1986; Hasbrouck, 1991a).

In addition to long-lived price effects caused by information conveyed in order flow, Lyons (2001) mentions the role of possible multiple equilibria in the determination of the exchange rate's level or its volatility. In some models, microstructure parameters are responsible for whether or not multiple equilibria are possible, and if so, which one of them is most likely to be achieved. Work on this issue was done, among others, by Hartmann (1998), Hau (1998), Portes and Rey (1998), Spiegel (1998), Rey (2001), and Jeanne and Rose (2002). The presence of multiple equilibria is of relevance here, because if they indeed depend on microstructure parameters, those parameters show permanent effects, since stable equilibria are by nature long-lived.

Keeping all these aspects in mind, it becomes clear why order flow is a vital part of microstructure finance. Order flow is the variable that guides researchers to the essence of the entire approach and is hence a crucial part of every micro model.

[25] Whether or not this is the case is investigated in chapter 4 of this work.

1.3 (Bid-Ask) Spreads

As explained above, market makers usually do not know whether the customers they are approached by want to purchase or sell a specific currency, say euro against U.S. dollars. Consider a customer who wants to trade USD against EUR. The market maker, not knowing yet which side of the transaction his counterpart might take, will quote a rate, he is willing to buy (so-called *bid* price) a certain amount of EUR and another rate he is willing to sell (so-called *ask* price) this amount of EUR to the customer.[26] As a result, the bid price will always be lower than the ask price. The difference between bid and ask is called *bid-ask spread*.

In the euro area, it is common to use indirect quotation with four decimal places to express the exchange rate between EUR and USD. Thus, euro is base currency and its value is expressed in units of U.S. dollars.[27] The bid-ask spread is measured, with respect to the quotation rule, in pips of U.S. dollars, i.e. USD 0.0001.[28] Spreads represent expenses for a marker maker's counterpart, because if she purchases euro against U.S. dollars at the market maker's ask price and sells it immediately at the market maker's bid price, she will suffer a loss amounting to the spread.

As mentioned above, market makers quote spreads to get compensation for providing immediacy in a specific currency pair without having a primary interest in investing in these currencies. Usually, spreads are believed to compensate for actually three cost components of the market maker, i.e. transaction costs, inventory costs, and costs of hedging against asymmetric information, alternatively termed *adverse selection costs*. The importance of these elements of costs is highlighted in Chordia et al. (2000). As they show for stocks traded on New York Stock Exchange (NYSE), variations in average trading costs account for more than 50 percent of variations in quoted bid-ask spreads.

---

[26] These quotes usually hold good for a certain range of amount only, which has to be mentioned by the trade-initiator in advance.

[27] At 19 October 2007, EUR / USD reference rate was €1 = $1.4288 (as published at www.ecb.int).

[28] As an example, consider the bid price for one EUR is USD 1.4286 and the ask price for one EUR is USD 1.4290, the bid-ask spread is four pips.

A number of studies identify further determinants of bid-ask spreads. Ito and Hashimoto (2006) argue that trading activity in FX markets, measured by the number of deals transacted, might be a major driving factor, since it is negatively correlated with spreads. In line with these findings, Chakravarty and Sarkar (1999) show that liquidity is also a potential spread determinant in Fixed Income markets. According to them, liquidity is negatively correlated with spreads, too. While Cheung and Chinn (2001) confirm this finding only for extraordinary circumstances, Breedon and Vitale (2004) find evidence that the bulk of the strong correlation between order flow and exchange rates is indeed due to liquidity effects rather than information.

Many microstructure models, such as the approach of Huang and Stoll (1997), treat transaction costs as the residual of the other two cost components. Transaction costs are usually assumed to be fix for a specific range of amount dealt (following hence a step function) and thus subject to economies of scale within that range. The larger the amount dealt within a specific range, the lower the fraction of transaction costs per unit traded is going to be. In contrast, the higher the respective range, the wider the spread should be. However, this seemingly positive relation between spreads and deal size is rather due to inventory and informational reasons and is not predominantly based on transaction costs. Thus, transaction costs are usually assumed to be negatively correlated with deal size.

To get compensation for inventory costs, the market maker should increase the respective fraction of the spread with deal size, since he is exposed to a higher inventory risk. As mentioned above, market makers, in general, are managing their inventories in order to get back to a net zero position, at least at the end of each trading day. Econometrically, inventory time series thus show mean reversion properties that, as mentioned by Lyons (1995), indicate substantial inventory control. To manage inventories this way, market makers have two tools at their disposal, the interdealer market[29] and so-called *price*

[29] Undesired inventory positions can be set off by using the interdealer market, i.e. trading at another dealer's price. Price shading, in contrast, is inventory management by changing one's own quotation.

shading.[30] Only the latter refers to spreads. Price shading can be explained best by using the following example.

Consider a market maker who is approached by a customer, purchasing from him EUR 5 millions against USD. Before that transaction, the market maker has achieved his desired inventory and holds a net zero position. In order to offset the undesired short-position of EUR 5 millions (and not trading via the interdealer market), the market maker can try to attract euro-sellers (or USD-buyers) while further euro-buyers (dollar-sellers) should be discouraged from trading with him. Thus, the market maker has the incentive to increase his ask price and his bid price accordingly. In doing so, the market maker increases probability that the next customer will sell him euro against U.S. dollars, while he reduces probability of further euro purchases, because these are now relatively unattractive. Hence, buyer-initiated transactions will tear prices up and seller-initiated trades will push them down.

Of course, price shading does not necessarily influence bid-ask spreads. In the above-mentioned example, the exchange rate increases as euro-purchasers approach at our market maker. Hence, primarily the mid-rate is influenced by price shading. Spreads are subject to price shading, if this is done in a rather aggressive way, i.e. the market maker increases his bid price even more than he increases his ask price. In this case, the mid-rate still increases and there is an additional spread widening.[31] However, even if spread remains unchanged, inventory costs are one of the standard cost components of spreads, at least from a theoretical point of view. Empirical studies, though, do not find strong evidence for this so-called *inventory-control channel.*[32]

[30] Early works on price shading as a tool for inventory control are those of, among others, Amihud and Mendelson (1980), Ho and Stoll (1983), and O´Hara and Oldfield (1986).

[31] According to Heidle and Li (2004), informed market makers at Nasdaq indeed signal their private information (in their study, it is information about analysts' reports) by using only one of their two prices (the bid price or the ask price), resulting in narrower (wider) spreads following positive (negative) reports.

[32] Lyons (1995) was the first to find empirical evidence for this argumentation. Earlier studies, e.g. Madhavan and Smidt (1991), Laux (1993), and Manaster and Mann (1996) as well as more recent contributions like, among others, Osler et al. (2006), and the work at hand do not find strong empirical evidence for the inventory-control channel, although their data sets are comparably powerful to the one analysed by Lyons (1995).

Costs of hedging against asymmetric information, influencing exchange rates and spreads via the so-called *adverse selection channel*, are the last one of standard spread components. This channel, too, implies a positive correlation between the sign of order flow and the direction of exchange rate changes. If a market maker realises that his end-users predominantly purchase euro against U.S. dollars, he might infer that private information of these counterparts are in general in favour of the euro. As a result of that, the market maker increases his price of euro by increasing both the bid and the ask price. Adjustment of the exchange rate is not necessarily accompanied by a change of the spread in the first place. However, spreads should adjust with respect to potential asymmetric information, too.

Standard models of market making under asymmetric information suggest that spreads should widen with increasing probability that the counterpart has informational advantages, i.e. private information. As a consequence, spreads are often believed to be positively correlated with deal size, since increasing volume is assumed to correspond with increasing informational content of the transaction. Additionally, presumably well-informed customers should get wider spreads (and thus face higher transaction costs) compared to worse informed counterparts, because the market maker is exposed to higher adverse selection risk while trading with well-informed customers.

Although this argumentation seems to be convincing at a first glance, it suffers from a severe shortcoming. If a counterpart has private information that is exploitable in the foreign exchange market, it is rational for her to trade in accordance to these information as long as the market maker's quotation leaves any room for profits. In turn, standard models ultimately suggest that market makers should quote spreads to prevent *any* transaction with informed counterparts. This is because as long as an informed customer is willing to trade at a specific quotation, the market maker will always suffer from the counterpart's informational advantage, provided that there is no uncertainty within the customer's information. Obviously, this argumentation makes standard propositions of asset pricing under asymmetric information not seeming very realistic. Nevertheless, many early empirical studies, e.g. Hasbrouck (1988), and Lyons (1995), among others, support the view that spreads widen with increasing probability that a specific counterpart has private information.

In contrast to the above-mentioned standard view on spreads, Osler et al. (2006) suggest that these traditional considerations about determinants of bid-ask spreads may be superposed by two additional channels, namely strategic dealing and market power. Taking strategic dealing considerations into account, a market maker has an incentive to quote narrower spreads to better informed counterparts in order to maximise probability that the respective customer will trade with him. This is because the market maker seeks to exploit the information conveyed in observed informed order flow for own speculative purposes. Market power, in contrast, forces the market maker to quote narrower spreads to better informed agents, since they have, in general, a stronger bargaining position compared to worse informed customers due to their informational advantages and their good overview of competing quotes and recent market conditions. If a market maker wants to transact with this group of agents, he has to quote competitive spreads.

As shown in Pasquariellô (2000), spreads seem to be determined not only by "hard facts" like different components of costs, but are subject to some kind of time-of-day effects, too. Although he confirms that trading costs indeed influence spreads significantly, Pasquariellô (2000) finds a hump-shaped pattern in quoted bid-ask spreads during the worldwide FX trading day. Furthermore, inventory management is shown to be more relevant during the trading morning, while information gains in importance during afternoon trading. This finding, which is indicating potential regional differences in FX trading, is in contrast to Barner et al. (2005), who find that informed traders tend to transact during the trading morning.

So, what is the explanation for academia's intensive interest in bid-ask spreads? According to Lyons (2001), spreads receive that much attention in microstructure finance for three reasons. From a scientific point of view, spreads are a core element of many data sets and are thus easily exploitable for hypothesis testing. In this way, spreads are superior to other aspects that are relevant to microstructure theory, e.g. information flow or belief dispersion.

The second reason is a rather practical one. Lyons (2001) relates it to the aforementioned cost aspects of spreads. Investigating trading costs and anything related to it is a natural field of interest for econometricians and practitioners as well. The third reason highlighted in Lyons (2001) is based on historical incident. To separate itself from literature on trading under rational expectations, microstructure finance focused on spreads, since they are closely connected to trading mechanisms. While works on trading under rational expectations abstract from anything related to trading systems and usances, one field in microstructure finance focuses on how these mechanisms might influence prices. To analyse this, one has to concentrate on how prices are determined and thus has to investigate spreads.

Bid-ask spreads, however, are only one subfield within microstructure finance. As mentioned above, many models, for example the one presented in Kyle (1985), being one of the best-known approaches in the field, do not even consider spreads. However, in this work, spreads are an important tool for analysing information-theoretic hypotheses.

1.4 Private Information

During previous chapters, the term *private information* emerged repeatedly. To avoid any misunderstanding, it seems helpful to clarify what this term means in the work at hand's context.

In line with Lyons (2001, p. 26), private information here has two defining criteria. It is

1. *not known by all agents; and*
2. *produces a price forecast with lower conditional variance compared to a prediction that is based on public information only.*

Because of 2., private information should be helpful for a dealer's own speculative trading. In particular, Lyons (2001) defines two subcategories of private information based on Frenkel and Mussa's (1985) and Obstfeld and Rogoff's (1996) conclusion that exchange rates can be seen as asset prices.[33] The

[33] This conclusion has become a standard assumption in exchange rate economics. Therein, the exchange rate is the present value of market participants' expectations concerning present and future economic conditions in the respective economic areas, so that price

first of Lyons' subcategories refers to private information regarding the size of a terminal payoff[34] (V) within a multi-period trading model; the second relates to interim prices realised before the terminal payoff is achieved. This distinction is in the spirit of Rubinstein (2001), who distinguishes uncertainty about fundamentals from uncertainty about market participants' preferences. While the former is linked to the first of Lyons' (2001) subcategories, the latter refers to the second. With this interpretation of private information at hand, the micro approach does not need bubbles or any form of irrationality to explain exchange rate dynamics. Thus, it seems to be worthwhile to take a closer look on these subcategories mentioned here.

Private information regarding V is often investigated by analysing central bank interventions. As Peiers (1997) argues, a dealer, who is approached by a central bank, clearly receives private information about the central bank's view on the exchange rate's fundamental value.[35] Alternatively, Lyons (1997) points out the role of dispersed private information regarding particular fundamentals relevant to exchange rates that are available long before statistics on those fundamentals are publicly available. This, too, can be seen as private information on a terminal payoff's value. Of course, any information regarding V has immediate influence on any price that is realised before V is achieved.

The second of Lyons' (2001) subcategories refers directly to interim prices. While the first subcategory influences these prices indirectly via new information on the terminal payoff, interim prices are now directly affected by private information. The second subcategory consists of any transitory or permanent risk premium determining variable like risk preferences or traders' trading constraints.[36] Obviously, these variables have no influence on the terminal payoff V, but are important in determining prices up to then. Information on these features of the trading environment are both not publicly available and

---

changes are largely unpredictable since they reflect primarily new information, which alter these expectations.

[34] According to Lyons (2001), in foreign exchange markets, V is related to future monetary fundamentals, e.g. interest rates differentials.

[35] Information induced by central bank interventions is a vital part of the so-called coordination channel, by which central banks might influence exchange rates via announced interventions. The coordination channel is empirically supported in Reitz and Taylor (2006).

[36] Saar (1999), and Cao et al. (2006) provide further insights.

producing better forecasts and thus meet the above-mentioned criteria of private information.

In contrast to Lyons (2001), this work does not predominantly focus on the second subcategory of private information. Instead, both of these subcategories are more or less equally weighted. Information on a terminal payoff are a vital part of, for example, the Madhavan and Smidt (1991) model that is in focus of chapter 3. Nevertheless, the second subcategory of private information is particularly important in foreign exchange markets, too. Because of this, chapter 4 focuses intensively on this kind of private information.

1.5 Theoretical Frameworks

The microstructure approach provides a third theoretical way to understand the determination of nominal exchange rates. Both of the alternatives, the Goods Market Approach and the Asset Market Approach, solely consider macroeconomic variables to influence a currency's external value. Consequently, most of them are hardly based upon microeconomic theory. The Goods Market View's fundament, for example, is the conviction that identical goods cannot be sold at the same time at different prices at different locations when arbitrage is possible.[37] For single products, this rule is known as *law of one price*. It is one of the most fundamental convictions in macroeconomics. For open economies and multiple goods, this law refers to the assumption of *purchasing power parity* (PPP). According to this, one euro should have, in equilibrium and after exchanged into U.S. dollars, the same purchasing power in the U.S. as it has in the euro area. Whenever the (exchange rate-adjusted) price level in Europe is higher than it is in the U.S., Europe is believed to import goods from the United States, since U.S. products are relatively cheap. As a result of this, demand for U.S. dollars will increase. Europeans purchase USD against euro, resulting in an appreciation of the dollar. This, in turn, makes U.S. goods more expensive for Europeans again and adjusts the euro's former purchasing power advantage. Obviously, this setting abstracts from costs of carriage and assumes that all goods are tradable across re-

[37] A textbook introduction to the Goods Markets Approach can be found in Mankiw (2007), among others.

spective currency-areas. Despite these simplifications, PPP is a quite valuable indicator in the long run with an information half-life of approximately five years (Rogoff, 1996; Lyons, 2001).

The Asset Market Approach, being the second macroeconomic view to exchange rate determination, has many facets. Only one group of them, so-called *General Equilibrium* (GE) *models*, have a proper microfoundation that links the exchange rate to demand (tastes) and supply (technologies) in the respective currency-areas. These GE models are generalisations of flexible-price monetary models (FPM) (e.g. Frenkel, 1976, and Mussa, 1976) or sticky-price monetary models (SPM) (e.g. Dornbusch, 1976), both of them hardly based upon microeconomic theory. GE models were employed to many fields, one of them being welfare analysis of alternative exchange rate regimes, as done, for example, by Devereux and Engel (2001), a second being the short-run relation between fundamentals and exchange rates, as done in Evans and Lyons (2007a).

The fourth approach within the group of Asset Market models, the so-called *Portfolio Balance Model* (PBM), is able to allow for a risk premium between currencies that is due to imperfect substitutability between domestic and foreign assets. This is possible because PBMs are neither assuming PPP nor uncovered interest parity[38] (UIP) to hold. UIP, focusing on financial markets, is similar to the PPP-view to goods markets. Whenever interest rates abroad are higher than domestic rates, investors will buy foreign bonds, resulting in an appreciation of the foreign currency that balances this difference out. Thus, UIP holds when a currency's expected rate of depreciation is equal to the difference between interest rates on domestic and foreign bonds. With the exception of Evans and Lyons (2007a), at least one of these parity conditions (PPP or UIP) is presumed by those other three asset market models (FPM, SPM, GE), but not in PBMs.

Risk premia are a crucial feature of PBM. The models argue that investors hold a portfolio of domestic bonds, foreign bonds (divided by the exchange

---

[38] A textbook description of UIP is provided, among others, by Bain and Howells (2003, p. 289).

rate[39]) and money that represents their total wealth. Demand for each of these assets depends on the domestic nominal interest rate, the foreign nominal interest rate, and the expected percentage change of the exchange rate (that is, for simplicity, often assumed to be zero). In combination with the foreign nominal interest rate, the latter expresses the expected return on an investment in foreign bonds. In addition, demand for all assets is positively correlated with total wealth. The exchange rate is driven by changes in relative asset supply within the respective currency-areas that have both short-run and long-run effects.[40] Now, consider an increasing supply of domestic bonds due to increasing government debt. As a result of this, domestic bond supply exceeds demand. To restore equilibrium, demand for domestic bonds has to be encouraged. This can be done by increasing domestic interest rates that affects demand for domestic bonds directly, or by a depreciating exchange rate of the domestic currency. The changing exchange rate affects demand for domestic bonds indirectly via an increasing wealth. When allowing for non-zero expectations on exchange rate changes, investors will expect a depreciating exchange rate, resulting in this wealth-effect. Consequently, they will adjust their expectations immediately and increase their demand for foreign assets, resulting in a higher demand for foreign exchange. Because of that, the exchange rate responds immediately, too. Here, investors view domestic bonds as imperfect substitutes for foreign bonds and claim compensation for higher risks associated with an investment in these assets. This compensation is the above-mentioned risk premium. The exchange rate, thus, is a tool for rebalancing actual disequilibria.[41] Evans and Lyons (2002b) find distinct empirical evidence for price effects due to imperfect substitutability.

As mentioned above, all these macro approaches provide virtually no guidance for high-frequent exchange rate dynamics. Here, the third theoretic approach, the Microstructure Approach to exchange rates, is by far most promising. Thus, the following section is to complete this introduction to micro-

[39] Nominal value on foreign bonds is in foreign currency and the exchange rate's base value is domestic currency.

[40] Long-run effects affect goods markets and the balance of payments.

[41] Contributions to the Portfolio Balance Model are provided in, among others, Kouri (1976), and Allen and Kenen (1980).

structure finance by providing an overview of the most important theoretical frameworks.[42] Figure 1.3 summarizes the various theoretical approaches.

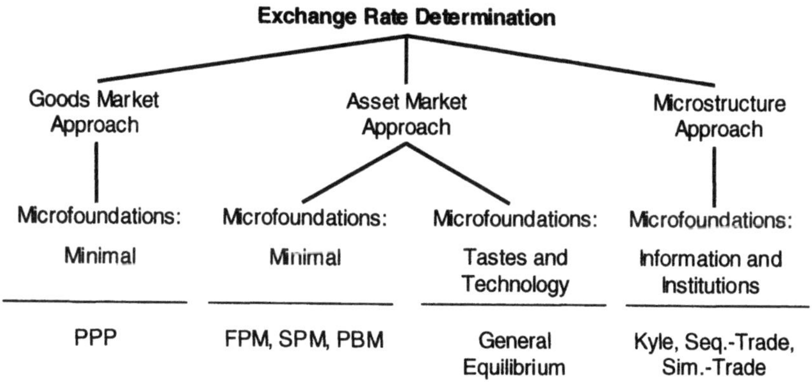

Figure 1.3
Three approaches to explain exchange rate determination and the respective models. PPP denotes purchasing power parity model. FPM denotes flexible-price monetary model. SPM denotes sticky-price monetary model, PBM denotes portfolio balance model. Kyle denotes Kyle (1985) model. Seq.-Trade denotes sequential-trade model. Sim.-Trade denotes simultaneous-trade model. Source: Lyons (2001, p. 168), slightly modified.

Basically, microstructure models can be distinguished according to the kind of market they analyse, which, in turn, depends on the accomplishment of the best available price. On the one hand, in so-called *quote-driven* or *dealer markets*, the best available price is defined by dealer quotes. On the other hand, so-called *order-driven* or *auction markets* accomplish the best price by submitted orders. Figure 1.4 provides an overview. Anyway, one should not be misleaded by terms. Both order-driven models and quote-driven approaches fit to microstructure theory. In the latter, too, order flow still induces price changes and not vice versa, because of the aforementioned information theoretical implications.

The following models are not subject to empirical investigations in this work. Rather, these approaches serve here as an overview of some of the most influential theoretical works in the field, which paved the way for further im-

[42] A detailed treatment of the theories and implications of the microstructure approach can be found in O'Hara (1995) and in a survey by Madhavan (2000).

provements of the microstructure approach. Empirical sections of this work deal with, among others, the Madhavan and Smidt (1991) model and the Huang and Stoll (1997) model in order to investigate the market maker's pricing behaviour. Nevertheless, both of them can be seen as special cases of subsequent theories. In order to provide a comprehensive introduction to the microstructure approach, it seems to be appropriate to mention at least the essential features of these basic models.

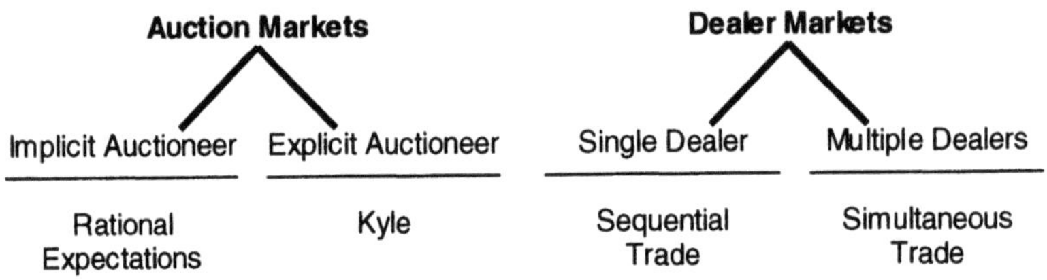

Figure 1.4
Four types of microstructure models, Source: Lyons (2001, p. 64).

The rational expectations model is only of minor interest here, because it is not a microstructure model in narrower sense. According to Lyons (2001), this approach is primarily useful from a didactical point of view, since its shortcomings can make the necessity of the microstructure approach clear. However, even though Wolinsky (1990) get at a closer link between microstructure theory and rational expectations modelling, this work will not take a closer look on this approach for mainly one reason: rational expectations models are based on an implicit auctioneer outside the model and thus cannot account for pricing behaviour of actual market participants. These kinds of models often refer to a hypothetical, so-called *Walrasian auctioneer*, who sets prices and executes orders. All orders submitted to this auctioneer are preliminary until he has determined the market-clearing price. Orders are then executed at this price and no trading occurs at prices other than that. In contrast to this, the focus of the work at hand is explicitly on (endogenous) pricing behaviour of market makers. Thus, rational expectations models do not seem to offer any gaining of insights in this case.[43] The three remaining approaches shown in figure 1.4, in contrast, are worthwhile a closer look.

1.5.1 The Kyle (1985) model

In contrast to rational expectations models, Kyle's (1985) approach explicitly accounts for a price setting process within the model. Since the price setter is not just an auctioneer, but takes own trading positions, Lyons (2001) defines him to be a market maker. In order to find the appropriate price, this market maker has to use available information that is, in turn, determined by order flow, to which the market maker has exclusive access. By this feature, the model gets an explicit informational dimension and is thus interesting in this work's context.

Obviously, the informational environment of the Kyle (1985) model is not very realistic. It assumes that order flow is the only source of information about fundamentals for the market maker, who is the only one who provides liquidity in the respective risky asset among all market participants. This assumption does not describe the decentralised structure of foreign exchange markets very well. However, as mentioned in section 1.1, a market maker's customers do not always trade for informational reasons, but also in accordance to their liquidity needs. This fact complicates the "vote counting" process of the market maker to learn about fundamentals. The Kyle (1985) model accounts for this complication. However, the problem is simplified by distinguishing between orders from informed traders,[44] X^I, and orders from uninformed traders, X^U. Informed traders, here, are defined by their (private) information about relevant fundamentals. Hence, they trade for informational reasons and behave strategically, i.e. they take the impact of their own orders on price into account. Uninformed traders, in contrast, trade for liquidity reasons only and show non-strategic behaviour.

The Kyle model deals with the first category of private information (private information regarding the size of a terminal payoff) as defined by Lyons (2001)

[43] Nevertheless, one of the most important conclusions of rational expectations models is that order flow does convey information.

[44] In its basic version, the model assumes that there is only one informed trader.

and described in section 1.4. However, because it is a one-period model, there is no room for private information of the second type. The terminal payoff, V, of the risky asset (here the exchange rate) is assumed to be a normally distributed random variable with zero mean and variance σ_V^2. V is paid at the end of the period after all trading is done. The informed trader, who is assumed to be risk-neutral, observes the true value of V before any trading takes place. She then approaches the market maker to trade in accordance to her private information.

The market maker as well as the uninformed market participants cannot observe the true value of V. Because of that, the market maker's problem is that he faces orders from one informed trader, which he cannot identify among the entirety of market participants, and many uninformed and non-strategic counterparts at the same time. His task is to find a market-clearing price, S, that holds good for both types of customers. Here, it is important to mention that the informed trader cannot observe uninformed order flow and is thus not able to condition her order on the market-clearing price. At least, the market maker will choose S in a way that it will offer the market maker himself an expected profit of zero. This assumption prevents the model from being subject to monopoly power aspects and can be justified by market-entry considerations. Taking all those information into account, S has to be the expected value of V given observed order flow X^I and X^U. Mathematically, this is

$$S = E(V \mid X^I + X^U). \tag{1.1}$$

Uninformed order flow is, by definition, independent of V. Because of that, it is convenient to assume X^U to be normally distributed with mean zero and variance σ_U^2 that is independent of σ_V^2. In equation (1.1), X^U is thus exogenous, but X^I is depending on the informed trader's trading strategy. The informed and strategic customer will choose X^I in order to maximise her expected profit. She will achieve this by choosing X^I to maximise the following

$$E(X^I(V - S) \mid V). \tag{1.2}$$

Equation (1.1) and (1.2) are closely linked to each other. If the informed trader was non-strategic, she would simply take S as given while maximising (1.2). This is not the case in Kyle's (1985) setting. The informed trader behaves strategically and knows that her order flow, X^I, affects S via equation (1.1). Because X^U has a zero mean, the market maker might infer X^I from observed total order flow. However, focusing only on order flows magnitude disregards X^U's and X^I's variance. Because of that, the market maker will set S according to

$$S = \lambda (X^I + X^U), \tag{1.3}$$

where λ is strictly positive and given by

$$\lambda = 0.5\left(\sigma_V^2 / \sigma_U^2\right)^{0.5}. \tag{1.4}$$

λ conveys the so-called *signal-to-noise-ratio*, i.e. $\left(\sigma_V^2 / \sigma_U^2\right)$. Because of (1.3) and (1.4), order flow's impact on price will be "great" ("small") as variance of uninformed demand is relatively small (great) compared to the terminal payoff's variance, i.e. the signal-to-noise-ratio is large (small). Since the informed trader observes the true value of V without any uncertainty, variance of X^I equals variance of V. If, as described, uninformed demand's variance is small, X^U is more likely to be small or even zero and consequently, observed order flow is more likely to convey information.

Remember, the informed trader knows the distribution of X^U, though she does not know X^U before submitting her own order. Nevertheless, the informed trader can infer the influence of X^I on S, so her trading strategy, aiming to maximise her profits, is non-trivial. In equilibrium, the informed trader will choose X^I according to

$$X^I = \beta V, \tag{1.5}$$

where β, too, is strictly positive and defined by[45]

$$\beta = \left(\sigma_U^2 / \sigma_V^2\right)^{0.5}. \tag{1.6}$$

The more the informed trader is able to camouflage her order in uninformed order flow, the more she will react to her private information concerning V. Hiding an informed order in total order flow is easiest when variance of unin-

---

[45] For derivations of equations (1.4) and (1.5) see Kyle (1985).

formed demand is "great" relative to the terminal payoff's variance, i.e. when the signal-to-noise-ratio's reciprocal β is large. The informed trader's trading strategy thus depends on the same two parameters as the market maker's pricing rule does.

There are several important insights of the Kyle model. One of the most interesting results in this context here is the fact that market makers indeed learn about fundamentals via observed order flow as described in equation (1.3). Further, it gets obvious to which degree the informed trader's private information is revealed by equilibrium price. As shown in Appendix A.1, because of the informed agent's strategy, equilibrium price reveals exactly half of her private information, regardless of V and X^U. Because equilibrium price is common knowledge after trading took place, private information partially becomes public information and is hence revealed during the trading process.

Kyle's considerations paved the way for many microstructure models. However, even though the model was often extended, e.g. in order to allow for uninformed traders behaving strategically (Admati and Pfleiderer, 1988), allowing the informed trader to be risk averse (Subrahamanyam, 1991), and considering multiple informed traders in a multi-period environment (Holden and Subrahamanyam, 1992), there are still quite a few shortcomings of the model that limit its applicability, especially to foreign exchange markets. As Lyons (2001) emphasises, there are primarily three aspects to criticise.

Firstly, the Kyle model cannot account for strong inventory management that can be observed empirically. Because of that, the model is not able to analyse possible inventory effects on price. This is a potential shortcoming since order flow's signal-to-noise ratio decreases if a larger fraction of (market-wide) order flow is due to inventory management and does not convey information.

In addition to that, the model does not capture bid-ask spreads, because it is set up as a so-called *batch-auction*, where all orders are executed at a single price. Although Madhavan (1996), among others, suggests to estimate an "implicit" spread, this feature remains to be problematic.

Lastly, Lyons (2001) criticises the model for not being able to account for price impacts of individual orders. This is probably the most severe shortcoming of Kyle's approach. In the this work's context, price impacts of different types of counterparts as well as of different order sizes receive explicit attention during empirical investigations. To explain dealer behaviour as subject to information or market power considerations, it is necessary to investigate every single transaction. This is not possible in the batch auction setting of the Kyle model, so this approach is not suitable for detailed empirical analysis here.

In addition to the above-mentioned criticism, the fact that the model assumes only a single market maker to set prices does obviously not provide a realistic environment of foreign exchange markets. Furthermore, it is now widely accepted that exchange rates are determined in the interdealer market. Because there is no interdealer market in this setting, the model misses a potentially crucial feature of exchange rate determination.

1.5.2 The Glosten and Milgrom (1985) model (The sequential-trade model)

Even though the Kyle (1985) model was criticised for focusing on a single dealer in the last section, Glosten and Milgrom (1985) assume only one dealer, or market maker, too. Their approach is one of the best known models within the sequential-trade literature. The model considers one risk-neutral market maker[46] and many uninformed traders. In contrast to Kyle (1985), Glosten and Milgrom (1985) allow for multiple, risk-neutral informed traders. In addition, informed traders are not behaving strategically – a major shortcoming compared to Kyle (1985). Non-strategic behaviour of informed traders is due to the model's feature that both the informed and uninformed traders join a single pool of counterparts to the market maker from which they are drawn sequentially and randomly. The random selection prevents informed traders from adjusting their demand strategically in the way described by the Kyle model.

[46] The assumption of a market maker being risk-neutral is a first point of criticism here, too.

Informed traders are once more defined by their private information about the true value of a single risky asset's terminal payoff. By assumption, this value can either be high, denoted V^H, or low, denoted V^L. Neither the market maker nor uninformed traders have these information. The market maker's only information regarding the terminal payoff is unconditional probability of V^H, denoted p, and V^L, given by $(1-p)$. In addition, the market maker knows the fraction, q, of traders' entirety that is informed. Consequently, a fraction of $(1-q)$ traders is uninformed. Informed traders will buy (sell) with probability 1 if the actual value of V is high (low). In contrast, probability of uninformed traders to buy (sell) is by definition independent of V and often assumed to be 0.5 for reasons of simplification.[47]

Every single trade involves the market maker and one counterpart, who is drawn from an unchanging pool of traders. As a consequence of this, probability that a specific counterpart is an informed trader, q, remains constant, regardless of how many informed traders have already approached the market maker in earlier periods. Whenever the market maker is approached by a customer, he quotes a bid-ask spread. This spread is said to hold good for a single standardised transaction of one unit of the risky asset. The bid price, i.e. the price the market maker is willing to pay for one unit of the risky asset, is equal to the market maker's expectation concerning the terminal payoff, V, conditional on the next approaching trader wants to sell, and vice versa for the ask price. Formally, this is

$$\begin{aligned} \text{Bid} &= E[V \mid \text{next trader sells}] \\ \text{Ask} &= E[V \mid \text{next trader buys}] \end{aligned} \tag{1.7}$$

After the market maker quoted his spread, the trader reveals her side of the transaction, i.e. she tells the market maker whether she wants to buy at the ask-price or whether she is going to sell at the bid. Alternatively, she can decide not to trade at all. After the trader has made her trading-statement, the transaction is executed (given she actually decides to trade) and the market maker updates his expectations concerning the value of the terminal payoff.

[47] This simplification directly corresponds to Kyle's (1985) assumption that expected uninformed order flow is zero. It is reasonable, because uninformed order flow is usually assumed to arise from idiosyncratic shocks, e.g. hedging demand.

The binomial tree depicted in figure 1.5 shows every possible combination of the traders' type (informed or uninformed), direction of the transaction (trader buys or trader sells), and value of the terminal payoff (V^H or V^L). Because the market maker knows constant values of p and q, he is able to quote a spread on basis of these possible combinations by using Bayes' Rule, a well known formula to review probabilities in the presence of new data, introduced by Thomas Bayes (1763, 1764).

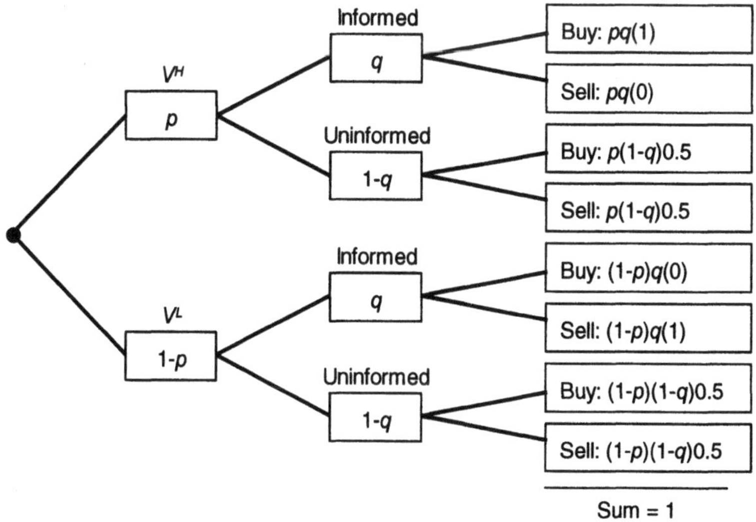

Figure 1.5
Overview of all possible trade types (binomial tree) within the sequential-trade model and respective probabilities. An informed trader buys (sells) with probability 1, if V is high (low). An uninformed trader is assumed to buy (sell) with probability 0.5, regardless of the terminal payoff's value. Probability of V being high is p, while q denotes probability that a trader who approaches the market maker is informed. Source: Lyons (2001, p. 90).

By conducting Bayes' Rule, the market maker is able to calculate probability that V is high or low conditional on the next trader wants to buy or sell. Because of that, the market maker is able to quote a bid price and an ask price according to equation (1.7) and will be regret-free, regardless of the direction the next trader is actually going to trade.

Conducting Bayes' Rule is quite easy in this setting, because the market maker is given all the information he needs to do so. The following example is for clarification. Given the above mentioned information concerning p, q, and probability that an uninformed trader trades in a specific direction, consider the market maker's bid price. According to equation (1.7), it is the expected value of V conditional on the next trader wants to sell. Because the market maker does not know whether the next counterpart is informed or not, he has to take both possibilities into consideration. Thus, equation (1.7) has to be expanded to

$$\text{Bid} = E[V \mid \text{sell}] = (V^L)\cdot\text{Prob}\{V^L \mid \text{sell}\} + (V^H)\cdot\text{Prob}\{V^H \mid \text{sell}\} \tag{1.8}$$

Assume V^L equals 2 (units of money), while V^H equals 10 (units of money). The market maker knows these values. In addition, consider probability for V being V^L is 0.5 and a fraction of 25 percent of all traders is informed. Consequently, $p = 0.5$ and $q = 0.25$. At last, an informed trader will sell (buy) with probability 1 whenever V is low (high), while an uninformed trader will buy with probability 0.5, regardless of V. All these information are in the data set of the market maker.

According to Bayes' Rule, probability that V is low given the next trader wants to sell equals probability that V is low times probability that a sell occurs when V is low relative to overall probability that the next trader sells. Formally, this is

$$\text{Prob}\{V^L|\text{sell}\} = \frac{\text{Prob}\{V^L\}\cdot\text{Prob}\{\text{sell}|V^L\}}{\text{Prob}\{V^L\}\cdot\text{Prob}\{\text{sell}|V^L\} + \text{Prob}\{V^H\}\cdot\text{Prob}\{\text{sell}|V^H\}}. \tag{1.9}$$

Probability of V being V^L is 0.5. If V was actually equal to V^L, informed traders sell with probability 1 and uninformed traders sell with probability 0.5. Because 25 percent of all traders are informed and 50 percent of the remaining 75 percent will sell, the numerator in equation (1.9) can be written as $(0.5) \cdot (0.25 + 0.5 \cdot 0.75) = 0.3125$. The left term of the sum in the denominator of equation (1.9) is obviously identical to this. For the second term, one has to be aware that probability of V being V^H is 0.5, too. None of the informed traders would sell, if V was indeed V^H, but 50 percent of uninformed traders would do so. Thus, for the second term of the sum one can write (0.5)(0 + 0.5

$\cdot$ 0.75) = 0.1875. Hence, probability that V equals V^L given that the next trader wants to sell is 0.3125 / (0.3125 + 0.1875) = 0.625. Multiplying this result by 2, being the actual value of V^L, yields 1.25 (units of money) for the first term of equation (1.8).

For the second term of (1.8), calculations are in accordance to those described in equation (1.9) and are thus not shown here. In addition, because V can only be V^L or V^H, probabilities of these two states have to sum up to 1. Hence, probability of V being V^H given the next trader wants to sell is (1 – 0.625 =) 0.375. Multiplied by the actual value of V^H, 10, the second term of equation (1.8) equals 3.75. Consequently, the market maker's regret-free bid price is 1.25 + 3.75 = 5 (units of money). Here, as mentioned above, it becomes clear that the market maker indeed suffers losses from trading with informed counterparts given that V is actually V^L and thus equals 2. This is because the market maker buys an asset for five units of money that is actually worth two units. However, the market maker gains profits from trading with uninformed customers, since his ask price (calculations not shown here) is seven units of money. Hence, the market maker sells an asset that is actually worth two units of money for seven units to uninformed customers. As shown in Appendix A.2, this pricing behaviour exactly results in an overall profit of zero for the market maker.

After the next trader has actually sold, the market maker will adjust his expectation concerning the realisation of V with respect to the probabilities calculated above. The sequential-trade model thus is an approach in the manner of Bayesian Updating. Since the dealer uses all available information for setting his price, there is no estimate of price better than the dealer's price unless one has superior information.

The sequential-trade model by Glosten and Milgrom (1985) bears some interesting insights, which are highlighted by Lyons (2001). First of all, the existence of a bid-ask spread is possible even in an environment with a competitive risk-neutral market maker. It arises from the fact that the market maker, aiming for an expected profit of zero due to same considerations as in Kyle (1985), knows that he will suffer losses while trading with informed counterparts. In order to balance these losses out, he has to make profits when he trades with uninformed counterparts. Spreads, thus, do not need market power, trading costs or risk-aversion of the market maker, but can be sufficiently justified by the existence of information asymmetries.

Second, market makers learn from every single transaction and update their expectations concerning the terminal payoff after every trade. Although the dealer can not identify whether a counterpart is informed or not, knowledge of *p* and *q* enables the market maker to infer the probable value of the terminal payoff after observing a sequence of transactions. Hence, and this is the model's third important insight, Glosten and Milgrom (1985) really describe a process of price *discovery* rather than price *determination*, as it is often used in standard macro models. This is exceptionally interesting, because price adjustment and trading happens even though there are no news arriving.[48] At last, the explicit consideration of bid-ask spreads is a further advantage of the sequential-trade model.

However, although the Glosten and Milgrom (1985) approach provides many helpful insights, it has its limitations, too. The most severe shortcoming of the model is its random selection of traders approaching the market maker. As a consequence of this, timing and sequencing of order arrivals are random, too, and are thus not exploitable for informative reasons. In fact, a sequence of higher frequent orders is usually seen to bear more information than a sequence of orders approaching the market maker at lower frequencies. This is mainly because in information-efficient markets, information aggregation should happen quite rapidly, so important news should induce an increasing trading-frequency. Liquidity-driven trading, in contrast, is not seen to be closely related to transaction frequencies. Furthermore, Barner et al. (2005) reveal in an experimental study that early contracts tend to be initiated by informed agents, who tender limit orders. The authors hence conclude that information aggregation is path dependent, called *the fundamental coordination principle of information transfer in competitive markets*.

[48] According to Romer (1993), this information-revelation process of trading might provide a rational explanation of dynamics during the stock market crash in October 1987 that occurred even without fundamental news.

Another shortcoming of the Glosten and Milgrom (1985) approach is the fact that trading volume is limited to one unit. Nowadays, it is broadly accepted that information content of order flow increases with deal size. Allowing for varying order sizes would help the market maker in identifying the counterpart as being informed or uninformed. This could improve the information aggregation process in this environment.[49] The non-strategic behaviour of informed traders in this model was already criticised above.

Lastly, as mentioned by Lyons (2001), the sequential-trade model, too, does not account for dealers' risk aversion and thus cannot take inventory and risk-management considerations into account. The consequence arising from this, namely an upward-biased signal-to-noise-ratio of the model due to absence of liquidity-driven trading of informed agents, was already mentioned in section 1.5.1. Nevertheless, this problem might be resolved quite easily by introducing an additional probability for informed traders who are trading for informational reasons instead of liquidity purposes, hedging or inventory reasons. Doing so would necessitate to reconsider *q*, because in this case it could no longer be interpreted as the fraction of dealers being informed. However, it becomes clear that expanding the model this way necessitates further assumptions, which improve the theoretic environment only slightly in order to be more realistic, but cause a significant gain in complexity.

1.5.3 The simultaneous-trade model

Up to here, all previous models assume a single market maker to set prices and execute transactions. Obviously, this feature does not describe foreign exchange markets very realistically. The simultaneous-trade model, considering a multiple market maker environment, thus seems to provide a superior theoretic framework. Because of the existence of many market makers, inter-dealer trading gets into the focus of the approach. Even more, because trades happen simultaneously, market makers bear risk of potential inventory shocks, since they cannot condition their own trades on other dealers' trans-

[49] However, Huang and Stoll (1997) argue that traders have an incentive to split up their informed orders into a number of standardised transactions in order to camouflage its information content.

actions. Additionally, market makers are now assumed to be risk averse, not risk-neutral as they are in Glosten and Milgrom (1985) and Kyle (1985). Hence, hot potato trading, playing an important role in foreign exchange markets as explained in section 1.1, becomes a crucial part of the model. By that, it is possible to show that interaction between private information and dealers' risk-aversion actually lowers the signal-to-noise ratio of order flow and thus reduces the information revealed by price. In addition, dealer inventories, too, become potential sources of private information, not only customer order flow.

These features indeed make simultaneous trade models very interesting to study. However, as Lyons (2001) already pointed out, there are still not many approaches yet that are really able to capture FX market's special features in a multiple-dealer environment, even though there has been much work on multiple-dealer theory up to now, e.g. Ho and Stoll (1983), Biais (1993), Leach and Madhavan (1993), Perraudin and Vitale (1996), Vogler (1997), Hau (1998), and Viswanathan and Wang (1998), among others. As a consequence of this and in contrast to the previous two kinds of models mentioned here, there is no specific workhorse in the field of simultaneous-trade modelling. Thus, the following explanations draw heavily on the model introduced in Lyons (1997).

As in previous approaches, modelling simultaneous trading among multiple dealers requires game theory. Specifically, the following model is a two-period simultaneous-move game with N dealers[50] and one risky asset that has a terminal payoff, V, at the end of period two (when the game ends). V is distributed normally with mean zero and variance σ_V^2. Every market maker observes customer order flow that originates from an equally-sized customer base for any single dealer. The entire group of customers over all dealers is large and consists of competitive counterparts like central banks, corporate treasurers, fund managers, speculators, etc., who are said to be risk-averse and non-strategic.

The game starts at the beginning of period one with the arrival of a publicly observed macro announcement, y, and a private signal for each dealer (indexed by i), denoted w_i. This private signal should not be misinterpreted as in-

[50] The term *dealer* is tantamount to *market maker*.

formation arising dealer i from customer order flow. Rather it is knowledge about customers' trading habits, i.e. cognition about customers' sensitivities in trading activity to specific news. Both signals y and w_i are assumed to be normally distributed with mean V and variance σ_y^2 and $\sigma_{w_i}^2$, respectively, but are independent of each other.

Customer order flow, X_i, appears after all dealers quoted a price, S_{i1}, in period one. X_i, too, is independent of y and w_i. Since no other dealer can observe customer order flow of any other market maker, X_i is private information to i. It is assumed to be normally distributed with mean zero and variance σ_X^2.

After dealer i has received and executed all orders from his customers at price S_{i1}, the market maker offsets his inventory position via the interdealer market, resulting in T_{i1} that denotes dealer i's net outgoing orders to other dealers in period one. Before proceeding, it seems to be helpful to note some important further aspects.

Quoting S_{i1} happens simultaneously and independently among all dealers. Every market maker is forced to quote a price. S_{i1} is a single price, not a bid-ask spread. This is a potential point to criticise. However, as Lyons (2001) stresses, adding spreads to the model's customer trading component is quite easy, but introducing spreads to interdealer trading makes the model significantly more complex, since price dispersion becomes possible despite of the no-arbitrage condition. Spreads are thus omitted here. It is more important to note that S_{i1} holds good for any amount and any customer and any dealer. All quotes are available to all dealers, so search costs for dealers are assumed to be zero. In addition, rational quotes have to be identical across dealers to avoid arbitrage opportunities. Like quoting, trading is simultaneously and independently, too. A feature worth mentioning with respect to trading is that dealer i does not trade only with one customer and one dealer. X_{i1} is the net of the entire customer order flow and T_{i1} is the sum of outgoing order flow of dealer i that is feasibly traded with more than one other dealer, even though every dealer quotes the same price.

Finding T_{i1} is of particular interest. Remember, every dealer is assumed to be risk-averse and thus has a desired inventory position, I_{i1}^*, in the risky asset.

As mentioned above, many empirical investigations treat I_{i1}^{*} to be zero. Whenever market makers are assumed to be risk-averse, this is realistic and often confirmed in interviews with foreign exchange dealers. However, the model does not necessarily treat I_{i1}^{*} to be zero and thus can capture speculative trading of market makers, as it is going to be described below. To find T_{i1}, the market maker has to have an expectation concerning incoming interdealer order flow, T'_{i1}, which will simultaneously arrive while he submits T_{i1} to other dealers. The market maker's expectation on T'_{i1} is conditional on the data set available to him while submitting T_{i1}. Let $\Omega_{T_{i1}}$ denote this data set, this is formally

$$T_{i1} = I_{i1}^{*} + X_i + E[T'_{i1} \mid \Omega_{T_{i1}}]. \tag{1.10}$$

Obviously, a dealer has to repurchase (resale) the risky asset when customer trading dropped (raised) his actual inventory below (above) desired inventory. Finding T_{i1}, however, is complicated by the fact that T'_{i1} is uncertain. After all orders are transacted, all dealers observe net market wide interdealer order flow, denoted Z. For Z, one can write[51]

$$Z \equiv \sum_{i=1}^{N} T_{i1}. \tag{1.11}$$

With the arrival of Z, period one ends.

In period two, there is no new signal, neither public nor private, and no customer order flow happens for any of the market makers. Period two thus is entirely about interdealer trading, specifically, hot potato trading. Whenever dealer i guessed incoming interdealer order flow during period one wrong, he does not hold his desired inventory. The market maker then has suffered an inventory shock. Because dealers are assumed to be risk-averse in this

[51] According to Lyons (2001, p. 99), specifying X without stochastic noise maximises the transparency difference between customer trading and interdealer trading. In reality, interdealer trading is indeed more transparent than customer trading, but it is still not complete. The effects of changing transparency are analysed, among others, in Lyons (1996).

setting, they have an incentive to trade once more via the interdealer market in period two.

The second period starts with dealers' quotes. The quoted price of dealer i, S_{i2}, again holds good for any amount and any dealer approaching this market maker.[52] In the second round of quoting, there is one aspect of pricing particularly worth considering in greater detail. As argued above, because of the no-arbitrage argument, quoted prices are identical across all dealers. Hence, prices can only reveal public information, because if private information are used to determine price, quotes of different dealers would have to differ, too. S_{i1} thus can only be based on y, because y is the only common information available when quoting happens in period one. S_{i2}, in contrast, is determined by two pieces of public information, y and Z. Z is correlated with X_i and w_i and is thus a means to aggregate private information in the market place. But Z does not, by assumption, convey all information about the X_i's and the w_i's. In addition, even though customer order flow is a source of private information for dealers, it is assumed to be a noisy signal and hence, neither X_i nor Z reveal the true value of V to any single dealer. Because of that, dealers are not as well informed as informed traders are in Kyle (1985) and Glosten and Milgrom (1985). This is of particular importance for information efficiency of price here, because with an exact knowledge of V, no interdealer trading would happen, since all market makers knew the terminal payoff's value just after customer trading. Since dealers are assumed to be rational speculators in this setting, no market maker holding a long (short) inventory position in the risky asset after customer trading would be willing to get his inventory back to zero, if he knew that V is higher (less) that S_{i1}.

After the quoting procedure, interdealer trading starts once more. It is, again, simultaneously and independently among market makers. Dealer i will submit outgoing orders with an amount of T_{i2} to other dealers, aiming to get his inventory position to the desired level I_{i2}^*. T_{i2} is hence determined by

[52] Detailed information on equilibrium quoting strategies can be found in Lyons (2001, p. 100 et sqq.).

$$T_{i2} = I^*_{i2} + E[T'_{i2} \mid \Omega_{T_{i2}}] - I^*_{i1} + T'_{i1} - E[T'_{i1} \mid \Omega_{T_{i1}}], \tag{1.12}$$

where $T'_{i1} - E[T'_{i1} \mid \Omega_{T_{i1}}]$ is the inventory shock, dealer *i* suffered in period one. The dealer hence chooses his outgoing volume in order to offset the inventory shock he suffered in period one and expected interdealer inflow during period two. In addition, T_{i2} has to set off the change in *i*'s desired inventory between period one and period two, namely $I^*_{i2} - I^*_{i1}$, both of which are exogenous in the model. By this, the model becomes capable of speculation-driven changes in desired inventory.[53] Obviously, it is again uncertain that dealer *i* actually realises his desired inventory, since expectation errors are possible. Uncertainty concerning interdealer order flow thus causes risk sharing among market makers to be incomplete.[54] To ensure an equilibrium in this setting, dealers are, as stated earlier, not only assumed to be risk-averse, but to be rational speculators, too. Hence, dealers are not always seeking to hold a net zero inventory position.

Analysing the simultaneous-trade model with respect to outgoing order sizes of market makers provides some important results. One of them is the fact that order flow initiated by dealer *i* is insofar informative as it originates from his own customer order flow, X_i. Information in customer order flow, in turn, is not considered unless it is reflected in interdealer transactions. Consequently, the information aggregation process in simultaneous-trade models consists of two stages. But even though interdealer trading is the crucial part of the model's two types of trading, it is responsible for lower information efficiency of price due to a shrinking signal-to-noise ratio compared to the Kyle (1985) model and the Glosten and Milgrom (1985) model.

To clarify, consider *i*'s desired inventory position in period one is zero and expected incoming interdealer order flow is zero as well. Hence, T_{i1} has to offset X_i entirely to bring the dealer's inventory position back to the desired level. As X_i conveys information about customers' expectations concerning the risky

[53] Dealer's speculative motives are not modelled, so changes in desired inventory are exogenous.

[54] As a consequence of this, inventory models, such as the approach introduced by Madhavan and Smidt (1991) that is going to be estimated in chapter 3 of the work at hand, should provide useful insights.

asset's terminal payoff, T_{i1} is fully informative in this case. However, as soon as expected incoming interdealer order flow or market-wide desired inventory is not zero, the signal-to-noise ratio of T_{i1} (and hence Z) is reduced.[55] This is, at least in the former of these two alternatives, due to the fact that interdealer trading then becomes subject to expectation driven trading, which, in turn, in exposed to information conveyed in $\Omega_{T_{i1}}$. This is particularly worrying, since it is the interdealer market that is widely seen to be the place where prices are actually determined in FX markets.

During hot potato trading in period two, there, too, is information driven trading, since dealers are not only assumed to be information intermediaries, but are rational speculators as well. Hence, any private information not reflected in S_2 will trigger speculative trading in period two. Indeed, information driven speculative trading *could* enhance information aggregation in period two, but does actually not, since the net of interdealer flow remains omitted, as there is no third round of quoting in the game. The game ends with the revelation of the terminal payoff V that becomes common knowledge immediately.

As stated earlier, desired inventory does not has to be stable between period one and period two. This is because of market makers' role as rational speculators. Private information not reflected in S_2 will trigger speculative trading in period two, but does not lead to further information aggregation due to the structure of the game. Instead of a further revelation of interdealer order flow and a third round of quoting, V is paid and speculators profit (or suffer) from the difference between S_2 and V.

Before discussing advantages and potential shortcomings of the simultaneous-trade model, it seems to be helpful to comprehend the findings up to here briefly. As it is shown, (i) customer order flow is a source of private information for market makers, but it does not fully reveal the true value of the risky asset's terminal payoff to them. (ii) During interdealer trading, private information are aggregated in the market place, but only insofar as interdealer trading is originated in customer order flow. (iii) Since market makers are assumed to

[55] The assumption of risk-averse market makers usually prevents I^*_{i1} from being unequal to zero.

be risk-averse, customer trading is not the only driving force of interdealer flow, resulting in a lower information revelation through trading. In addition, (iv) because market makers are also rational speculators, any private information not reflected in price is a source of speculation during period two trading.[56] (v) Information revealed by interdealer order flow during the second period does not contribute to higher information efficiency of price, since there is no further quoting until the game ends.

There is another interesting feature in this setting worth mentioning. As commonly known, risk-aversion means that an agent is indeed willing to take increasing risk, but only if expected profits increase as well. In addition, dealers are assumed to be rational speculators here. So far, risk-aversion was usually interpreted as being the rationale for a desired net-zero inventory position and hence, I_{i1}^{*} was usually seen to be zero, as mentioned above. In fact, strategic dealers, though risk-averse, might have an incentive to choose I_{i1}^{*} different to zero and hence alter T_{i1} compared to the volume proposed by the "old" interpretation of risk-aversion. By this, dealers are able to camouflage their private information until pricing is done in period two and can maximise their potential profit from their information advantage via T_{i2}. As a consequence of this, information revelation by price is further shrinking. Being a rational speculator hence distorts market makers' function of being an information intermediary. This effect is further accelerated by dealers' strategic behaviour, since they know that their interdealer flow reveals information and hence have an incentive to camouflage their private information in order to profit from it during the second period or when V is paid at the end of the game.

Obviously, the simultaneous-trade model provides a superior perspective on foreign exchange markets compared to the two approaches mentioned previously. As it shows, hot potato trading is a rational feature of trading, arising from the existence of multiple risk-averse and strategic market makers. Hot potato trading, despite of its importance for risk-sharing among market participants, as well as strategic behaviour of market makers, actually distort information aggregation through trading. As pointed out by Lyons (2001), strategic

[56] The effects of strategic market makers with asymmetric information are investigated in Calcagno and Lovo (2006).

behaviour and hot potato trading in fact enable us to explain, why prices do not adjust immediately.

The model can be criticised for its relatively short view of only two periods with two times of quoting and only one revelation of information of net interdealer flow, Z. Because of that, Evans and Lyons (2000) extend this approach by considering interday trading. Additionally, Lyons (2001) criticises three further issues. First, as mentioned above, there is no spread, but the model would definitely gain complexity, if bid and ask prices were added, because the no-arbitrage argument was no longer valid to rule out price dispersion. Second, aggregation of private information only happens via Z, but dealers are likely to communicate information via quoted spreads, too. Possibility of learning via prices is ruled out in the model because of the no-arbitrage argument. Last, simultaneous trading is closely linked to brokered trading, but the model is not capable of explaining how dealers choose specific trading mechanisms. This is particularly important, because direct interdealer trading is much less transparent than brokered interdealer trading is.[57]

1.6 Recent theoretical developments

In recent years, theoretical and empirical literature on microstructure finance advanced significantly. Theoretical models today have expanded their view from a pure analysis of market makers' pricing behaviour to explicit investigations of bargaining power, the evolution of volatility, and micro-level learning, among other issues. In doing so, a number of studies is directly linked to earlier works that have become standard to the literature up to now. Interesting contributions to the literature on Bayesian models are those of Dunne (2000) and Owens (2005), for example. Dunne (2000) enhances the Madhavan and Smidt (1991) model by allowing for interdependencies among trading periods, which were assumed to be independent of each other before. Owens (2005), in contrast, modifies the approach introduced by Easley and O'Hara (1992) by considering variations in expected adverse selection costs under random arrival and assimilation of information.

[57] For further theoretical and empirical insights on trading mechanisms see, among others, Werner (1997), and Bjønnes and Rime (2000), respectively.

Further improvements in research of dealers' price setting behaviour and expectation revisions are achieved by, for instance, Bauwens and Giot (2000). They introduce a logarithmic version of Engle and Russel's (1998) autoregressive conditional duration (ACD) model to achieve greater flexibility in investigating how bid-ask spreads, volume and trading intensity contribute to dealers' revisions of beliefs.

As mentioned above, microstructure theory expanded its view in recent years and does now cover a broad set of fields of application. Theory on bargaining and market power, for example, benefits significantly from works by Duffie et al. (2004) and Green et al. (2007). These studies provide theoretical (and empirical) background on how bargaining power and costs for comparison shopping affect pricing and market makers' markups when they are trading with heterogeneously informed customers. Since the foreign exchange market structure is relatively opaque and information asymmetries are hence very likely to exist, it is in all likelihood that market power actually affects transaction prices.

Improvements in understanding driving factors of volatility were made by the work of Renault and Werker (2006), among others. As they show for stock prices, there are instantaneous causality effects between the time elapsing between two quotes and price volatility. Up to this work, it was not possible to identify such causality effects seperately from Granger causal relationships. In addition, they find that these time-effects on volatility are the stronger the less liquid is the specific underlying.

Empirical literature mainly benefited from increasing availability of tick-by-tick data sets, covering various financial markets. Despite of the theoretic advances mentioned above, standard microstructure models like those of Madhavan and Smidt (1991) and Huang and Stoll (1997) have not become less important to empiricists. A number of recent studies like Osler et al. (2006), among others, use these standard models to reassess earlier empirical findings as presented in Lyons (1995), for example. Interestingly, more recent works' conclusions are often in contrast to results shown in earlier studies, specifically with respect to the prominence of inventory considerations and hedging against asymmetric information. These findings partly have strong implications for the understanding of the functionality of financial markets, as it is going to be shown in subsequent chapters.

The work at hand starts its empirical investigation by analysing two standard models in microstructure finance, namely the Madhavan and Smidt (1991) model and the Huang and Stoll (1997) model, in order to get a deeper understanding of how dealers actually quote prices. In later chapters, more recent models like the approach introduced by Green et al. (2007) are analysed to answer the question whether or not this pricing behavhiour is due to market power considerations. To do so, two data sets, each of them covering an entire trading year at an average-sized German bank, are analysed. Before starting with the emprical investigation in chapter 3, chapter 2 introduces these data sets in greater detail.

Appendix to chapter 1

A.1.1 Information revelation by price within the Kyle (1985) model

Equation (1.3) in the text defines price to be

$$S = \lambda (X^I + X^U). \qquad \text{(A.1.1)}$$

Given information about λ shown in equation (1.4), this can be re-written as

$$S = 0.5\left(\sigma_V^2 / \sigma_U^2\right)^{0.5}\left(X^I + X^U\right). \qquad \text{(A.1.2)}$$

Equation (1.5) in the text defines $X^I = \beta V$, so by taking equation (1.6) into consideration, one can write

$$S = 0.5\left(\frac{\sigma_V^2}{\sigma_U^2}\right)^{0.5}\left[\left(\frac{\sigma_U^2}{\sigma_V^2}\right)^{0.5} V + X^U\right]. \qquad \text{(A.1.3)}$$

Expanding the bracket then yields

$$S = 0.5\left(\frac{\sigma_V^2}{\sigma_U^2}\right)^{0.5}\left(\frac{\sigma_U^2}{\sigma_V^2}\right)^{0.5} V + 0.5\left(\frac{\sigma_V^2}{\sigma_U^2}\right)X^U$$

$$S = 0.5V + 0.5\left(\frac{\sigma_V^2}{\sigma_U^2}\right)X^U$$

$$S = 0.5V + \lambda X^U. \qquad \text{(A.1.4)}$$

As shown in equation (A.1.4), S conveys exactly half of the terminal payoff's value. As the informed trader is the only one who knows V, this indicates that half of her private information is revealed in price.[58]

[58] An alternative way to show this result is provided in Lyons (2001, p. 83).

A.1.2 Profits and losses for market makers within the Glosten and Milgrom (1985) model – an example

As mentioned in the text, the dealer's bid price is five units of money, say euro, and his ask price is seven euro. 25 percent of customers are informed and hence, 75 percent are not. Let V be V^L and hence equal two euro.

Under these conditions, all of informed customers will sell the asset. Additionally, half of uninformed traders will sell as well. Whenever the market maker sells at his bid, he will suffer a loss of three euro, since he purchases an asset for five euro that is actually worth two euro. Hence, the market maker suffers overall losses of

$$\text{Loss} = 0.25 \cdot 3 + 0.75 \cdot 0.5 \cdot 3 = 1.875 \text{ euro.} \quad \text{(A.2.1)}$$

In contrast, half of uninformed traders buy the asset from the market maker, resulting in a profit of five euro per transaction for the dealer. Thus, the market maker's profit is given by

$$\text{Profit} = 0.75 \cdot 0.5 \cdot 3 = 1.875 \text{ euro.} \quad \text{(A.2.2)}$$

Hence, it is shown that the market maker will earn zero profits, as it is proposed by the model.

2. Data

The data set analysed in this study consists of all EUR / USD spot transactions of a German bank from October 1st, 2002, until September 30th, 2003, as well as from October 1st, 2004, until September 30th, 2005. Sub-periods differ substantially in terms of trading activity with the second being much more active than the first. However, results are qualitatively similar for both data sets.

The market maker investigated here works for an average-sized bank in Germany, whereas "average-sized" is with respect to FX trading volume. Nevertheless, as mentioned in Osler et al. (2006), relative size of a dealer should not play a significant role in foreign exchange, because the market is extremely competitive. In such an environment, any single successful dealer should be an appropriate representative of the entirety of successful dealers. Hence, the fact that the bank is of medium size among market participants, but rather small compared to dealers investigated in some other studies like Lyons (1995), Yao (1998), and Evans and Lyons (2005c) is unlikely to be much of a shortcoming here. Furthermore, Cheung and Chinn (2001) find market convention to be the predominant driving force of currency spreads. Thus, dealers should show quite similar patterns in their behaviour, regardless of their actual market share in FX trading. Lastly, the findings that are to be presented here are in line with those of Osler et al. (2006), at least with respect to spread variations across different types of transactions. As they mention, the patterns they identify are confirmed by market participants they have spoken to. The head of FX trading at the bank analysed here confirms the following findings, too. Thus, the data set investigated herein is appropriate to provide important insights into foreign exchange trading as a whole.

Each trade record contains the following information:

1. currency pair (which is EUR / USD for all transactions),
2. date and exact time stamp of the trade,
3. direction of the transaction (buy or sell),

4. transaction price,

5. market price from the interdealer market (taken from Reuters),

6. deal size,

7. customer code,

8. initiator of the trade.

As mentioned in Lyons (1995), and Bjønnes and Rime (2003), using actual transaction prices is superior to analysing indicative quotes, as done in earlier studies like Goodhart and Figliuoli (1991), Bollerslev and Domowitz (1993), and Bessembinder (1994). This is because transaction prices describe market conditions and trading activity more precisely, since indicative quotes are not actually transactable prices and thus show larger spreads and different behaviour under varying market conditions over time.

In addition to transaction prices, the data set conveys interdealer market prices, which were recorded simultaneously when orders were executed. This reference quote is a mid price calculated from the respective bid and ask prices provided by Reuters. The bids and asks themselve, however, are not explicitly recorded. Calculating the spread between transaction price and interdealer mid-quotes enables the bank's risk controlling department to monitor a dealer's performance more precisely. In the context of this study, it provides a proximate variable for the respective bid-ask spread of a transaction. Doing so assumes that the market maker's quoted mid-price is equal to the interdealer market mid-quote. This, of course, is a simplification, so the analysis of those "directly observed" spreads is only one of three approaches to investigate dealer behaviour in chapter 3.

The data used herein consists of spot transactions only. The minor fraction of outright-forward trades is skipped from the data set, since there are no real-time records of international interest differentials to calculate forwad premia. In addition, swap-trades are removed from the data set, because they have no order flow consequences. If a market maker agrees in an FX swap, he, for example, purchases USD now (so-called *spot-forward swap*) or in some days time (so-called *forward-forward swap*) and contemporaneously, he agrees to sell this amount of USD in some months time. Order flow of FX swaps hence is zero. All remaining orders within the data set were traded either via direct or brokered trading, while brokered trading was done via Electronic Broking Services (EBS), which is the predominant brokerage system in EUR / USD interdealer trading.

Compared to similar transaction records used in the literature up to now, the data set at hand bears some advantageous properties to subsequent analyses. In contrast to Lyons (1995), who is focussing on interdealer trading only, each counterpart here has an unique customer code that enables one to investigate a dealer's behaviour when he is approached by different types of customers. Hence, the data is comparable in preciseness to Carpenter and Wang (2003), and Osler et al. (2006). The customer code is even more accurate than the one used in Bjønnes and Rime (2003). While they are only able to distinguish between customer trading and interbank trading, data at hand identifies several types of counterparts like banks, corporate clients, internal customers, and mutual- or hedge funds. As done in Osler et al. (2006), counterparts are aggregated to commercial customers, i.e. corporate clients, financial customers, i.e. mutual- and hedge funds, and banks. Internal customers remain a separate group for several reasons. On the one hand, a bank's internal trading guidelines might bar its traders from making considerable profits with internal counterparts, resulting in a preferential treatment of internal customers. On the other hand, internal departments might be expected to transact their needs for foreign exchange with the bank's own FX traders. If this was the case, the market maker could exploit a superior bargaining position vis-à-vis internal customers to quote less favourable prices to these counterparts, even though they are in fact financial customers.

In addition to treatment of internal counterparts, there is another difference in aggregating customers compared to Osler et al. (2006) worth mentioning. Since there are only a few transactions with mutual- and hedge funds in the data, interbank transactions are added to the group of financial customers. At a first glance, this seems problematic, since Sager and Taylor (2005) argue that the logic of information aggregation implies that customer-, i.e. end-user order flow, is consistently more important to exchange rate determination than interdealer flow.[59] However, as argued by the simultaneous-trade model, banks do not only trade for liquidity reasons, but are speculators as well. Because of that, they exploit private information that originated from their own end-user order flow in interbank trading, too. Additionally, banks conduct their own FX research. Since research-quality differs across market makers, some of them might have superior forecasting ability compared to their competitors. Hence, adding banks to the group of financial customers is appropriate in this case.

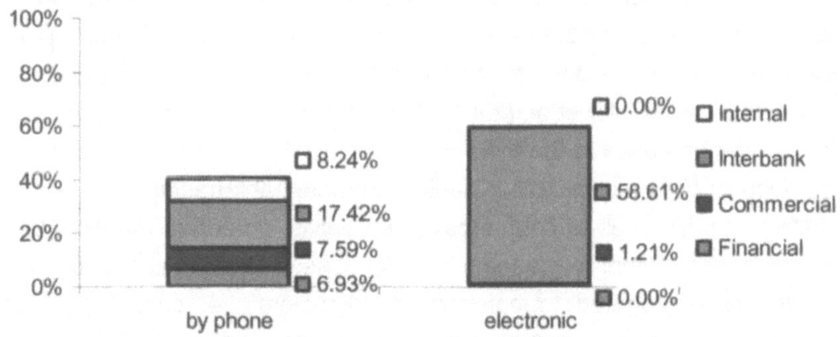

Figure 2.1
Distribution of transactions (by trading volume) via phone and EBS across different counterparts at an average-sized German bank between October 1, 2002, and September 30, 2003.

Figures 2.1 and 2.2 provide information on trading activity (by trading volume) across different trading systems (telephone and EBS) and various types of counterparts. In 2002 / 2003, the market maker's trading activity was dominated by EBS transactions, which accounted for a total of 59.82 percent of the entire trading volume. Within EBS trading, interbank transactions were by far the most voluminous group. Actually, interbank trading made the bulk of the dealer's trading activity, accounting for more than 76 percent of entire trading volume (incoming and outgoing flows). Mutual- and hedge funds accounted for 6.93 percent of total volume, which were entirely traded by phone. The share of commercial customer trading was 8.8 percent, 86.25 percent of

[59] Empirical evidence on that can be found in Lyons (1995), Ito et al. (1998), and Bjønnes and Rime (2001).

which were transacted by phone (corresponding to 7.59 percent of total volume). Internal customers, who accounted for 8.24 percent of overall volume, transacted every single euro by phone and none via EBS.

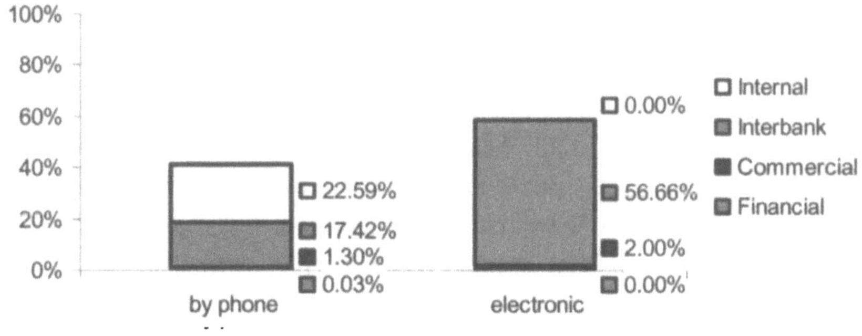

Figure 2.2
Distribution of transactions (by trading volume) via phone and EBS across different counterparts at an average-sized German bank between October 1, 2004, and September 30, 2005.

In 2004 / 2005, trading structure remained almost unchanged compared to 2002 / 2003. Still, the dealer's trading activity was dominated by interbank transactions via EBS, which accounted for more than every second euro transacted. The share of telephone based interbank trading remained stable compared to 2002 / 2003 at 17.42 percent of total volume. Financial customers' relevance was reduced (measured by trading volume) to only 0.03 percent of total transaction volume. All of these trades were transacted by phone, as it was the case in 2002 / 2003. Commercial customers, too, decreased in trading activity. While 1.3 percent of total trading volume were traded by phone, another 2.0 percent were transacted via EBS, resulting in an overall share of 3.3 percent for commercial customers (compared to 8.8 percent in 2002 / 2003). Internal counterparts, in contrast, gained in importance. In 2004 / 2005 they accounted for a total of 22.59 percent of trading volume, which were entirely traded by phone.

Compared to other studies, the data set at hand covers a much longer trading period. In 2002 / 2003, the sample spans 255 trading days and another 250 trading days are covered by the 2004 / 2005 sub-sample. Other works' data sets, for example the ones used in Yao (1998, 25 trading days), Lyons (1995, 5 trading days), Bjønnes and Rime (2003, 5 trading days), and Osler et al. (2006, 87 trading days), are by far shorter with respect to the time period they cover. The fact that the data set used herein spans two sub-periods is particularly benefitial, since it allows one to analyse possible differences between these two periods.

Unfortunately, the data set suffers a familiar drawback. The dealer who is analysed here trades various currencies against one FX portfolio. For example, he is able to purchase USD against EUR in one transaction and can offset his long position in USD by selling dollars against, e.g. British Pounds Sterling (GBP). Because the dataset at hand conveys only transactions in EUR against USD, the resulting inventory time series does not show common properties like, e.g. strong mean reversion, since these features refer to the bank's overall inventory position. Furthermore, the dealer's spot inventory is also affected by swap transactions as well as exercised currency options. Obviously, these facts result in a biased USD inventory position.[60] However, the head of currency trading confirmed that, in line with common standards, the bank's overnight position aggregated over dealers and currencies is negligible. Furthermore, EUR / USD is by far the most actively traded currency pair at this bank. Thus, as proposed by Lyons (1995) and unless stated otherwise, inventory positions are set equal to zero at the beginning of each trading day whenever inventory calculations are necessary.

For most of the analyses conducted in this work, the focus is on incoming trades only. Following common practice, a transaction is termed *incoming* when it is initiated by the market maker's counterpart, regardless of whether the respective customer is an end-user or a bank. To analyse a dealer's pricing behaviour, it is straightforward to focus on incoming trades only. With the exception of chapter 4.4, where outgoing trades as means for speculative trading are investigated, this will always be the case during the following investigations.

---

[60] Since the dataset at hand focuses on one currency pair only, even portfolio-orientated approaches for calculating FX inventory positions as suggested, among others, by Bjønnes and Rime (2003), are not practical here.

In contrast to incoming orders, outgoing trades are initiated by the market maker himself and may represent his demand for liquidity or an attempt to exploit private information gathered from incoming (customer[61]) order flow. Outgoing trades are one tool for market makers to manage their inventory (the alternative is price-shading). While submitting an order, the market maker is willing to trade at another dealer's price to set off his undesired inventory instead of changing his own price in order to induce further customer order flow (as he would do in price-shading). Unfortunately, the data set is not powerful enough to distinguish between outgoing flow due to liquidity reasons and outgoing orders that are speculation-driven. This problem is of specific relevance in chapter 4.4.

Order flow, as usual, is calculated from the perspective of the deal initiator. Thus, trades get a positive sign if the trade initiator purchases and a negative sign if the initiator sells a specific currency. In this way, there is no difference between incoming and outgoing transactions.

Within the 2002 / 2003 sub-sample, data contains 12,612 transactions, 11,830 of which are incoming. As in Reitz et al. (2007), these 11,830 incoming orders represent intraday transactions only, i.e. the number is adjusted for overnight price changes. Almost 49 percent of all incoming orders were submitted by banks, representing a fraction of 75 percent of total incoming volume. Mutual funds and hedge funds account for barely 1.5 percent of incoming orders, but they gain in importance for the bank due to their large average deal size, resulting in a share of seven percent of incoming flows. Commercial customers (i.e. corporate clients), in contrast, account for 44 percent of all incoming trades. However, because average trading volume of corporate clients is much smaller than volume of financial customers, their share in total incoming volume is only 9.2 percent. Table 2.1 summarises these descriptive statistics for the 2002 / 2003 sub-sample.

[61] "Customer" is put into parentheses here, because in this study banks are treated as customers as well.

Table 2.1: Trading activity and size distribution of incoming orders at an average-sized German bank

255 trading days between October 1, 2002, and September 30, 2003

	Financial Customer	Commercial Customer	Internal Customer	Interbank	All Customers
incoming transactions	189	5,229	639	5,773	11,830
percent	1.6%	44.2%	5.4%	48.8%	100.0%
per trading day	0.7	20.5	2.5	22.6	46.4
turnover (EUR mill.)	841	1,118	1,044	9,049	12,052
mean size (EUR mill.)	4.4	0.2	1.6	1.6	1.02
median (EUR mill.)	0.7	0.04	0.3	1.0	0.5
standard deviation	18.0	1.2	6.5	2.0	3.3
Share (%)					
below € 0.1 million	24.3	79.9	31.5	2.8	38.8
€ 0.1 – 0.5 million	22.8	14.7	28.5	4.7	10.7
€ 0.5 – 1.0 million	16.4	1.8	14.0	3.8	3.7
€ 1.0 - € 20.0 millions	32.3	3.6	24.7	88.7	46.7
€ 20 millions and above	4.2	>0.01	1.3	>0.01	0.02

The dealer analysed in this study is quite similar to the one investigated by Osler et al. (2006) with respect to his customer structure. Interestingly, trading activity differs enormously across single month' during the sample. As shown in figure 2.3, the last quarter of 2002 is very calm with only 40 to 60 incoming orders a month. The market maker's trading activity accelerates in February 2003 and remains on a relatively high level in both number of incoming transactions and trading volume throughout the rest of the sample. If one focuses on the period between February and September 2003, the number of incoming orders per trading day increases to 68. Average trading volume per transaction, however, remains virtually unchanged.

Unfortunately, there is no convincing explanation for low trading activity at the beginning of the 2002 / 2003 sub-sample. Of course, trading volume in December is usually lower than throughout the rest of the year, but figures for October and November are considerably low, too, even when compared to trading activity during the 2004 / 2005 sub-sample.[62] However, since the last quarter of 2002 accounts for only a small fraction of the entire number of transaction, this structural break in trading activity should not be too much of a problem, since robustness-checks based on a sample spanning the period from February to September 2003 show qualitatively comparable results.

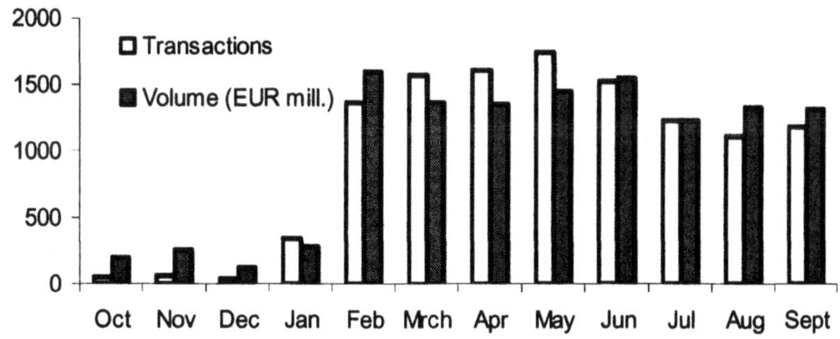

Figure 2.3
Number of incoming transactions (spot) and volume traded at an average-sized German bank between October 1, 2002, and September 30, 2003.

Lastly, figure 2.4 depicts EUR / USD transaction prices between October 2002 and September 2003. Due to the expansionary stance of the Federal Reserve Bank's monetary policy in the aftermath of the New Economy hype during the late 1990's and 9/11 terrorist attacks, the dollar suffered an interest rate disadvantage vis-à-vis the euro. This environment made the euro ascending against the greenback. In addition, ongoing concerns about the U.S. current account deficit provided further arguments for dollar sceptics.

During the second sub-sample at hand, covering trading activity between October 1, 2004, and September 30, 2005, the structure of the bank's customer base did not alter significantly. However, overall trading activity increased enormously. Over the entire sample, the market maker traded 22,596 transactions in EUR / USD, 21,296 of which were incoming and intraday. Despite of this acceleration in trading activity, the structure of the bank's customer base as well as trading properties within the specific groups of counterparts remained qualitatively unchanged compared to the earlier sub-sample. As

[62] See figure 2.5 below.

table 2.2 depicts, average sizes of the customer groups' incoming orders as well as their respective size distributions did not change much over time. Considerable changes happened only to the relative importance of interbank trading, since the share of banks in FX trading increased from 48.8 percent in 2002 / 2003 to more than 55 percent in 2004 / 2005, account of all remaining types of customers. Thus, banks, being the most important group of counterparts in 2002 / 2003, reinforced their leading position even more.

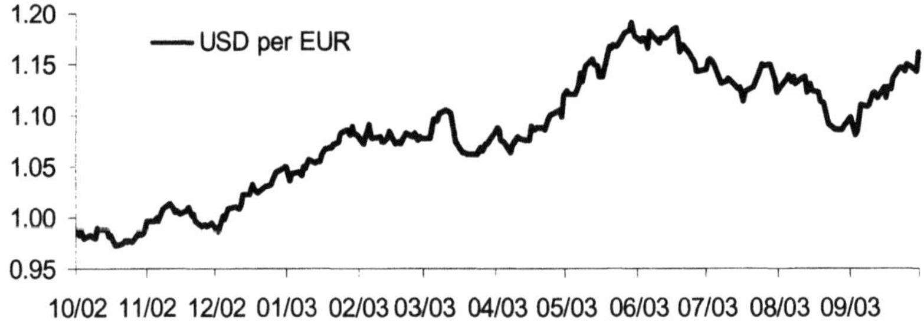

Figure 2.4
U.S. dollars per euro spot exchange rate between October 1, 2002, and September 30, 2003.

Even though size distribution moved towards an increasing importance of transactions between one and 20 millions, absolute turnover with financial customers decreased. With one transaction arriving every second trading day, this group of customers is virtually of no relevance for the bank at hand. This is deplorable, since financial customers are commonly seen as the best informed customer group of all (Osler et al., 2006). This view is supported by the fact that mean size of transactions is largest for financial customers, given that transaction volume is believed to be positively correlated with information content. This might be a first indication that the market maker here is probably gathering relatively weak private information.

As shown in figure 2.5, there was no such calm trading period in 2004 / 2005 as there was in the beginning of the 2002 / 2003 sample. However, number of transactions and trading volume are quite volatile throughout the year. Transaction volume is at its maximum in January 2005, after the euro had approached its interim peak against the U.S. dollar in December 2004 with an exchange rate above $1.36 per euro. With the exception of December and August, when trading volume is small in both of the two sub-samples because of Christmas and holiday-season, there is virtually no pattern in incoming order flow during the year.

Table 2.2: Trading activity and size distribution of incoming orders at an average-sized German bank

250 trading days between October 1, 2004, and September 30, 2005

	Financial Customer	Commercial Customer	Internal Customer	Interbank	All Customers
incoming transactions	131	8,388	885	11,892	21,296
percent	0.6%	39.4%	4.2%	55.8%	100.0
per trading day	0.5	33.6	3.5	47.6	85.2
turnover (EUR mill.)	458	2,057	2,275	17,491	22,281
mean size (EUR mill.)	3.5	0.2	2.6	1.5	1.05
median (EUR mill.)	1.7	0.04	0.6	1.0	1.0
standard deviation	5.8	1.5	5.5	1.6	2.1
Share (%)					
below € 0.1 million	6.1	77.4	23.4	2.6	32.9
€ 0.1 – 0.5 million	12.2	15.0	22.3	4.2	9.3
€ 0.5 – 1.0 million	13.7	1.7	11.3	1.1	1.8
€ 1.0 - € 20.0 millions	66.4	5.9	41.7	92.0	55.8
€ 20 millions and above	1.6	<0.01	1.3	0.1	0.2

As stated before, the euro approached its interim high up to then during the 2004 / 2005 sub-sample. Within this period, structural arguments as well as rather cyclical arguments regarding U.S. interest rate hikes alternated each other. The euro's strength during the fourth quarter of 2004 was said to result from the dollar's weakness that was due to concerns about the U.S. "twin-deficit", leading to general scepticism vis-à-vis the U.S. economy's stability that was even boosted by expensive oil. In 2005, concerns stepped aside and the Fed's interest rate hikes attracted notice of market participants.

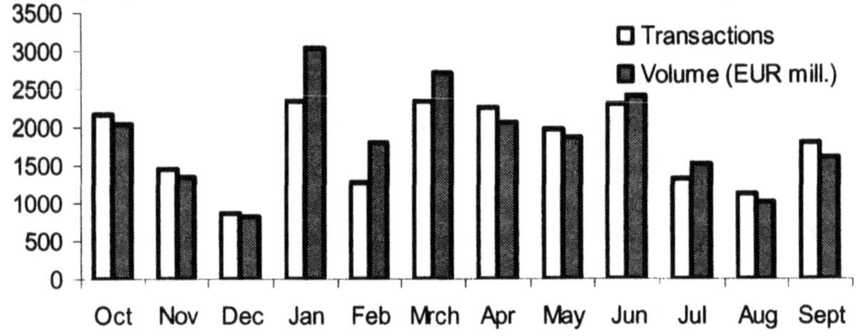

Figure 2.5
Number of incoming transactions (spot) and volume traded at an average-sized German bank between October 1, 2004, and September 30, 2005.

In addition to those rather dollar-optimistic arguments, the euro area hit the news with some negative reports, leading to further euro depreciations. One of the most severe "bad news" for the euro was the rejection of the European constitution and rumours that some countries might opt out of the European single currency. This led to further rising doubts about the euro, resulting in an depreciation that led quotations back below $1.20 within six month.

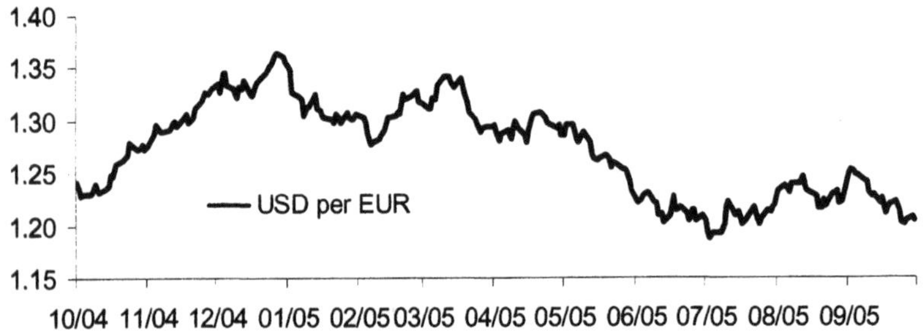

Figure 2.6
U.S. dollars per euro spot exchange rate between October 1, 2004, and September 30, 2005.

3. Dealer behaviour

If, as they do, macro models perform poorly in explaining high-frequent exchange rate dynamics, there is a need to look at foreign exchange markets from a different angle. Given the numerous contributions to the microstructure approach, it seems perspicuous to analyse dealers' behaviour in order to understand price discovery in currency markets. However, a fundamental postulate to come to this view is to recognise and internalise Lyons' (2001) perception that in free-floating exchange rate regimes, the exchange rate is determined exclusively by FX dealers. Thus, it is crucial to understand dealers' pricing behaviour in order to realise exchange rate dynamics.

As stated earlier, bid-ask spreads are important to evaluate a currency dealers' pricing behaviour. Standard microstructure literature suggests that these spreads are mainly driven by three components, namely adverse selection costs, inventory costs,[63] and order processing costs, with adverse selection costs being the predominant one. Theoretical background on this is provided by the above-mentioned contributions by Glosten and Milgrom (1985) and Kyle (1985). Adverse selection costs are said to increase with likelihood that a given counterpart has superior information. In addition, because trade size is often believed to be positively correlated with an order's information content, adverse selection costs are usually assumed to rise with deal size, at least when trading is anonymous (Easley and O'Hara, 1987; Glosten, 1989). However, Sager and Taylor (2006) point out that market makers know their major customers, so they are usually able to infer their counterparts' likelihood of being well informed.

Standard models of market making under asymmetric information thus suggest that spreads should be widest for large trades with financial customers, because adverse selection costs are at their maximum for these kinds of orders. This hypothesis is directly testable by using transaction data as done in this study. The Madhavan and Smidt (1991) model and the Huang and Stoll (1997) model became well-known workhorses for this purpose and are used

---

[63] Formal models of price shading to control inventory were developed by Amihud and Mendelson (1980), Zabel (1981), Ho and Stoll (1983), and O'Hara and Oldfield (1986).

in various studies up to now.[64] Before starting with empirical investigation in section 3.2, theoretical background on the Madhavan and Smidt (1991) model and the Huang and Stoll (1997) model is introduced in section 3.1. Chapter 3.3 provides an interim conclusion on dealer behaviour.

3.1 Theoretical background

3.1.1 The Madhavan and Smidt (1991) model

The informational environment of the Madhavan and Smidt (1991) model consists of both, public information and private information. While the former does not necessarily induce trading, trading itself provides private information to the respective market maker and may hence cause price changes. The market maker will use both sources of information to update his beliefs concerning the terminal payoff of the traded asset, that is foreign currency here.

Consider an environment with one riskless bond and one risky asset that has a stochastic terminal payoff at the end of the model's horizon, denoted *T*. The terminal payoff can be seen as full information price of the risky asset, denoted $\tilde{\upsilon}$. As mentioned in the description of the simultaneous-trade model in chapter 1.5.3, prices can only reflect public information because of the no-arbitrage argument. This feature is reflected in the Madhavan and Smidt (1991) model by the fact that the authors assume the market maker to observe all trading activities and to adjust his quotes, even though he is not directly involved in a particular transaction. The result of this is that full information price is composed by a series of publicly known increments, d_t, which are realised just after trading took place in period *t*, so that $\tilde{\upsilon} = \sum_{i=0}^{T} \tilde{d}_i$, with $d_0 > 0$ being a commonly known constant. Obviously, in any period $t < T$, the risky asset's interim value υ_t is given by $\upsilon_t = \sum_{i=0}^{t} d_i$. Since d_i is assumed to be distributed normal with mean zero, υ_t is a random variable at *t* before $\tilde{d}_t$ is realised. Without taking transaction costs and private information into ac-

[64] Further theoretical models in the field were developed by Ho and Macris (1984), Roll (1984), Choi et al. (1988), Glosten and Harris (1988), Foster and Vishwanathan (1990a, 1990b), George et al. (1991), and Hasbrouck (1993).

count, the asset's price at t, S_t, equals the asset's value after the last public information was announced, i.e. υ_{t-1}. Because d_t is an innovation, the best forecast for the next period's price given the recent price is the recent price itself. This is one major feature of a price being a martingale.

The Madhavan and Smidt (1991) model explicitly accounts for aforementioned inventory- and adverse selection or, more precisely, information components of asset prices. Thus, every market maker within the multi-dealer framework of the model sets his respective bid price and ask price in accordance to

$$S_t = \mu_t - \gamma(I_t - I^*) + \psi D_t, \tag{3.1}$$

where μ_t is the market maker's conditional expectation of $\tilde{\upsilon}_t$, I_t is his recent inventory level, whereas I^* denotes the dealer's desired inventory, that is usually assumed to be zero due to dealers' risk aversion.[65] Thus, $\gamma(I_t - I^*)$ describes the inventory response effect, measured by $\gamma \geq 0$, indicating the market maker's adjustment of price due to the deviation of recent from desired inventory. Whenever $I_t > I^*$ ($I_t < I^*$), the marker maker will lower (increase) his price to attract buyers (sellers), who bring back his inventory to the desired level. Obviously, this part of the pricing equation implies inventory control via quote shading, not via the interdealer market. Lastly, D_t is an indicator variable for the trade's direction that is +1, if the trade initiator buys, and –1, if the trade initiator sells the asset to the market maker. ψ can be interpreted as compensation for execution costs per unit of the risky asset or as rent elements. Both measures of dealer's price-setting sensitivities, γ and ψ, are assumed to be constant. For reason of completeness one should bear in mind that quoted price is usually said to hold good for any amount, but it is possible to create a quote schedule with different quotations for varying trade sizes, too. For simplicity, we abstract from the latter during subsequent analyses.

---

[65] As shown in Appendix A.3.1.5, assuming I^* to be constant is not crucial to the model. Relaxing this assumption makes the model capable of speculative motives of inventory management. It results in a slight modification of the econometric equation. However, it is useful to understand the basic version of the model first, before one concentrates on this manipulation of the basic Madhavan and Smidt (1991) model.

Unfortunately, equation (3.1) is not directly testable, because one cannot observe μ_t. The evolution of the market maker's expectations thus becomes a crucial part of the approach. To model a dealer's beliefs, Madhavan and Smidt (1991) assume that all market participants observe a noisy public information signal, $\tilde{y}_t$, concerning the true value of the next increment, d_t, just before time t. Remember, υ_t is composed of a series of d_t, and the asset's value during the last period, υ_{t-1}, is public information. Consequently, a signal concerning d_t can be written as

$$\tilde{y}_t = \upsilon_t + \tilde{\varepsilon}_t, \tag{3.2}$$

where $\tilde{\varepsilon}_t$ is a white noise error term. By defining y_t to be the realisation of $\tilde{y}_t$, the dealer's expectation about υ_t prior to t is distributed normal with mean y_t and variance σ_ε^2 that is variance of $\tilde{\varepsilon}_t$ in equation (3.2).

Analogue to the public signal in (3.2), the private signal about υ_t, $\tilde{w}_t$, is noisy, too. It is observed by the dealer at t and is formally given by

$$\tilde{w}_t = \upsilon_t + \tilde{\omega}_t, \tag{3.3}$$

with $\tilde{\omega}_t$ being a white noise disturbance term. Once more, Madhavan and Smidt (1991) define w_t to be the realisation of $\tilde{w}_t$. Since both the public and the private signal are thus drawn from a normal distribution, the posterior mean (m_t) of the market maker's distribution is given by[66]

$$m_t = \theta w_t + (1-\theta) y_t, \tag{3.4}$$

where $\theta = \sigma_\varepsilon^2 / (\sigma_\varepsilon^2 + \sigma_\omega^2)$. The market maker's posterior expectation, m_t, thus is a weighted average of both the private signal and the public signal.

The market maker's source of private information is order flow, so there is a need to model the dealer's counterparts' behaviour. Madhavan and Smidt (1991) assume that order quantity, Q_t, of any counterpart approaching the

[66] See DeGroot (1970, 169), among others, for details. An alternative description based on portfolio theory of this so-called Bayesian updating rule is provided in Appendix A.3.1.1.

market maker is a function of the deviation between the respective counterpart's conditional expectation of $\tilde{\upsilon}_t$, m_t, and the market maker's quoted price, S_t, as well as of the counterpart's liquidity demand, L_t. This is formally

$$Q_t = \alpha(m_t - S_t) - L_t, \tag{3.5}$$

where α denotes customer's sensitivity to a subjective "mispricing" by the market maker. The term is assumed to be a positive constant.

Liquidity trading does not convey any useful private information for the market maker, so L_t can be interpreted as an error term, which is distributed normal with mean zero and constant variance σ_L^2. Potential presence of liquidity trading makes order flow a noisy source of information. However, if not liquidity driven, Q_t conveys information about the counterparts' expectations on the risky asset's true value. Thus, the market maker is able to construct a statistic, denoted $\hat{\upsilon}(Q_t)$, which yields him private information about υ_t, provided that Q_t is observed. This statistic is given by[67]

$$\hat{\upsilon}(Q_t) \equiv \frac{\alpha S_t + Q_t - \alpha(1-\theta)y_t}{\alpha\theta}. \tag{3.6}$$

As shown in Appendix A.3.1.2, there is an alternative representation to the statistic defined by equation (3.6). Since $\hat{\upsilon}(Q_t) \equiv \upsilon_t + \omega_t - (\alpha\theta)^{-1}L_t$ is equivalent to (3.6), it becomes clear that $\hat{\upsilon}(Q_t)$ can be interpreted as realisation of a random variable with mean υ_t and variance $\sigma_\omega^2 + (\sigma_L/\alpha\theta)^2$. Because both the private information signal ($\hat{\upsilon}(Q_t)$) and the public signal (y_t) are normally distributed, the market maker's posterior mean on the asset's fundamental value can now be written as

$$\mu_t = \zeta y_t + (1-\zeta)\hat{\upsilon}(Q_t) \tag{3.7}$$

with $\zeta \equiv \sigma_{\hat{\upsilon}}^2/(\sigma_\varepsilon^2 + \sigma_{\hat{\upsilon}}^2)$, where $\sigma_{\hat{\upsilon}}^2$ denotes variance of $\hat{\upsilon}(Q_t)$, i.e. $\sigma_{\hat{\upsilon}}^2 = \sigma_\omega^2 +$ $(\sigma_L/\alpha\theta)^2$. As shown in Appendix A.3.1.3, substituting equation (3.6) into

[67] See Appendix A.3.1.2 for its deviation.

(3.7) yields an alternative representation for (3.7) that conveys a particularly interesting term for subsequent analysis

$$\mu_t = \pi y_t + (1-\pi)(S_t + \alpha^{-1}Q_t), \qquad (3.8)$$

where $\pi \equiv (\zeta + \theta - 1)/\theta$ is the aforementioned crucial parameter. Because $\zeta \in (0,1)$ and $\theta \in (0,1)$, it is $\pi \in (0,1)$, too.[68] As Madhavan and Smidt (1991, p. 104) outline, π *summarizes a number of aspects of market quality and information.* The higher the volume of liquidity trading, the less precise is information conveyed in private signals, and the higher the accuracy of public information, the higher π is going to be. Because of that, calculating π provides valuable information on the most important market conditions that make market makers behave the way they do.

Taking Madhavan and Smidt's (1991) modelling of market makers' expectation formation concerning the risky asset's fundamental value into account, equation (3.1) can be rendered more precisely. Thus, substituting (3.8) into equation (3.1) yields

$$S_t = \pi y_t + (1-\pi)[S_t + \alpha^{-1}Q_t] - \gamma(I_t - I^*) + \psi D_t. \qquad (3.9)$$

According to equation (3.9), price in *t* depends on a variety of signals. First, there is a public information signal, y_t, representing the market maker's beliefs prior to *t*. Second, the market maker uses a private information signal observed in *t*, Q_t, that is quantity of order flow. Third, the deviation between the market maker's actual and desired inventory is another determinant of S_t, and lastly, the market maker has to cover transaction costs, represented by ψD_t, for which he has to get compensation for.

Because y_t is unobservable, the authors deploy a small artifice. They assume that the market maker's beliefs prior to *t* are equal to his posterior beliefs in period *t-1* minus an error term, denoted η_t, that is due to the unpredictable, but publicly observed increment d_t. Posterior expectation in *t-1* conveys both the public signal (prior to *t-1*) and the private signal at *t-1*, so previous period's price can be written as

[68] See Appendix A.3.1.3 for a demonstration.

$$S_{t-1} = y_t - \gamma(I_{t-1} - I^*) + \psi D_{t-1} - \eta_t \tag{3.10}$$

with $\eta_t \equiv y_t - \mu_{t-1}$. Rearranging (3.10) yields a proxy for the market maker's prior expectation y_t, which is given by

$$y_t = S_{t-1} + \gamma(I_{t-1} - I^*) - \psi D_{t-1} + \eta_t. \tag{3.11}$$

Now, there are explicit representations for every single term within the pricing equation. The last step is to substitute equation (3.11) into (3.09) to get a complete econometric model that is going to be the benchmark for following analyses. Formally, this is[69]

$$\Delta S_t = \kappa + \lambda Q_t - \frac{\gamma}{\pi} I_t + \gamma I_{t-1} + \frac{\psi}{\pi} D_t - \psi D_{t-1} + \eta_t \tag{3.12}$$

with $\Delta S_t \equiv S_t - S_{t-1}$, $\kappa \equiv -\gamma(1 - 1/\pi)I^*$, and $\lambda \equiv (1-\pi)/(\alpha\pi)$. λ represents the information effect, i.e. the exchange rate's response to order size. Alternatively, π provides a measure of information asymmetry, too, but it is not directly observable in the reduced form of the model, which is given by

$$\Delta S_t = \beta_0 + \beta_1 Q_t + \beta_2 I_t + \beta_3 I_{t-1} + \beta_4 D_t + \beta_5 D_{t-1} + \eta_t, \tag{3.13}$$

where β_0, β_1, β_2, β_3, β_4, and β_5 are the coefficients to be estimated and $\eta_t = \tilde{\varepsilon}_t - \zeta\varepsilon_{t-1}$ is a stochastic disturbance term. From equation (3.12) one can infer various coefficient restriction, namely $\beta_0 < 0$, $\beta_1 > 0$, $\beta_2 < 0$, $\beta_3 > 0$, $\beta_4 > 0$, $\beta_5 < 0$, $|\beta_2| < \beta_3$, and $\beta_4 < |\beta_5|$.

If one uses, as will be during the empirical investigation of this model, Hansen's (1982) Generalized Method of Moments (GMM) technique to estimate the respective coefficients, π is not directly observable. However, as highlighted above, this parameter takes a prominent part within the model. Here, an artifice is employed to get an idea about π. By deploying a Wald test, one can infer whether $|\beta_2|$ and β_3 as well as β_4 and $|\beta_5|$ are significantly different from each other, respectively. If they were, this would be an indication that π is significantly different from unity. Whenever this is the

[69] See Appendix A.3.1.4 for the maths.

case, the respective market maker uses his source of private information, i.e. order flow, to form his expectation μ_t, as described by equation (3.8). By calculating $\beta_3/|\beta_2|$ and $|\beta_5|/\beta_4$, one gets a proximate measure for π. The lower this parameter, the more valuable is private information perceived by the market maker, so (1 - π) is the fraction of the agent's expectations that is based on order flow.

3.1.2 The Huang and Stoll (1997) model

One of the main differences between the Madhavan and Smidt (1991) model and the approach of Huang and Stoll (1997) is the latter's conviction that customers are aware of the fact that order flow or, more precisely, order quantity reveals information to the market maker. Hence, in a standard microstructure environment, strategically behaving customers have an incentive to split large orders into a number of smaller, standardised transactions to hamper the market maker in inferring the order's information content via deal size.[70]

In every single one of the model's time periods, quoting happens at the beginning of the respective period *t*. All quotes consist of a bid price and an ask price, so it is easy to calculate a quoted midpoint, denoted M_t. Every quote is observed by all market participants, so M_t is, after quoting was done, common knowledge. Huang and Stoll (1997) assume that quote midpoints consist of the traded asset's true, albeit unobservable, value, V_t, as well as of the market maker's recent inventory. Since they are convinced that dealers have an incentive to camouflage information content of order flow by trading standardised deal sizes, the market maker's inventory is modelled as the sum of trades up to period *t-1*, whereas every single trade is of standard volume one unit. Because of that, D_t is a trade indicator that is +1 in case the trade initiator purchases and –1 whenever the trade initiator sells the asset. Thus, under the aforementioned assumption, D_t can be used to calculate the market maker's inventory position, so M_t is formally given by

[70] Remember, standard microstructure models suggest that spreads increase with probability that the initiating counterpart is well informed.

$$M_t = V_t + \beta \frac{BA}{2} \sum_{i=1}^{t-1} D_i \,, \qquad (3.14)$$

where BA is the constant bid-ask spread and β is the percentage of the half-spread that represents inventory holding costs. Assuming the spread to be constant provides a helpful simplification, because it enables equation (3.14) to hold good for the ask price, the bid price, and the midpoint.

Just before t, V_t is determined. This fundamental value does not, by assumption, include any transaction costs. Recent period's fundamental value is hence assumed to depend on the previous period's fundamental value, V_{t-1}, and an adverse selection component, represented by the previous trade's initiator's trading direction, D_{t-1}. The fundamental value's representation is completed by a public information shock, denoted ε_t, which is assumed to be a white noise error term. Thus, one can write

$$V_t = V_{t-1} + \alpha \frac{BA}{2} D_{t-1} + \varepsilon_t \qquad (3.15)$$

with α being the proportion of the half spread that compensates for adverse selection.

By defining $\Delta M_t \equiv M_t - M_{t-1}$ and $\Delta V_t \equiv V_t - V_{t-1}$, one can write the change of the midpoint between $t-1$ and t as $\Delta M_t = \Delta V_t + \beta(BA/2)D_{t-1}$. So, after equation (3.15) is rearranged to $\Delta V_t = \alpha(BA/2)D_{t-1} + \varepsilon_t$, equation (3.16) shows that M_t changes in accordance to adverse selection costs and inventory costs of the previous trade, that is

$$\Delta M_t = (\alpha + \beta)\frac{BA}{2} D_{t-1} + \varepsilon_t \,. \qquad (3.16)$$

As mentioned above, Huang and Stoll (1997) assume bid-ask spreads to be constant. Thus, they define traded price, S_t, to be

$$S_t = M_t + \frac{BA}{2} D_t + \eta_t \,, \qquad (3.17)$$

where η_t conveys rounding errors as well as deviations between observed half-spread, i.e. $S_t - M_t$, and constant half-spread, $BA/2$.

Taking all these information into consideration, getting to a testable econometric model is straightforward.[71] It is given by

$$\Delta S_t = \frac{BA}{2}(D_t - D_{t-1}) + \lambda \frac{BA}{2} Q_{t-1} + e_t, \tag{3.18}$$

with $\lambda \equiv \alpha + \beta$ and $e_t \equiv \varepsilon_t + \Delta\eta_t$. Obviously, $1-\lambda$ represents the proportion of the half-spread attributable to order processing costs in this model. Unfortunately, it is not possible to calculate parameters for adverse selection costs (α) and inventory holding costs (β) separately in this basic framework. However, Bjønnes and Rime (2003) suggest a slight modification of the model to overcome this shortcoming. They re-write equation (3.14) as

$$M_t = V_t + \beta \frac{BA}{2} I_t \tag{3.19}$$

with $I_t = \sum_{i=1}^{t-1} D_i$. As shown in Appendix A.3.2.2, the testable model can then be written as

$$\Delta S_t = \alpha \frac{BA}{2} D_{t-1} + \beta \frac{BA}{2} \Delta I_t + \frac{BA}{2}(D_t - D_{t-1}) + e_t. \tag{3.20}$$

Because of this slight modification, we will use the term *modified* Huang and Stoll (1997) model henceforth.

3.2 Empirical evidence

All models presented in chapter 3.1 are baseline models to the following analyses, since they do not account for different order sizes or different types of customers as potential driving factors of market makers' pricing behaviour. Thus, those baseline models are seen as benchmarks for respective model variations.

---

[71] See Appendix A.3.2.1 for the maths.

During subsequent analyses, orders are said to be "large" when trading volume exceeds EUR 500,000. All transactions below this quantity are, consequently, "small" orders. When distinguishing by types of counterparts, the group of commercial customers consists of importers and exporters, who are trading foreign exchange to meet their needs from international trading activities in real goods and services. Commercial customers are presumed to be relatively less informed than financial customers, because they have usually no detailed knowledge about current market conditions and competing price quotations of different market makers. This results in a relatively weak bargaining position of commercial customers vis-à-vis a market maker.

In contrast to Osler et al. (2006), financial customers here do not only consist of hedge funds and mutual funds, but of other banks, too. This is because there are only a few "real" financial customer transactions in the dataset. Furthermore, banks themselves conduct FX research and act as speculators, so there are some similarities to fund managers. Nevertheless, interbank trades are more likely to be liquidity-driven than is fund initiated order flow. Consequently, interbank transactions should convey less useful information. This fact becomes quite an important argument when interpreting the overall findings in the concluding chapter of this work. Lastly, as mentioned in chapter 2, the group of internal customers represents further departments at our trader's bank that are involved with foreign exchange like, for example, the bank's FX swap trading desk.

All estimation in chapter 3 is done by using Hansen's (1982) Generalized Method of Moments (GMM) estimator. The advantage of this technique is that it adjusts standard errors for heteroskedasticity and serial correlation of unknown form by using Newey and West (1987) correction of the covariance matrix. The set of instruments always equals the set of regressors here, implying that parameter estimates parallel OLS estimates (Bjønnes and Rime, 2005). A short introduction to GMM estimation is to be found in the Annex of this work.

3.2.1 The Madhavan and Smidt (1991) model

Table 3.1 depicts empirical results on the baseline Madhavan and Smidt (1991) model as well as on spread variations across deal sizes and counterparty types during the 2002 / 2003 sub-sample. It is already the baseline model that describes the dealer's pricing behaviour quite accurately. By using the standard Madhavan and Smidt (1991) model, it is possible to explain 23 percent of volatility in tick-by-tick price changes at the respective dealer within this earlier sub-period. As table 3.2 shows for 2004 / 2005, adjusted R^2 even increases to 29 percent.

The coefficient on the lagged direction indicator provides an estimate of the dealer's average half spread across all kinds of transactions. Compared to other studies by Lyons (1995) (0.92 pips), and Bjønnes and Rime (2005) (2.95 pips), an average half spread of 5.82 pips is relatively large. However, this finding is likely to be due to fixed order processing costs in a dealing environment dominated by small deal sizes.[72] This view is supported by results of the modified models, especially the one that accounts for different order sizes, which will be discussed in greater detail a little later.

An important result of the baseline model, which is supported in both the modified models as well as the 2004 / 2005 sub-period, is the fact that all coefficients on inventory variables are not statistically significant. This finding is in line with other recent studies such as Bjønnes and Rime (2005), and Osler et al. (2006). Lyons (1995), in contrast, actually finds such an influence of inventory-based price shading. One probable explanation for this contradiction between earlier and recent studies might be a more intensive use of electronic brokerage systems nowadays. As Bjønnes and Rime (2005) point out, electronic brokerage systems enable dealer's to offset undesired inventory via the interdealer market instead of shading prices. As highlighted in chapter 2, the dealer at hand uses EBS intensively, not at least to unload undesired inventory. Inventory management via (electronic) outgoing transactions has primarily two advantages to the market maker, namely direct and indirect costs. Interdealer trading via EBS or Reuters Dealing 3000 is less expensive and

[72] Schultz (2001) and Harris and Piwowar (2006) find transaction costs to decrease with deal size for corporate bonds and municipal bonds, respectively.

much faster than price shading. In addition, it reduces dealers' uncertainty about inventories, since the dealer himself is the initiator of respective order flow.

Table 3.1: *Baseline MS model and spread variations across deal sizes and customer types 255 trading days between October 1, 2002 – September 30, 2003 (11,830 obs.)*

	Baseline Model	Size Dummies		Counterparty Dummies	
Constant	0.21 (0.11)*		0.15 (0.11)		0.08 (0.11)
Deal Size Q_{it}	0.34 (0.13)**	Large	0.06 (0.08)	Commercial	0.94 (0.17)***
		Small	20.2 (2.10)***	Financial	0.09 (0.09)
				Internal	0.29 (0.14)**
Inventory I_t	-0.01 (0.07)	Large	-0.03 (0.07)	Commercial	-0.04 (0.07)
		Small	-0,03 (0.07)	Financial	-0.04 (0.07)
				Internal	0.03 (0.09)
Lagged Inventory I_{t-1}	0.001 (0.07)	Large	0.04 (0.07)	Commercial	0.03 (0.07)
		Small	0.02 (0.07)	Financial	0.05 (0.07)
				Internal	-0.16 (0.12)
Direction D_t	6.48 (0.2)***	Large	2.13 (0.21)***	Commercial	9.47 (0.19)***
		Small	11.5 (0.26)***	Financial	2.04 (0.21)***
				Internal	14.8 (1.08)***
Lagged Direction D_{t-1}	-5.82 (0.2)***	Large	-1.17 (0.15)***	Commercial	-9.84 (0.20)***
		Small	-10.3 (0.26)***	Financial	-0.94 (0.15)***
				Internal	-14.3 (1.50)***
Adjusted R^2	0.23		0.33		0.34

Notes: Dependent variable is change of currency price measured in pips between two incoming orders. Standard errors in parentheses. Baseline model is given by equation (3.13). Estimation method is GMM with Newey-West (1987) correction. Set of instruments equals set of regressors, implying that parameter estimates parallel OLS estimates (Bjønnes and Rime, 2005). * (**, ***) denotes significance at the 10% (5%, 1%) level.

In addition to inventory management via interdealer trades instead of quote shading, Madhavan and Smidt (1991) point out that weak inventory effects might also be due to speculative motives in market maker's inventory management. If this was the case, desired inventory would no longer be constant, but becomes a function of the asset's expected fundamental value and recent price. How this could affect the model is explained in Appendix A.3.1.5.

In contrast to coefficients on inventories, deal size has significant explanatory power for the dealer's price changes, indicating that order flow indeed does convey information. Results imply that there is a potential incentive for market makers to expand spreads to hedge themselves against asymmetric information. However, subsequent paragraphs will argue that there is indeed an asymmetric information component in spreads, but it seems to be superposed by further channels, which influence dealers' pricing behaviour.

At last, parameter π gets into focus of the analysis. Even though this calculation can potentially be done via both pairs of parameters β_2 and β_3 as well as β_4 and β_5, we concentrate on ratio $|\beta_5|/\beta_4$, since β_2 and β_3 are not statistically significant. First of all, a Wald test conducted to the baseline model indicates that $|\beta_5| \neq \beta_4$, implying π is significantly different from unity and hence, dealers seem to be aware of potential information asymmetries. Thus, the market maker adjusts his expectation about the currency's fundamental value to a proportion of 89.8 percent in accordance to public information, while only 10.2 percent of the adjustment are, on average, due to order flow information.

Even though the baseline model offers valuable results, analysing modified models that account for deal sizes and different types of counterparts provides further useful insights. Within the 2002 / 2003 sub-sample, adjusted R^2's increase to 0.33 and 0.34, respectively. In 2004 / 2005, modified models actually are able to explain 46 percent (deal size) and 45 percent (counterparts) of transacted intraday exchange rate changes' volatility.[73]

Absolute values of coefficients on lagged trade direction indicators provide a direct measure of half spreads here. Hence, as shown in table 3.1 and in line with findings in Osler et al. (2006), presumably well informed order flow, identified by deal size or customer type, obtains lower bid-ask spreads. While half spread for small incoming orders is 10.3 pips, large orders are quoted only 1.17 pips. All spread estimates are highly statistically significant. This finding holds good for customer type-based estimates, too. Financial customers, being the presumably best informed group of counterparts, get tightest half

[73] See table 3.2 for details.

spreads (0.94 pips). Commercial customers are quoted an average half spread of 9.84 pips. However, internal customers suffer an even wider half spread (14.3 pips). Although the baseline model's half spread estimate seems relatively large, spread estimates of these modified models appear to be reasonable when compared to those reported in previous studies.

All those findings are, however, in contrast to standard interpretations of pricing behaviour under asymmetric information. As mentioned earlier, Osler et al. (2006) suggest dealers' strategic behaviour and market power to be the driving forces of this result and hence to be these channels, which superpose traditional adverse selection arguments. These "new" interpretations are heavily supported by the data at hand. However, up to now, one cannot predict which one of the two alternatives is the one that *primarily* determines pricing strategies, but this will be in focus of subsequent chapters.

As in the baseline model, inventory coefficients in augmented models are once more statistically insignificant, providing further support for inventory management via interdealer trading instead of price shading. Besides all these promising findings, there is one result that remains puzzling. In both sub-samples at hand, coefficients on deal size are only significant for potentially uninformed order flow, regardless of whether information content is measured by trade volume or counterparty type. One possible explanation for this might be that introducing dummy variables that account for informational differences take all explanatory power from order quantity of well informed order flow, supporting Huang and Stoll's (1997) view that customers with superior information have an incentive to camouflage their orders' information content by choosing a standardised deal size. In other words, a customer's identity is a sufficient indicator to enable the market maker to infer his counterpart's informational superiority or inferiority. Hence, market makers do not have to take deal size into account as soon as they are aware of the customer's identity. Due to the fact that potentially well informed financial customers tend to transact large trades in the context of this study, this argumentation should provide a rationale for deal size coefficient's lack of significance on large trades.

However, statistical significance of small deal sizes and commercial customers' order flow remains surprising. If commercial customers tend to transact primarily small trades, as they do, there should not be significant information content in their deal flow, neither when differentiated by deal size nor by customer type. Hence, there is no obvious and convincing explanation for these results so far.

Lastly, π is once more in the focus of the analysis. For large deals, π indicates that the market maker puts 45 percent weight on order flow information when he adjusts his expectations after transacting more than EUR 0.5 million. After executing a small order, the proportion of order flow contributing to the market maker's expectation updating is only ten percent. For both kinds of transaction classes, Wald tests have shown that π is significantly different from unity.

As reported in table 3.2, results for 2004 / 2005 broadly confirm findings of the previous sub-sample. Coefficients of determination are even better than in 2002 / 2003 with adjusted R^2's well above 40 percent for augmented models. Coefficients on trade direction are all highly significant and potentially well informed order flow obtains lower spreads than uninformed customers. This, once more, supports the view of Osler et al. (2006) and their strategic dealing and market power hypotheses.

Results for π are in line with aforementioned findings. First of all, π is significantly different from unity for both classes of deal size as well as for commercial and financial customers. The market maker uses 18 percent of order flow to adjust his expectation when the previous order was small, but backs 59.5 percent of his beliefs with observed order flow whenever the respective order was large.

When concentrating on different types of counterparts, results for 2002 / 2003 are again confirmed in 2004 / 2005. For commercial and internal counterparts, it is not possible to reject the Null of coefficients on recent and lagged inventory being equal at common levels of significance. Thus, there is no indication for asymmetric information vis-à-vis these kinds of customers and the market maker does not seem to use observed order flow with these counterparts to adjust his expectations. In contrast to this, financial customers' order flow accounts for roughly 67 percent of the dealer's expectations adjustment and is statistically significant.

Table 3.2: *Baseline MS model and spread variations across deal sizes and customer types 250 trading days between October 1, 2004 – September 30, 2005 (21,296 obs.)*

	Baseline Model	Size Dummies		Counterparty Dummies	
Constant	-0.04 (0.04)		-0.05 (0.04)		-0.09 (0.04)**
Deal Size Q_{it}	1E-3 (1E-3)	Large	-6E-4 (16E-4)	Commercial	0.57 (0.16)***
		Small	21.5 (17.1)***	Financial	8E-4 (8E-4)
				Internal	-4E-3 (3E-3)
Inventory I_t	6E-4 (1E-3)	Large	-2E-4 (13E-4)	Commercial	3E-4 (8E-4)
		Small	3E-4 (9E-4)	Financial	5E-4 (7E-4)
				Internal	1E-3 (2E-3)
Lagged Inventory I_{t-1}	-8E-4(9E-4)	Large	-7E-4 (9E-4)	Commercial	-6E-4 (6E-4)
		Small	-5E-4 (6E-4)	Financial	-1E-3 (8E-4)
				Internal	1E-9 (1E-9)
Direction D_t	5.53 (0.1)***	Large	2.27 (0.08)***	Commercial	9.02 (0.11)***
		Small	11.0 (0.15)***	Financial	2.19 (0.09)***
				Internal	11.5 (0.75)***
Lagged Direction D_{t-1}	-4.51 (0.1)***	Large	-0.92 (0.08)***	Commercial	-8.40 (0.12)***
		Small	-9.06 (0.14)***	Financial	-0.72 (0.07)***
				Internal	-11.8 (0.83)***
Adjusted R^2	0.29	0.46		0.45	

Notes: Dependent variable is change of currency price measured in pips between two incoming orders. Standard errors in parentheses. Baseline model is given by equation (3.13). Estimation method is GMM with Newey-West (1987) correction. Set of instruments equals set of regressors, implying that parameter estimates parallel OLS estimates (Bjønnes and Rime, 2005). * (**, ***) denotes significance at the 10% (5%, 1%) level.

So far, the Madhavan and Smidt (1991) model provides useful insights to the dealer's pricing behaviour. With R^2's well above 40 percent, results are exceptionally promising. As it is shown, market makers are aware of potential asymmetric information in FX markets, but adverse selection risk is actually priced in contrast to standard interpretations of micro models. Results presented above indicate a negative correlation between probability that a counterparty has superior information and bid-ask spreads. So, a natural next step is to see whether these findings are confirmed by the Huang and Stoll (1997) model, too.

3.2.2 The Huang and Stoll (1997) model

Results for the Huang and Stoll (1997) model, as shown in table 3.3 and table 3.4, broadly support findings of the Madhavan and Smidt (1991) approach. In both sub-samples, average half spreads for large deals are lower than half spreads for small order sizes and well informed financial customers obtain narrower spreads than both commercial and internal customers, respectively. This finding thus seems to be robust across different models, various time periods and different market makers, as reported in other studies like Osler et al. (2006).

Table 3.3: *"Modified" HS model and spread variations across deal sizes and customer types*

255 trading days between October 1, 2002 – September 30, 2003 (11,830 obs.)

	Baseline Model	Size Dummies		Counterparty Dummies	
Half Spread ($BA/2$)	6.19 (0.1)***	Large	3.70 (0.12)***	Commercial	7.72 (0.14)***
		Small	8.41 (0.18)***	Financial	3.56 (0.12)***
				Internal	11.9 (0.69)***
Information (α)	2.25 (2.8)	Large	115.7 (5.07)***	Commercial	-42.0 (2.41)***
		Small	-39.5 (2.57)***	Financial	116.7 (5.3)***
				Internal	-56.5 (9.98)***
Inventory (β)	4.95 (1.5)***	Large	-6.75 (1.45)***	Commercial	3.91 (2.23)*
		Small	1.60 (0.92)*	Financial	-3.42 (1.30)***
				Internal	2.37 (1.23)*
Adjusted R^2	0.29	0.40		0.42	

Notes: Dependent variable is change of the currency price measured in pips between two incoming orders. Standard errors in parentheses. Baseline model is given by equation (3.20). Estimation method is GMM with Newey-West (1987) correction. Set of instruments equals set of regressors implying that parameter estimates parallel OLS estimates (Bjønnes and Rime, 2005). Coefficients α and β are measured in percent of half spread. * (**, ***) denotes significance at the 10% (5%, 1%) level.

The fact that it is primarily financial customers' and high volume order flow that conveys information is once again supported by a highly statistically significant and positive coefficient α. Information content of small trades as well as of orders initiated by commercial or internal customers basically are informative "in the wrong direction". Results hence confirm findings in Fan and Lyons (2002), who observe different behaviour across different types of end-users, too. All these results hence support Osler's (1998) conclusion that commercial customers are ultimate liquidity providers in FX markets, resulting in commercial customers' order flow being some kind of a contra-indicator for future price movements. The market maker has no need to hedge against superior information when trading with these counterparts and can reduce spreads with respect to informational aspects instead.

As indicated by β coefficients, inventory considerations seem to have only moderate influence on this dealer's price setting behaviour. Inventories are only insofar driving the market maker's quotes as they result from large trades or financial customers' order flow.

Table 3.4: *"Modified" HS model and spread variations across deal sizes and customer types*

250 trading days between October 1, 2004 – September 30, 2005 (21,296 obs.)

	Baseline Model	Size Dummies		Counterparty Dummies	
Half Spread (*BA/2*)	10.9 (0.2)***	Large	4.69 (0.19)***	Commercial	17.2 (0.41)***
		Small	18.3 (0.30)***	Financial	3.92 (0.19)***
				Internal	20.9 (1.61)***
Information (α)	-1.42 (2.7)	Large	60.7 (4.57)***	Commercial	-26.4 (3.00)***
		Small	-21.6 (2.11)***	Financial	71.2 (3.37)***
				Internal	-31.3 (6.04)***
Inventory (β)	10.23 (1.7)***	Large	-2.00 (1.54)	Commercial	0.44 (0.18)**
		Small	1.76 (0.12)***	Financial	-2.93 (1.16)**
				Internal	1.76 (0.91)*
Adjusted R^2	0.27	0.40		0.41	

Notes: Dependent variable is change of the currency price measured in pips between two incoming orders. Standard errors in parentheses. Baseline model is given by equation (3.20). Estimation method is GMM with Newey-West (1987) correction. Set of instruments equals set of regressors implying that parameter estimates parallel OLS estimates (Bjønnes and Rime, 2005). Coefficients α and β are measured in percent of half spread. * (**, ***) denotes significance at the 10% (5%, 1%) level.

Results for 2002 / 2003 are once more confirmed by estimates for 2004 / 2005. Informed order flow obtains narrower spreads than presumably less informed flows. Surprisingly, and in contrast to results of the Madhavan and Smidt (1991) model, spread estimates increase between the two sub-samples. In addition, there is no influence of inventories resulting from large trades now, as there was in 2002 / 2003, but there is significant explanatory power for inventories resulting from small trades. 1.76 percent of quoted half spreads on small trades are due to this component, but there is still information of "converse direction" in small orders.

3.2.3 The dynamics of directly observed spreads – an intuitive approach

As mentioned in chapter 2, the data set at hand conveys a quote-midpoint from the interdealer market at the time of the market maker's respective customer trade. Hence, by assuming that the quoted midpoint of the market maker vis-à-vis his customer is equal to the interdealer midpoint at this time, one can calculate a respective half spread for every trade from transaction price. This section hence is going to reassess the above-mentioned dynamics of bid-ask spreads across different types of customers by running the regression

$$\frac{BA_t^*}{2} = \beta_1 Q_t + \beta_2 CC_t + \beta_3 FC_t + \beta_4 IC_t + \varepsilon_t, \tag{3.21}$$

where $BA_t^*/2$ is the percentage half spread relative to the interdealer quote midpoint and Q_t is the respective order's size measured in EUR millions. CC_t, FC_t, and IC_t are dummy variables for commercial customers, financial customers, and internal counterparts, respectively. Dummy variables equal "+1" ("-1") when the respective counterpart purchases (sells) euro and "0" if there was no trade from this group of customers in period t. ε_t is a white noise disturbance term.

Table 3.5 shows estimation results for both sub-samples. All of the aforementioned findings are, again, confirmed therein, since every coefficient is highly significant, correctly signed and the specification explains up to 50 percent of the dependent variable's volatility. The deal size coefficient is showing a negative sign, implying that larger orders get narrower half spreads, highlighting potential information content of large orders and potential importance of dealers' strategic behaviour. Again, the percentage difference between interdealer midpoint and transaction price is lowest for financial customers. With an average midquote of €1 = $1.1155 in 2002 / 2003 and €1 = $1.2716 in 2004 / 2005, financial customers obtain an average half spread of 1.12 pips and

2.54 pips, respectively. Commercial customers (internal customers), in contrast, are quoted 10.0 pips (13.4 pips) in 2002 / 2003 and 8.9 pips (13.99 pips) in 2004 / 2005, respectively.

***Table 3.5:** Dynamics of directly observed half spreads*
255 (250) trading days between October 1, 2002 (2004) – September 30, 2003 (2005)
11,830 obs. (21,296 obs.)

	2002 / 2003	2004 / 2005
Deal size (Q_t)	-13.2 (5.35)**	-36.4 (5.19)***
Half spreads		
Commercial customers (CC_t)	0.09 (1E-3)***	0.07 (7E-4)***
Financial Customers (FC_t)	0.01 (1E-3)***	0.02 (1E-4)***
Internal Customers (IC_t)	0.12 (8E-3)***	0.11 (6E-3)***
Adjusted R^2	0.50	0.45

Notes: Dependent variable is difference between interdealer midquote and transaction price relative to the midquote. Coefficient on deal size is measured in percent of relative half spread. Coefficients on customers are measured in percent of interdealer midpoint. Standard errors in parentheses. The estimated model is given by equation (3.21). Estimation method is GMM with Newey-West (1987) correction. The set of instruments equals the set of regressors implying that parameter estimates parallel OLS estimates (Bjønnes and Rime, 2005). Coefficients are measured in percent of half spread. * (**, ***) denotes significance at the 10% (5%, 1%) level.

Even though this approach is rather intuitive and not backed by an explicit theoretical model, it supports findings of the Madhavan and Smidt (1991) model and the Huang and Stoll (1997) model presented in previous sections of this chapter. It thus seems to be appropriate to interpret the above-mentioned patterns in dealer behaviour as robust and to view them as the basis for subsequent analyses.

3.3 Interim conclusion: Reviewing market makers' pricing behaviour

Results on regressions presented in previous sections of chapter 3 show coefficients of determination that are particularly promising. Baseline models of the Madhavan and Smidt (1991) model and the Huang and Stoll (1997) model consistently explain more than 20 percent of volatility of permanent exchange rate changes at the bank at hand. When accounting for different deal sizes or types of customers, adjusted R^2's increase above 30 and even above

40 percent in most of analyses. These results are quite encouraging, since models conducted here obviously do not account for every potential driving force of exchange rates.[74] With very few exceptions, all coefficients are correctly signed and statistically significant. These findings provide strong empirical support for the view that exchange rates are mainly driven by microeconomic factors with trading taking a prominent part in the search for an appropriate price when information are dispersed across market participants. Hence, results are in line with a number of recent studies like, among others, Pasquariellô (2000), Evans and Lyons (2002a, 2007a), Payne (2003), Batten and Hogan (2005), Marsh and O'Rourke (2005), and Osler et al. (2006), although coefficients vary slightly.

However, results on information content of order flow are not without controversy. Flood et al. (1998) find search costs to be a significant spread component, Breedon and Vitale (2004) argue that it is liquidity rather than information[75] that is the main driving factor of order flow's short-run correlation with exchange rates, and McGroarty et al. (2005) present empirical evidence that random variations in volumes are more important than information at high frequencies. Actually, although *private information* was already defined in chapter 2, it is still uncertain, to which frequency the term *information* refers to. Does order flow convey information about short run exchange rate changes, as proposed by Batten and Hogan (2005), and Osler et al. (2006)? Or is order flow information related to rather medium term dynamics? Chapter 4 will investigate these questions intensively.

Results on the Madhavan and Smidt (1991) model evidence dealers' awareness of potential presence of asymmetric information and illustrate the role of private order flow information during the expectations adjustment process of the dealer investigated here. According to findings concerning term π, the market maker intensively uses observed order flow of financial customers to adjust his expectations about a currency's fundamental value, implying that he is aware of financial customers' potential information advantage. An inter-

[74] For example, Breedon and Vitale (2004) argue that liquidity is a major determinant of exchange rates dynamics, Lyons and Moore (2005b) highlight the role of cross-market relationships between different currency pairs. These findings leave space for future research.

[75] Chakravarty and Sarkar (1999) confirm this conclusion for Fixed Income markets.

esting next step, paving the way for further research, could be to investigate whether or not informed traders are able to generate systematic supernormal profits. Unfortunately, the data set at hand is not powerful enough to answer this question, since it covers only trading at a single bank. However, for stock markets, Da Silva Rosa et al. (2005) indeed find slight evidence that there exists a positive correlation between an investor's level of information and magnitude of abnormal profits she earns, but it seems that informed traders trade in response to supernormal profits rather than in anticipation.

In contrast to standard models of market making in the presence of asymmetric information, results presented here consistently suggest that market makers quote narrower spreads to presumably better informed order flow. Both of the above-mentioned models as well as the intuitive approach introduced in section 3.2.3 find this pattern in both of the sub-samples analysed here in unison. Thus, results at hand provide empirical support for findings of Osler et al. (2006) and their suggestion of two "new" channels by which pricing behaviour of market makers might be affected, i.e. so-called *strategic dealing hypothesis* and *market power hypothesis*.

Strategic dealing implies that informed incoming order flow has predictive power for short-run exchange rate movements. If this was the case, the market maker would have a strong incentive to subsidise informed order flow in order to maximise probability that this potentially informative order is executed with him. In this way, the dealer could observe informed flow and exploit it for his own speculative reasons. Market makers then would subsidise informed order flow by quoting narrower spreads. For government bond transactions, Hong and Warga (2000) present evidence that dealers indeed provide trading services for major institutional clients as non-profit business, highlighting potential strategic behaviour or market power in this segment, too.

If it was *market power* that governs the dealer's pricing behaviour, findings presented here suggest a relatively weak bargaining position of the market maker vis-à-vis financial customers, who force the dealer to quote narrow spreads, if he would like to transact any trade with these customers at all. Financial customers' superior market power could be due to their detailed knowledge of recent market conditions and competing quotes of various market makers, they can potentially transact with. The finding that large deals obtain narrower spreads than small deals would thus be due to financial customers' tendency to transact primarily large volumes. This explanation fits to descriptive statistics presented in chapter 2. The fact that the dataset at hand includes interbank trades to the group of financial customers does not bias results towards a better bargaining position of these counterparts. In contrast, hedge funds and mutual funds are managed that professionally that they can use the same information and trading systems, traders at banks have at their disposal. Even more, Osler et al. (2006) interpret fund managers to be the best informed players of all, because of their continuous and intensive communication with a variety of market participants. From a bargaining point of view, including interbank trades to the group of financial customers thus is appropriate or might even reduce this group's market power within the data set. The market power hypothesis will be in focus of chapter 5.

The last finding worth mentioning here is the consistent result that it is interdealer trading rather than quote shading that dealers use to manage their inventories. All these results are consistent with other recent studies like Bjønnes and Rime (2005) and Osler et al. (2006). This behaviour is due to the fact that electronic brokerage systems like EBS or Reuters Dealing 3000 provide market makers with fast and cheap tools for inventory management.

Appendix to chapter 3

A.3.1 The Madhavan and Smidt (1991) model

A.3.1.1 A portfolio-theoretic derivation of the Bayesian updating rule

As described in chapter 3.1.1, the market maker observes two noisy signals he can use to adjust his expectations concerning the risky asset's fundamental value. Both of these signals are, by assumption, drawn from a normal distribution. Actual expectations of the market maker can thus be interpreted as a "portfolio" of two risky signals and hence, the dealer will choose that combination of these signals that provides him the most accurate, i.e. variance-minimal, forecast of the risky asset's value.

Portfolio theory[76] tells us that a "two-asset" or, more precisely here, two-signal portfolio's variance, σ^2_{Port}, is given by

$$\sigma^2_{Port} = a^2_{\varepsilon}\sigma^2_{\varepsilon} + a^2_{\omega}\sigma^2_{\omega} + 2a_{\varepsilon}a_{\omega}Cov_{\varepsilon,\omega}, \qquad \text{(A.3.1)}$$

with a_{ε} and a_{ω} being the weight of the public information signal and the private information signal, respectively. σ^2_{ε} denotes variance of the public signal, σ^2_{ω} is private information signal's variance, and $Cov_{\varepsilon,\omega}$ describes covariance between these two kinds of signals.

Calculating the first derivative for a_{ε} and a_{ω} yields marginal risk associated with each of the two signals, respectively. An optimum is achieved when marginal risks are equal among all signals, so one can write

$$\frac{\partial\sigma^2_{Port}}{\partial a_{\varepsilon}} = 2a_{\varepsilon}\sigma^2_{\varepsilon} + 2a_{\omega}Cov_{\varepsilon,\omega} = 0$$

$$\frac{\partial\sigma^2_{Port}}{\partial a_{\omega}} = 2a_{\omega}\sigma^2_{\omega} + 2a_{\varepsilon}Cov_{\varepsilon,\omega} = 0$$

[76] See Markowitz (1952, 1959).

$$a_\varepsilon\sigma_\varepsilon^2 + a_\omega Cov_{\varepsilon,\omega} = a_\omega\sigma_\omega^2 + a_\varepsilon Cov_{\varepsilon,\omega}. \quad \text{(A.3.2)}$$

a_ε and a_ω necessarily have to sum up to one. Thus, by defining $a_\omega = \theta$ and $a_\varepsilon = 1-\theta$, equation (A.3.2) can be re-written as

$$(1-\theta)\sigma_\varepsilon^2 + \theta Cov_{\varepsilon,\omega} = \theta\sigma_\omega^2 + (1-\theta)Cov_{\varepsilon,\omega}. \quad \text{(A.3.3)}$$

Solving equation (A.3.3) for θ yields

$$\sigma_\varepsilon^2 - \theta\sigma_\varepsilon^2 + \theta Cov_{\varepsilon,\omega} = \theta\sigma_\omega^2 + Cov_{\varepsilon,\omega} - \theta Cov_{\varepsilon,\omega}$$
$$\sigma_\varepsilon^2 - Cov_{\varepsilon,\omega} = \theta\sigma_\omega^2 + \theta\sigma_\varepsilon^2 - 2\theta Cov_{\varepsilon,\omega}$$
$$\sigma_\omega^2 - Cov_{\varepsilon,\omega} = \theta(\sigma_\omega^2 + \sigma_\varepsilon^2 - 2Cov_{\varepsilon,\omega})$$

$$\theta = \frac{\sigma_\varepsilon^2 - Cov_{\varepsilon,\omega}}{\sigma_\varepsilon^2 + \sigma_\omega^2 - 2Cov_{\varepsilon,\omega}}. \quad \text{(A.3.4)}$$

Under the assumption that signals are independent of each other, this is the private signal's weighting factor mentioned in the text. However, equation (A.3.4) shows that this weighting strategy is optimal, even if signals co-vary.

A.3.1.2 Derivation of equation (3.6)

From equation (3.5) in the text, it is known that

$$Q_t = \alpha(m_t - S_t) - L_t \quad \text{(A.3.5)}$$

that can be rearranged to

$$\frac{Q_t}{\alpha} + S_t = m_t - \frac{L_t}{\alpha}. \quad \text{(A.3.6)}$$

Equation (3.4) defines m_t to be

$$m_t = \theta w_t + (1-\theta)y_t. \quad \text{(A.3.7)}$$

So substituting equation (A.3.7) into equation (A.3.6) yields

$$\frac{Q_t}{\alpha} + S_t = \theta w_t + (1-\theta)y_t - \frac{L_t}{\alpha}. \tag{A.3.8}$$

The private information signal, w_t, is known to be a random variable, drawn from a normal distribution and defined as

$$w_t = \upsilon_t + \omega_t. \tag{A.3.9}$$

Substituting equation (A.3.9) into equation (A.3.8) gives

$$\frac{Q_t}{\alpha} + S_t = \theta(\upsilon_t + \omega_t) + (1-\theta)y_t - \frac{L_t}{\alpha} \tag{A.3.10}$$

that can be rearranged to get

$$\frac{Q_t + \alpha S_t - \alpha(1-\theta)y_t}{\alpha\theta} = \upsilon_t + \omega_t - \frac{L_t}{\alpha\theta}. \tag{A.3.11}$$

The left term of equation (A.3.11) defines the statistic $\hat{\upsilon}(Q_t)$ known from the text, the right term of the equation reveals that this statistic can be interpreted as a normally distributed random variable with mean υ_t and variance $\sigma_\omega^2 + (L_t/(\alpha\theta))^2$.

A.3.1.3 Derivation of equation (3.8)

Consider equation (3.7) from the text. The market maker's expectation μ_t is given by a combination of a public information signal, y_t, and the statistic $\hat{\upsilon}(Q_t)$. As shown earlier, this is

$$\mu_t = \zeta y_t + (1-\zeta)\hat{\upsilon}(Q_t). \tag{A.3.12}$$

Equation (3.6) in the text defines $\hat{\upsilon}(Q_t)$ as

$$\hat{\upsilon}(Q_t) \equiv \frac{Q_t + \alpha S_t - \alpha(1-\theta)y_t}{\alpha\theta}, \tag{A.3.13}$$

so substituting equation (A.3.13) into equation (A.3.12) yields

$$\mu_t = \zeta y_t + (1-\zeta)\frac{Q_t + \alpha S_t - \alpha(1-\theta)y_t}{\alpha\theta}. \tag{A.3.14}$$

Rearranging equation (A.3.14) finally gives

$$\mu_t = \zeta y_t + \frac{(1-\zeta)}{\theta}\left(\frac{Q_t}{\alpha} + S_t - (1-\theta)y_t\right)$$

$$\mu_t = \zeta y_t + \left[\frac{1-\zeta}{\theta}\right]\frac{Q_t}{\alpha} + \left[\frac{1-\zeta}{\theta}\right]S_t - \left[\frac{1-\theta-\zeta+\zeta\theta}{\theta}\right]y_t$$

$$\mu_t = \left[\frac{1-\zeta}{\theta}\right]\left[S_t + \frac{Q_t}{\alpha}\right] + \left[\zeta - \frac{1-\theta-\zeta+\zeta\theta}{\theta}\right]y_t. \tag{A.3.15}$$

Now, consider the second term of the sum in equation (A.3.15). By enhancing the left parameter ζ in this bracket by θ/θ, one can write

$$\mu_t = \left[\frac{1-\zeta}{\theta}\right]\left[S_t + \frac{Q_t}{\alpha}\right] + \left[\frac{\zeta\theta-1+\theta+\zeta-\zeta\theta}{\theta}\right]y_t$$

$$\mu_t = \left[\frac{1-\zeta}{\theta}\right]\left[S_t + \frac{Q_t}{\alpha}\right] + \left[\frac{\theta+\zeta-1}{\theta}\right]y_t. \tag{A.3.16}$$

Before turning to the desired expression of equation (3.8), one has to check whether $(1-\zeta)/\theta + (\theta+\zeta-1)/\theta$ is really equal to one, because these terms are weights of the only two types of signals received by the market maker here. Thus, write

$$\left[\frac{1-\zeta}{\theta}\right] + \left[\frac{\theta+\zeta-1}{\theta}\right] \overset{!}{=} 1. \tag{A.3.17}$$

It is easy to see that ζ and 1 get cancelled, so there is only θ/θ left and this is indeed one. Hence, by defining $\pi = (\theta+\zeta-1)/\theta$ it is demonstrated that equation (3.8) is correct, so one can write

$$\mu_t = \pi y_t + (1-\pi)\left[S_t + \frac{Q_t}{\alpha}\right]. \tag{A.3.18}$$

A.3.1.4 Derivation of equation (3.12)

Equation (3.9) in the text defines price in period t to be

$$S_t = \pi y_t + (1-\pi)[S_t + \alpha^{-1}Q_t] - \gamma(I_t - I^*) + \psi D_t, \qquad \text{(A.3.19)}$$

while the market maker's prior expectation, y_t, is given by equation (3.11) as

$$y_t = S_{t-1} + \gamma(I_{t-1} - I^*) - \psi D_{t-1} + \eta_t. \qquad \text{(A.3.20)}$$

Substituting equation (A.3.20) into (A.3.19) yields

$$S_t = \pi[S_{t-1} + \gamma(I_{t-1} - I^*) - \psi D_{t-1} + \eta_t] + (1-\pi)[S_t + \alpha^{-1}Q_t] - \gamma(I_t - I^*) + \psi D_t$$
$$\pi(S_t - S_{t-1}) = \pi\gamma(I_{t-1} - I^*) - \pi\psi D_{t-1} + \pi\eta_t + \alpha^{-1}Q_t - \pi\alpha^{-1}Q_t - \gamma(I_t - I^*) + \psi D_t$$
$$\Delta S_t = \gamma(I_{t-1} - I^*) - \psi D_{t-1} + \frac{\psi}{\pi}D_t + \frac{Q_t}{\pi\alpha} - \frac{Q_t}{\alpha} - \frac{\gamma}{\pi}(I_t - I^*) + \eta_t$$
$$\Delta S_t = -\gamma\left(1 - \frac{1}{\pi}\right)I^* + \left(\frac{1-\pi}{\pi\alpha}\right)Q_t - \frac{\gamma}{\pi}I_t + \gamma I_{t-1} + \frac{\psi}{\pi}D_t - \psi D_{t-1} + \eta_t$$

$$\Delta S_t = \kappa + \lambda Q_t - \frac{\gamma}{\pi}I_t + \gamma I_{t-1} + \frac{\psi}{\pi}D_t - \psi D_{t-1} + \eta_t \qquad \text{(A.3.21)}$$

with $\kappa = -\gamma(1 - 1/\pi)I^*$, $\lambda = (1-\pi)/(\pi\alpha)$, and $\Delta S_t = S_t - S_{t-1}$.

A.3.1.5 Relaxing the assumption that desired inventory (I^*) is constant

Relaxing the assumption that desired inventory is constant only affects constant term κ of the model. To see how, assume that desired inventory I^* is a function of the difference between the market maker's beliefs regarding the asset's fundamental value and recent price. In this way, the model becomes capable of speculation-driven inventory management of the market maker. Whenever the dealer beliefs recent price to be unjustifiably high (low), he will desire a net short (long) position in the asset. Formally, this can be written as

$$I^* = \delta(\mu_t - S_t), \qquad \text{(A.3.22)}$$

where $\delta > 0$ is a constant that expresses market maker's risk aversion. The greater δ, the less risk averse he is. Substituting equation (A.3.22) into the pricing strategy given by equation (3.1) from the text, i.e.

$$S_t = \mu_t - \gamma(I_t - I^*) + \psi D_t \tag{A.3.23}$$

then yields

$$S_t = \mu_t - \gamma[I_t - \delta(\mu_t - S_t)] + \psi D_t. \tag{A.3.24}$$

By solving equation (A.3.24) for S_t, one obtains

$$S_t = \mu_t - \gamma I_t + \gamma\delta\mu_t - \gamma\delta S_t + \psi D_t$$
$$S_t + \gamma\delta S_t = \mu_t + \gamma\delta\mu_t - \gamma I_t + \psi D_t$$
$$S_t(1+\gamma\delta) = \mu_t(1+\gamma\delta) - \gamma I_t + \psi D_t$$

$$S_t = \mu_t - \frac{\gamma}{(1+\gamma\delta)} I_t + \frac{\psi}{(1+\gamma\delta)} D_t. \tag{A.3.25}$$

Relaxing the assumption that desired inventory is constant changes the model only insofar that desired inventory disappears from the pricing equation. As a consequence of this, the constant term κ disappears from the econometric model shown in equation (3.12). With the exception of κ, there is no change in the structure of the model at all.

A.3.2 The Huang and Stoll (1997) model

A.3.2.1 Derivation of equation (3.18)

Deriving a testable econometric equation from the Huang and Stoll model is straightforward. First of all, taking first differences in equation (3.17) yields

$$\Delta S_t = \Delta M_t + \frac{BA}{2}(D_t - D_{t-1}) + \Delta\eta_t, \tag{A.3.26}$$

where $\Delta S_t \equiv S_t - S_{t-1}$, $\Delta M_t \equiv M_t - M_{t-1}$, and $\Delta\eta_t \equiv \eta_t - \eta_{t-1}$. A definition for ΔM_t is already given by equation (3.16) in the text, that is

$$\Delta M_t = (\alpha + \beta)\frac{BA}{2} D_{t-1} + \varepsilon_t, \qquad (A.3.27)$$

so substituting equation (A.3.27) into equation (A.3.26) gives the testable model

$$\Delta S_t = (\alpha + \beta)\frac{BA}{2} D_{t-1} + \frac{BA}{2}(D_t - D_{t-1}) + \varepsilon_t + \Delta\eta_t$$

$$\Delta S_t = \frac{BA}{2}(D_t - D_{t-1}) + \lambda \frac{BA}{2} D_{t-1} + e_t \qquad (A.3.28)$$

with $\lambda \equiv \alpha + \beta$ and $e_t \equiv \varepsilon_t + \Delta\eta_t$.

A.3.2.2 Derivation of equation (3.20)

As shown during the derivation of equation (3.18) in Appendix A.3.2.1, one can write change of price between *t-1* and *t* as

$$\Delta S_t = \alpha \frac{BA}{2} D_{t-1} + \beta \frac{BA}{2} D_{t-1} + \frac{BA}{2}(D_t - D_{t-1}) + \varepsilon_t + \Delta\eta_t. \qquad (A.3.29)$$

Bjønnes and Rime (2003) define M_t to be

$$M_t = V_t + \beta \frac{BA}{2} I_t \qquad (A.3.30)$$

with $I_t = \sum_{i=1}^{t-1} D_i$. Because of that, the term $\beta(BA/2)D_{t-1}$ of equation (A.3.29) can be substituted by $\beta(BA/2)\Delta I_t$, resulting in the modified testable equation

$$\Delta S_t = \alpha \frac{BA}{2} D_{t-1} + \beta \frac{BA}{2} \Delta I_t + \frac{BA}{2}(D_t - D_{t-1}) + \varepsilon_t + \Delta\eta_t. \qquad (A.3.31)$$

4. Information content of order flow

One potential explanation for the dealer's pricing strategy described in chapter 3 is strategic behaviour caused by informational reasons. If trading was indeed the main mechanism to aggregate dispersed information, dealers take informational aspects into consideration when they quote prices. Whenever privately observed order flow is not liquidity-driven, but based on information, there is probably a chance for dealers to infer future exchange rate movements from customer order flow. Thus, quoting narrow spreads to potentially well informed customers is in fact subsidising informed order flow and investing in information to profit from in speculative trading afterwards.

Depending on the time horizon, there are two possible interpretations regarding order flow's information content. On the one hand, customers might have superior information about short-run exchange rate movements, the market maker would like to participate on. This view is rather short-term orientated and price movements should take place not too long after order flow occurred. On the other hand, end-user order flow might be a variable that describes recent macroeconomic conditions sooner than any other variable does. This, obviously, is a rather medium-term view to information aggregation via trading, since a single trade conveys only a marginal fraction of new information about the exchange rate's fundamental value. Hence, dealers have to observe cumulative order flow over a longer period (i.e. few hours or even days) to infer future exchange rate movements from recent order flow trends. After observing incoming customer order flow, dealers set off their inventory via the interdealer market, where the exchange rate actually adjusts. Since information in end-user transaction flow causes interdealer flows and market-wide interdealer flows determine exchange rates, it is straightforward to interpret end-user flows as a potential source of information concerning future exchange rate movements. From a theoretical point of view, there is now a broad consensus that it is indeed order flow that carries private information over to exchange rates.

The view that it is interdealer-trading that determines exchange rates is empirically supported by the work of Evans and Lyons (2002a), who find that 64 percent of daily DEM / USD returns can be primarily explained by interdealer flows. For daily returns in JPY / USD, the respective figure is 45 percent and thus only marginally weaker. Results in Evans and Lyons (2002b) confirm this result in general for various European currencies against U.S. dollar, even though coefficients of determination are lower and vary substantially between single currency pairs.

The study most comparable to section 4.1 is done by Killeen et al. (2006), who apply Johansen (1988, 1991) cointegration tests to daily order flow collected from EBS. Although they, too, find empirical support for the hypothesis that interdealer flows determine exchange rates, the view that order flow can help dealers improving their practical forecasting ability is still controversial. After analysing various data sets including the one used in Evans and Lyons (2002a), Sager and Taylor (2005) conclude that interdealer order flow has barely any explanatory power for future exchange rate returns. The usefulness of (publicly available interdealer) order flow information for practical exchange rate forecasting is thus generally weak. End-user, i.e. non-bank, order flow, however, may be an important source of private information, but only at very high frequencies.

If, as proposed by Evans and Lyons (2005c), order flow really conveys information about recent macroeconomic conditions, exploiting order flow information for speculative reasons would not be as easy as described above, since a single dealer's order flow is unlikely to predict market-wide flows during the next periods. But because end-user flows should be positively correlated with future flows of market-wide information, incoming customer orders are likely to be helpful in predicting rather medium-run exchange rate movements.

Subsequent sections of chapter 4 deal with information content of order flow in various ways. First of all, cointegration tests are deployed to investigate a possible "long-run" relationship[77] between our single dealer's customer order flow and the (market-wide) exchange rate. This is focus of section 1. Afterwards, short-run dynamics between these two variables are investigated by calculating the related error correction model in section 2. The more complex interpretation of information aggregation via trading described in Evans and

[77] In contrast to standard interpretations in macroeconomics, the term "long-run" in high-frequency economics refers to just a few hours or days.

Lyons (2005c) is analysed in chapter 4.3. This section deals with the model's theoretical background first before arguments are investigated empirically.

In section 4.4, the angle to information content of order flow is altered. As stated earlier, the strategic dealing hypothesis suggests that dealers subsidise well informed order flow to exploit private information conveyed therein for their own speculative trading. However, a necessary condition for the strategic dealing hypothesis to hold is that respective dealers are aware of order flow to be a potential source of information concerning future exchange rate movements. Consequently, even if order flow conveys information, strategic dealing would not be an appropriate explanation for a market maker's pricing behaviour, if the dealer does not use order flow information for speculative trading. Hence, inspired by Mende and Menkhoff (2005), an event-study is conducted to the bank's own speculative positions in order to investigate, whether or not the bank's speculation was actually profitable. Section 4.5 provides an interim conclusion.

4.1 Cointegration analysis

The major advantage of cointegration analysis compared to standard econometric regressions is the fact that an empiricist does not need time series to be stationary to investigate their relationship. Most economic time series are indeed not stationary. The aim of cointegration analysis is to identify a common stochastic trend among the variables in question. In other words, it is an attempt to identify a stable equilibrium, the economic systems tends back to whenever it is disturbed.

Basically, there are two ways to test for cointegration between two (or more) variables. The first of them is proposed by Engle and Granger (1987). Their approach's basic principle is to test whether the residual sequence of an econometric system is stationary. In contrast, Johansen's (1988, 1991) approach to cointegration proposes some kind of multivariate unit-root test-like procedure. Both the Engle and Granger (1987) as well as the Johansen (1988, 1991) methodology are to be explained and discussed in greater detail in the mathematical Annex.

In contrast to analyses conducted in chapter 3, this section uses *market spot rates* collected from Reuters instead of *dealt spot rates* for calculations. This is because the exchange rate is said to be determined at the interdealer market and not in transactions with a single dealers end-users. Hence, testing for cointegration between market spot rates and a single dealer's incoming order flow in fact tests whether this dealer's customer flow is a representative of market-wide transactions.

As a first step, all time series are tested for an existing unit root by using Augmented Dickey Fuller[78] (ADF) tests. Table 4.1 reports τ-statistics for cumulative incoming order flow from internal customers, financial customers, commercial customers, as well as a joint statistic on financial and commercial customers, termed *non-internal customers* here. It should be borne in mind that cumulative incoming order flow does not coincide with the dealer's inventory, which includes outgoing trades and is manipulated by setting it equal to zero at the beginning of each trading day. ADF τ-statistic for the exchange rate is -2.79. Hence, with a 10% critical value for unit root tests with constant and trend being –3.13, one cannot reject the hypothesis of an existing unit-root in any of the time series at hand. In addition, testing for unit-roots in first differences, there is strong evidence that all variables are I(1).[79] Consequently, cointegration analysis is an appropriate instrument here.

Investigations start with the Engle and Granger (1987) methodology to test for cointegration. Here, the spot exchange rate (S_t) is regressed against cumulative incoming order flow (X_i) received from customer-group i ($i \in$ {financial customer, commercial customer, internal customer, non-internal customer}), a constant (β_{i0}), and a linear trend, by using OLS estimates with Newey-West correction for heteroscedasticity. Formally, this is

$$S_t = \beta_{i0} + \beta_{i1} trend_{it} + \beta_{i2} X_{it} + \varepsilon_{it}, \tag{4.1}$$

where ε_{it} is the disturbance term that is to be tested for stationarity by using standard Augmented Dickey Fuller tests with automatic truncation lag selec-

[78] For the basic Dickey Fuller test, see Dickey and Fuller (1981). For ADF test, see Said and Dickey (1984).

[79] Test statistics not reported here.

tion based on Schwartz (1978) Information Criterion (SIC), as done above. When testing for cointegration this way, Enders (2004, p. 337) mentions that one should use MacKinnon's (1991) critical values to evaluate stationarity of the ε_{it}-series.[80] Results of equation (4.1) for both sub-samples are presented in table 4.1.

***Table 4.1:** Engle Granger cointegration test for exchange rates and cumulative incoming orders; 255 (2002 / 2003) and 250 (2004 / 2005) trading days between October 1 and September 30*

	Financial Customers	Commercial Customers	Internal Customers	Non-internal Customers
2002/2003	5964 obs.	5231 obs.	642 obs.	11195 obs.
ADF τ-Statistic	-1.74	-1.52	-2.10	-1.97
Constant	1.22 (6E-3)***	0.90 (0.006)***	1.26 (0.02)***	1.21 (0.01)***
Trend	3E-5 (1E-6)***	-3E-5 (1E-6)***	3E-4 (3E-5)***	1E-5 (6E-7)***
Cum. inc. orders	1.6 (0.14)***	-10.0 (0.22)***	5.6 (0.89)***	0.79 (0.09)***
ADF τ-statistic on ε_{it}	-2.98***	-5.99***	-3.71***	-2.85***
2004/2005	12026 obs.	8385 obs.	884 obs.	20411 obs.
ADF τ-Statistic	-2.03	-1.60	-1.98	-1.78
Constant	1.10 (4E-3)***	1.14 (4E-3)***	1.13 (0.01)***	1.20 (5E-3)***
Trend	-2E-5(2E-7)***	-2E-5(4E-7)***	-2E-4(8E-6)***	-6E-6 (3E-7)***
Cum. inc. orders	2.1 (0.07)***	-4.6 (0.22)***	0.18 (0.03)***	-0.01 (2.7E-3)***
ADF τ-statistic on ε_{it}	-2.29**	-2.62***	-2.78***	-2.42**

Notes: Unit root test: Number of lags included is calculated from sample size with SIC automatic truncation lag selection). τ-statistic of the level of exchange rate is –2.79. Dickey Fuller 10% critical value for unit root test with constant and trend: –3.13. MacKinnon (1996) critical values used for ADF-test on exchange rate- and order flow time series. MacKinnon (1991) critical values used for ADF-tests on ε_{it}. OLS estimates with Newey West correction. Cumulative incoming order flow is in € millions; coefficients are multiplied by 10,000. Standard errors in parentheses. * (**, ***) denotes significance at the 10% (5%, 1%) level.

As table 4.1 reveals, the null hypothesis of no-cointegration can be rejected at least at the 5% level in both sub-samples. All coefficients are statistically significant, but their signs indicate an interesting result. Coefficients on cumulative order flow from financial and internal customers are positively correlated with the exchange rate. However, the sign on cumulative order flow from commercial customers is negative. This finding is in line with Evans and

[80] Stationarity of exchange rate- and order flow series is evaluated by using MacKinnon's (1996) critical values.

Lyons (2005c), as well as Bjønnes et al. (2005), Marsh and O'Rourke (2005b), and Osler et al. (2006). Hence, commercial customers, on average, buy when the exchange rate depreciates and sell when currency prices increase. As argued by Osler (1998), this result is due to commercial customers' role as ultimate liquidity providers in FX markets.

Of course, market makers provide liquidity to financial customers in the first place whenever they demand a specific currency. But since dealers aim to limit their open positions, they have to "refinance" themselves from counterparts outside their own circle. According to Osler (2003, 2005), commercial customers provide liquidity by submitting so-called *take-profit orders*, i.e. conditional market orders that trigger buy (sell) orders whenever the exchange rate falls (increases) to a certain level. In addition, intra-day trading strategies are often used by these customers, too. Osler et al. (2006) thus argue that commercial customers' cumulative order flow has to be negatively correlated with exchange rates and does not reveal useful information once one knew order flow of financial customers.

In addition to commercial customers' role as ultimate liquidity providers in FX markets, which can be seen as a rather market-wide phenomenon, the market maker considered here told us in an interview that commercial customers, on average, sell (buy) foreign exchange when exchange rates increase (decrease) and that they are usually *at the wrong side of the market.* To him, this behaviour is mainly due to these customers' relatively weak knowledge of recent market conditions. When interpreting commercial customers' incoming order flow, at least at a single dealer level, one should always bear this argument in mind.

More detailed information on causalities running from order flow to exchange rates or vice versa may be provided by performing Granger-causality tests in a Johansen cointegration framework.[81] To do so, a first step is to estimate unrestricted VAR models of the form

[81] See Johansen (1988, 1991), Johansen and Juselius (1994), and this work's Annex for details.

$$\begin{pmatrix} S_t \\ X_{i,t} \end{pmatrix} = \begin{pmatrix} \beta_0^S \\ \beta_0^{X_i} \end{pmatrix} + \begin{pmatrix} \beta_1^S \\ \beta_1^{X_i} \end{pmatrix} trend_t + \sum_{j=0}^{J} \Gamma_j \begin{pmatrix} S_{t-j} \\ X_{i,t-j} \end{pmatrix} + \begin{pmatrix} u_t^S \\ u_t^{X_i} \end{pmatrix}, \quad (4.2)$$

where *i*, again, indicates the type of counterparty with $i \in$ {financial, commercial, internal, non-internal}. The number of lags, *J*, necessary to account for autocorrelation within the residuals, is determined by using Schwartz (SIC) and Hannan-Quinn (HQ) Information Criteria.[82] For financial and non-internal customers, both criteria recommend a lag length of four periods in 2002 / 2003, while for commercial and internal counterparts, *J* should be one. In 2004 / 2005, SIC suggests five lags for financials, while HQ recommends *J* to be seven. Since results for both alternatives are almost the same, we follow SIC, so *J* is set to be five. For commercials and internals, *J* is one, and for calculations using aggregated non-internal customers' cumulative order flow, *J* is set to be four again.

After that, Maximum Eigenvalue statistics and Trace statistics are calculated to test the null hypothesis of no-cointegration. Both test statistics indicate cointegration between the level of exchange rates and financial customers' and commercial customers' cumulative order flow in 2002 / 2003. In addition, cumulative flows of non-internal customers are cointegrated with exchange rates. In contrast, there seems to be no cointegration between respective variables in case of internal customers. Hence, internal customers are skipped from subsequent analyses.

Results for 2004 / 2005 are not that distinctive. Maximum Eigenvalue and Trace statistics again indicate cointegration for financial customers' cumulative order flow and exchange rates. For commercial customers, it is the Trace test statistic only that allows to reject the hypothesis of no-cointegration. Furthermore, cumulative incoming order flow of aggregated non-internal customers seems to be far from being cointegrated with exchange rate levels this time. As in 2002 / 2003, this result holds good for internal customers' cumulative order flow, too. Results for both sub-samples are reported in table 4.2.

[82] Results not reported here.

Table 4.2: Johansen cointegration test for exchange rates and cumulative incoming orders; 255 (2002 / 2003) and 250 (2004 / 2005) trading days between October 1 and September 30

	Financial Customers	Commercial Customers	Internal Customers	Non-internal Customers
2002 / 2003				
Max. Eigenvalue statistics	16.54†	18.50†	10.47	18.54†
Trace test statistics	18.54†	19.48†	12.71	20.82†
2004 / 2005				
Max. Eigenvalue statistics	14.34†	10.68	9.71	6.57
Trace test statistics	18.06†	16.68†	13.38	10.09

Notes: Max. Eigenvalue test: 5% critical value of the unrestricted cointegration rank test (Maximum Eigenvalue): 14.07 († denotes significance). Trace test: 5% critical value of unrestricted cointegration rank test (Trace): 15.41 († denotes significance).

Cointegration results thus differ by techniques used for investigation. While tests using the Engle and Granger (1987) methodology indicate cointegration with exchange rates for all types of cumulative order flow and in both subsamples, analyses based on Johansen's (1988, 1991) cointegration procedure are less promising. As explained in the mathematical Annex of this work, there are several reasons to put more trust into Maximum Eigenvalue- and Trace-tests than into the Engle and Granger (1987) methodology. Hence, one can conclude that it is, if at all, (disaggregated) financial and commercial customers' cumulative order flow that might convey useful information for future exchange rate movements and thus paves the way for possible strategic dealing behaviour of market makers.

4.2 Vector error correction models

As shown in chapter 4.1, there are some indications for a stable equilibrium between incoming cumulative order flow of financial and commercial customers and the level of exchange rates. Hence, whenever this equilibrium is disturbed, the economic system, i.e. the combination of cumulative order flow and exchange rates, tends to move in order to re-balance. During this process, adjustment dynamics can potentially be executed by just one or both of the system's variables. Here, the exchange rate *should* adjust with respect to cumulative order flow or vice versa. Questions of this kind can be answered by calculating the vector error correction model (VECM) related to equation (4.2) and conduct tests of weak and strong exogeneity of the respective variables.

The VECM related to the case at hand has the form

$$\begin{pmatrix} \Delta S_t \\ \Delta X_{i,t} \end{pmatrix} = \begin{pmatrix} \alpha^S \\ \alpha^{X_i} \end{pmatrix} \begin{pmatrix} 1 & \beta_{i,0} & \beta_{i,1} & \beta_{i,2} \end{pmatrix} \begin{pmatrix} S_{t-1} \\ 1 \\ trend_{t-1} \\ X_{i,t-1} \end{pmatrix} + \sum_{j=0}^{J} \Gamma_j \begin{pmatrix} \Delta S_{t-j} \\ \Delta X_{i,t-j} \end{pmatrix} + \begin{pmatrix} \varepsilon_t^S \\ \varepsilon_t^{X_i} \end{pmatrix} \tag{4.3}$$

for different types i of incoming order flow.

Results for 2002 / 2003 are shown in table 4.3. As revealed by the VECM's cointegration vector, cumulative order flow from financial customers is positively correlated with the exchange rate, highlighting the potentially dominating role of financial customers in exchange rate determination, while commercial customers' order flow shows a negative sign. Hence, results confirm findings of the aforementioned cointegration analyses based upon Engle and Granger (1987) methodology. However, this finding does not enable one to infer the direction of causality, so adjustment dynamics have to be analysed in greater detail.

Adjustment dynamics are described by error correction (ECM) coefficients. Regardless of the type of customer group, ECM coefficients between -0.05 and -0.21 indicate that, in general, the adjustment process is quite slow here. Information half life implied in an existing disequilibrium, calculated with respect to the average time relapsing between two trades of a specific group of customers, is hence relatively long, at least compared to other studies. However, remember that order flow here originates from customers of a single bank, whereas exchange rates should be driven by market-wide order flow. Hence, this finding is not too much of a surprise.

Although ECM coefficients are quite low, they differ substantially between customer groups. By every trade with a financial customer, departures from equilibrium are dissipated by 0.1 percent (for changes of the spot exchange rate) and 0.12 percent (for changes of cumulative order flow), respectively. By taking average trading frequency of financial customers into account, these figures correspond to an respective information half life of 81 hours and 67 hours. Hence, private information are slowly processed within the information aggregation mechanism that is compared to other studies like Batten and Hogan (2005), and Osler et al. (2006), among others. This finding, as well as existence of serial correlation at higher lags within residuals (documented by the Q statistic), implying a slow learning process, generally confirms predictions of Evans and Lyons (2004b, 2005c).

***Table 4.3:** Estimates of vector error correction model given by equation (4.3)*
255 trading days between October 1, 2002 and September 30, 2003

	Financial Customers		Commercial Customers		Non-internal Customers	
Cointegration eq.						
Constant	0.83		1.05		0.55	
$Trend_{t-1}$	2.9E-5 (5.98)***		-1.5E-5 (5.54)***		8.4E-5 (5.15)***	
X_{t-1}	6.3E-6 (5.94)***		-1.1E-5 (9.21)***		1.4E-5 (4.74)***	
Dependent variable	ΔS_t	ΔX_t	ΔS_t	ΔX_t	ΔS_t	ΔX_t
ECM coefficient	-0.10 (2.46)**	-0.12 (3.38)***	-0.19 (1.90)*	-0.21 (3.95)***	-0.05 (2.25)**	-0.15 (3.70)***
Half life (hours)	80.8	67.3	42.5	38.5	161.6	50.5
ΔS_{t-1}	-0.41 (39.4)***	-22.87 (1.73)*	-0.41 (39.2)***	-2.53 (0.50)	-0.41 (39.4)***	-26.81 (1.88)*
ΔS_{t-2}	-0.15 (13.9)***	-6.50 (0.46)	-0.15 (13.8)***	-3.40 (0.62)	-0.15 (13.9)***	-10.64 (0.70)
ΔX_{t-1}	0.12 (1.43)	0.13 (12.6)***	0.23 (1.09)	0.01 (0.48)	0.13 (1.75)*	0.11 (10.4)***
ΔX_{t-2}	0.01 (1.11)	0.11 (10.6)***	0.17 (0.80)	0.01 (0.01)	0.10 (1.34)	0.08 (7.77)***
Adj. R^2	0.14	0.04	0.001	0.14	0.14	0.04
Q(10)	1.16 (0.31)	3.55 (0.00)	1.05 (0.40)	2.00 (0.03)	1.12 (0.34)	3.03 (0.00)
Weak ex.	6.07**	11.40***	3.77*	15.59***	5.06**	13.66***
Strong ex.	10.07**	15.93***	5.71	17.57***	10.62**	17.99***

Notes: Coefficients of lagged cumulative order flow (X_{t-1}) in the cointegration equation are multiplied by 10,000; t-statistics in paretheses. ECM coefficients in ΔS_t equations are multiplied by 100, order flow variables are in € millions; t-statistics in parentheses. * (**, ***) denotes significance at the 10% (5%, 1%) level. Q(10) is Breusch-Godfrey test up to ten lags, p-values in parentheses. Weak ex. is weak exogeneity: χ^2-test statistic (1 df). Strong ex. is strong exogeneity: χ^2-test statistic (4 df).

As shown by weak and strong exogeneity tests, the adjustment process is driven by both the spot exchange rate and cumulative incoming order flow, at least in case of financial customers. Within the 2002 / 2003 sub-sample, the Null of weak and strong exogeneity can be rejected for both of these variables,[83] indicating that both time series are likely to be a function of the system's departure from equilibrium.

Interestingly, adjustment is more rapidly in case of commercial customers. Now, 0.19 and 0.21 percent of a departure from equilibrium are dissipated with every single trade, corresponding to an information half life for both of the variables of 43 hours and 39 hours, respectively. However, compared to Osler et al. (2006), this is still quite a long time. These results might be caused by the very few take-profit orders within the data set. Obviously, take-profit orders react very rapidly to price changes and are thus likely to reduce the average information half life enormously.

When taking a look at exogeneity tests, it becomes obvious that almost the entire adjustment process is driven by cumulative commercial customers' order flow, whereas exchange rate movements seem to be exogenous here. F-tests for weak exogeneity confirm t-tests' results for statistical significance of the ECM coefficient, indicating low-level exogeneity of exchange rate changes, but when taking Granger causality into account, it is only order flow that adjusts to existing disequilibria. This, again, is consistent with findings presented in Osler (1998) and Evans and Lyons (2005c).

At last, it is not surprising that the exchange rate adjusts even slower in case of aggregated order flow of financial and commercial customers. Both the magnitude of ECM coefficients and information half life suggest that. As mentioned in Reitz et al. (2007), this finding is likely to be due to the smoothing impact of commercial customers, who sell foreign exchange when the spot rate is rising and vice versa.

When looking at the 2004 / 2005 sub-sample, results generally confirm findings for the earlier period, even though they are not that clear as they are for 2002 / 2003. Cumulative incoming order flow from financial customers is

[83] A description of tests for weak- and strong-sense exogeneity is to be found in this work's Annex.

positively correlated with the exchange rate, whereas commercial customers' order flow bears again a negative sign within the VECM's cointegration equation. Because non-internal customers' cumulative order flow shows no signs of cointegration in 2004 / 2005, it is skipped from the analysis. Results are shown in table 4.4. It basically confirms weaker cointegration results shown in table 4.2.

***Table 4.4:** Estimates of vector error correction model given by equation (4.3)*
250 trading days between October 1, 2004 and September 30, 2005

	Financial Customers		Commercial Customers	
Cointegration eq.				
Constant	1.21		1.25	
$Trend_{t-1}$	-1.6E-5 (3.88)***		-2.5E-5 (3.16)***	
X_{t-1}	0.457 (-4.87)***		-10.49 (3.44)***	
Dependent variable	ΔS_t	ΔX_t	ΔS_t	ΔX_t
ECM coeff.	-0.01 (0.45)	-1.98 (3.33)***	0.01 (0.59)	-1.25 (-3.16)***
Half life (hours)	992.6	5.87	---	11.16
ΔS_{t-1}	-0.02 (-2.18)**	-58.81 (-2.68)**	-0.01 (-0.61)	-7.78 (-0.57)
ΔS_{t-2}	-0.01 (-0.90)	-25.43 (-1.16)	---	---
ΔS_{t-3}	0.02 (1.81)	-15.29 (-0.70)	---	---
ΔS_{t-4}	-0.01 (-0.32)	-16.25 (-0.74)	---	---
ΔX_{t-1}	3.0E-5 (7.15)***	0.19 (20.2)***	-9.4E-6 (-1.06)	0.01 (0.84)
ΔX_{t-2}	-2.2E-6 (-0.51)	0.10 (9.81)***	---	---
ΔX_{t-3}	-3.9E-6 (-0.91)	0.04 (4.42)***	---	---
ΔX_{t-4}	1.6E-7 (0.04)	0.03 (2.93)***	---	---
Adj. R^2	0.005	0.07	0.001	0.001
Q(10)	5.92 (0.21)	6.28 (0.18)	3.19 (0.53)	3.44 (0.49)
Weak ex.	0.07	4.09**	0.08	2.26*
Strong ex.	52.65***	10.00*	1.12	0.33

Notes: Coefficients of lagged cumulative order flow (X_{t-1}) in the cointegration equation are multiplied by 10,000; t-statistics in paretheses. ECM coefficients in ΔS_t equations are multiplied by 100, order flow variables are in € millions; t-statistics in parentheses. * (**, ***) denotes significance at the 10% (5%, 1%) level. Q(10) is Breusch-Godfrey test up to ten lags, p-values in parentheses. Weak ex. is weak exogeneity: χ^2-test statistic (1 df). Strong ex. is strong exogeneity: χ^2-test statistic (4 df).

In contrast to outcomes for 2002 / 2003, the spot rate's ECM coefficient is not at all statistically significant for financial customers, neither when tested by a t-test nor an F-test. Surprisingly, tests for strong exogeneity nevertheless indicate that the spot rate does adjust to deviations from equilibrium. Consequently, this adjustment process must be entirely driven by a Granger-causal relationship between the spot rate and cumulative financial customers' order flow.

For changes of financial customers' cumulative order flow, the ECM coefficient's magnitude is much greater than in 2002 / 2003 and thus adjustment happens more rapidly now. Tests for weak and strong exogeneity indicate that order flow adjusts, at least slightly, to departures from equilibrium. Taking results for both sub-samples into account, one can hence conclude that a single market maker's incoming order flow from financial customers is not as exogenous as micro theory believes it to be up to the present. Thus, financial customers do seem to exploit private information in FX trading, but react to exchange rate movements, too. Hence, this result basically supports findings in Taylor and Allen (1992). According to them, more than 90 percent of London-based currency traders rely on technical analysis in addition to their private and fundamental information. Since technical analysis often refers to trend-following trading strategies, dealers' reliance on technical trading can make financial customers' order flow subject to exchange rate changes.

What might be the reason for this deviation between financial customers' order flow's theoretic role and its empirical appearance in this study? Remember, the group of financial customers here consists not only of mutual and hedge funds, but includes other banks, too. In fact, interbank trading is the largest group of transactions within the financial customers segment (see chapter 2). Interbank trades, in turn, result from both the banks' own research driven trading and their hot potato trading that originates from trading with financial and commercial customers. Thus, incoming interbank order flow might react to exchange rate changes, because the originating bank's commercial customers do so.

As a consequence of this argumentation, incoming interbank order flow should be seen as a combination that conveys signals which are both positively and negatively correlated with information. At the bank at hand, actual correlation between financial customers' order flow and the exchange rate depends on the fraction of "real" financial customer order flow at the respective bank our market maker transacts with. The fact that financial customers' order flow is basically positively correlated with exchange rates indicates that the majority of interbank trading results from financial customer trading at our dealer's customer banks.

As shown in table 4.2, the cointegration relationship between cumulative incoming order flow and exchange rates in case of commercial customers is only weak. Hence, meagre results presented in table 4.4 are not surprising. As expected, exchange rate changes are exogenous for commercial customers, so there is not much of a difference compared to findings for 2002 / 2003. However, in contrast to earlier results, there are only weak indications that it is cumulative order flow that drives the adjustment process whenever a disequilibrium exists. The ECM coefficient is statistically significant, but only with respect to a t-test, even though calculations for information half life imply quite a rapid speed of adjustment. An F-test for weak exogeneity, however, indicates that the Null of exogenous changes in cumulative order flow can only be rejected at the ten percent level. Taking Granger causality into account, there are no indications that commercial customers' order flow is endogenous.

Nevertheless, even though results for 2004 / 2005 are not as clear as they are for 2002 / 2003, they generally confirm earlier findings. Hence, results presented here do not support the view that dealers subsidise trades with financial customers in order to gain informational advantages exploitable in future trades, as originally proposed by Leach and Madhavan (1992) and applied to FX markets by Osler et al. (2006). None of the tests shows an adjusted R^2 greater than 14 percent, so the VECM is able to explain only a small fraction of total return variance. Furthermore, lagged order flow coefficients are, in general, insignificant for exchange rate changes, indicating a lack of Granger causality running from order flow to exchange rates. Only once, within the 2004 / 2005 sub-sample, such a causal relationship exists, leading to a rejection of the hypothesis of strong exogeneity of exchange rate changes for financial customers, although the ECM coefficient is statistically insignificant.[84]

---

[84] Results do not change qualitatively when one re-runs the model with cumulative trade indicators instead of cumulative order flow. In doing so, one accounts for the fact that trad-

All these findings support the view of Sager and Taylor (2005) that even financial customers' cumulative order flow is not exploitable to predict short-run exchange rate changes for a single market maker, because a single bank's customer order flow is not a systematic and time-invariant predictor of market-wide end-user order flow. Hence, there is no need to subsidise potentially well-informed customer order flow at a single bank for informational reasons and thus, the strategic dealing hypothesis is not supported here. As mentioned in Osler et al. (2006), dealers' pricing behaviour in FX markets is rather governed by usance than by bank- or dealer-specific factors, so it is unlikely that results presented here are due to the data at hand. To further confirm this conclusion, subsequent sections of chapter 4 provide additional tests of order flow's forecasting power to reassess above-mentioned findings.

4.3 The Evans and Lyons (2005c) model of micro-based exchange rate forecasting

A standard working proposition in microstructure theory is that dealers aim to hold net zero positions in FX inventories at the end of each trading day. Even though this assumption is realistic, generally confirmed in interviews with traders, and describes dealers' risk aversion properly, the dealer investigated here mentions that he indeed keeps at least minor open positions over night. Relaxing the assumption concerning market makers' inventory management hence offers the opportunity to interpret open positions between two trading days as some kind of medium-term speculating in FX markets. Keeping the long information half life of the VECM in the previous section of chapter 4 in mind, the market maker at hand might use observed cumulative order flow to exploit information conveyed therein not for short-run, but for rather medium-term speculative trading over night or over a few days. If observed order flow really ensures an superior forecasting power compared to publicly available macroeconomic information, the dealer would indeed have an incentive to subsidise well-informed order flow by narrowing bid-ask spreads and thus to behave strategically. In order to come to a final conclusion about the strategic

---

ers do not care much about exact amounts of order flow, but are more interested in "vote counting", i.e. general trends in order flow.

dealing hypothesis being the driving force for dealers' pricing behaviour, these aspects should be analysed, too.

Up to the present, much effort has been put to various attempts to forecast spot exchange rates out-of-sample.[85] With the exception of some promising findings in micro-based studies like Evans and Lyons (2005c), and Ito and Hashimoto (2007), among others, results, though, are mixed. In general, forecastability is the worse the higher is frequency. Clarida and Taylor (1997), and van Tol and Wolff (2005), for example, employ forward exchange premia in an error correction framework to forecast spot exchange rates out-of-sample. Although Clarida and Taylor (1997) actually are able to outperform random walk predictions, van Tol and Wolff (2005) are not, indicating that forecasting power of their approaches is not stable over time. Wright (2003) suggests to use Bayesian averaging techniques over a variety of different forecasting models to come to an out-of-sample prediction. He finds that this approach is more accurate than any single one of the models used for averaging and is even able to slightly outpredict a random walk most of the times, while his technique never does much worse than a naive forecast.

There are some further successful studies in forecasting exchange rates. Sosvilla Rivero and Garcia (2005) use financial market data, so-called *inflation-indexed bonds*, to derive inflation expectations and conduct these in an expectations-augmented version of the purchasing-power-parity (PPP) model. Interestingly, they are able to outperform a random walk on a five-days horizon. Alquist and Chinn (2007), too, can outperform naive predictions by using Gourinchas and Rey's (2005) measure of external imbalances. This is specifically impressive since their model is obviously macro-based and they are actually forecasting exchange rates on a quarterly horizon, which is quite a high frequency for purely macroeconomic models.

How forecasts actually affect price changes is investigated in DeGrauwe and Rovira Kaltwasser (2007). They find evidence for the existence of both a fundamental and a non-fundamental (or bubble) equilibrium. From a theoretical

[85] In addition to point predictions of future exchange rates, a number of studies aims to forecast exchange rate volatility (Balaban, 2004, among others) or even try to forecast currencies' densities like, among others, Sarno and Valente (2005).

point of view, their model is exceedingly interesting, since it uses a different concept of rationality instead of the rather restrictive traditional *rational expectations approach*. Therein, agents realise that the world is much too complex to understand it in its entirety and hence, they use quite simple heuristics to forecast exchange rates. Within this theoretical environment, DeGrauwe and Rovira Kaltwasser (2007) show that probability to find either one of these two possible equilibria or to switch between them depends on the number of forecasting rules conducted by market participants. As a consequence of this, the exchange rate cyclically moves around its fundamental value and is subject to excess volatility, just as observed empirically.

Despite of these quite promising results, currency traders themselves are, in general, sceptical. In a survey done with U.S.-based currency dealers, Cheung and Chinn (2001) reveal that 60 percent believe that there is only low predictability of exchange rate returns intraday. Even on longer horizons, only one third of their respondents are convinced that predictability in FX markets is high.

As in Evans and Lyons (2005c), subsequent analyses compare *ex-ante* forecasting performances of a micro-based model against both a standard macro model and a driftless random walk. Since VECM analyses have shown that order flow conveys, if at all, information about medium-term exchange rate movements, forecasting horizons from one day to ten trading days are investigated here. For every model and every forecasting horizon, the mean squared prediction error (MSE) is calculated and results are compared by using a test introduced by Diebold and Mariano (1995). Additionally, Evans and Lyons' (2005c) projection statistic is calculated to reassess outcomes.

All tests presented here can be seen as further empirical examinations of Meese and Rogoff's (1983a, 1983b) conclusion that structural macro models cannot outperform a naive random walk. But while their contribution in fact focuses more on concurrent explanation than on ex-ante forecasting, analyses presented here forecast future exchange rate movements by using recently available data.

The remainder of this section is as follows. In section 4.3.1, theoretical background on the models compared herein, especially on Evans and Lyons'

(2005c) micro-based model, is provided. Afterwards, section 4.3.2 introduces basic principles of model-comparison techniques as well as a justification for why interbank transactions are included to financial customers' order flow, although Evans and Lyons (2005c) do not do this. Empirical results are presented in chapter 4.3.3.

4.3.1 Theoretical background

One explanation for unpredictability of exchange rates is that currency prices follow a random walk because they are driven by some unobservable fundamentals that itself follow a random walk process. Engel and West (2004, 2005) provide a valuable alternative to this view. They show that the exchange rate follows a process arbitrarily close to a random walk, if it is driven by potentially observable fundamentals that are I(1) (though not necessarily random walks) and the discount factor in the present value equation approaches unity. This is because an I(1) process can be seen as a combination of a random walk and a stationary component. Whenever the discount factor is near one, market participants put most of weight on fundamentals far into the future. Since expectations concerning these kinds of fundamentals are dominated by the random walk component, exchange rates follow a random walk process, too. In addition, forecasting based on deviations between the exchange rate and current macro fundamentals gets even more complicated by the fact that there are usually no real-time estimates of fundamentals available; and even if they are, ex-post values might differ significantly from real-time estimates. Evans (2005) addresses this problem in greater detail.

Based on these insights, Evans and Lyons (2005c) focus on expectational surprises as driving factors of exchange rate dynamics. By using a micro-based model, they are able to show that there exist some kind of non-public information, which are useful in forecasting this surprise component of exchange rate changes. In fact, their results show that exchange rates are indeed driven by fundamentals and these non-public signals provide information about the current state of the macro-economy. Hence, Evans and Lyons' (2005c) model provides a rationale for Engel and West's (2004) firm evidence that exchange rates are helpful in predicting future macroeconomic fundamentals (which are publicly observed with a time lag), because non-public signals are useful to do so. Macro models, in contrast, predict exactly the opposite.

As in Evans and Lyons (2005c), the micro model investigated here is a stylised version of the one developed in Evans and Lyons (2004b). There, the authors model information aggregation in FX markets via the trading process within a dynamic general equilibrium (DGE) setting with an enriched information structure that distincts their approach from earlier models of this kind. To understand the model, consider the present value representation of exchange rates, well known from the asset market approach. According to this, the (log-nominal) exchange rate is determined by the present value of expected future fundamentals. Formally, this is

$$s_t = (1-b)\sum_{i=0}^{\infty} b^i E_t f_{t+i}\,, \tag{4.4}$$

where s_t is the log-nominal exchange rate, f_t are exchange rate driving fundamentals, and b is a discount factor. Precise definitions of f_t and b depend on the macro model in question. The small but powerful difference of Evans and Lyons' (2005c) model is that their micro approach focuses on micro-level learning, so they work within an asymmetric-information framework instead of a symmetric-information setting, which would be typical for macro models. Consequently, they re-write equation (4.4) as

$$s_t = (1-b)\sum_{i=0}^{\infty} b^i E_t^m f_{t+i} \tag{4.5}$$

with E_t^m denoting expectations conditional on the market maker's information at the beginning of period t.

As shown in Appendix A.4.1, iterating equation (4.5) forward yields

$$s_t = E_t^m f_t + \frac{b}{1-b} E_t^m \Delta s_{t+1}. \tag{4.6}$$

Solving equation (4.6) for Δs_{t+1} and allowing for forecast revisions, i.e. taking changes in expectations into account, then gives

$$\Delta s_{t+1} = \frac{1-b}{b}(s_t - E_t^m f_t) + \varepsilon_{t+1}^m \tag{4.7}$$

with

$$\varepsilon_{t+1}^m \equiv (1-b)\sum_{i=0}^{\infty} b^i (E_{t+1} - E_t) f_{t+i+1} \tag{4.8}$$

being the present value of the market makers' forecast revisions of future fundamentals. This surprise component given by equation (4.8) is the driving force of innovations in spot exchange rates when b is approaching unity.

It is a central building block of micro models that market makers are assumed to revise their forecasts with respect to observed order flow. Whenever market makers observe order flow that is significant in both volume and correlation, they use these observations to revise their expectations. This is, as stated before, because order flow conveys information about the state of the macro-economy that is not available from other sources at the time.

The conviction that order flow is strongly correlated with information flow is empirically supported in a number of studies; two of the best-known are contributions by Evans and Lyons (2002a, 2002d). However, as animadversion on Meese and Rogoff (1983a), their analyses are more about concurrent correlations than about ex-ante forecasting, too. In Evans and Lyons (2005c), the authors are more interested in whether observed order flow until period *t-1* is correlated with the arrival of information between *t* and *t+1*. The fact that they find evidence for order flow's ex-ante forecasting power indicates that the group of market makers as a whole does not observe the entirety of market-wide transaction flows contemporaneously, because if this was the case, innovations in spot exchange rates would only be correlated with unanticipated flows during period *t* and not with earlier flows. Of course, market makers do not observe all transaction flows, not at least because customer flows are private information.

As Evans and Lyons (2005c) point out, forecasting power of micro-based models shows two critical features. First, transaction flows must contain relevant information about fundamentals that, in turn, originate from superior information of specific end-users (e.g. hedge funds) or from allocative trading that signals the current state of the macro-economy. Second, ex-ante forecasting power necessitates a time lag between order flow and exchange rate movements.

Evans and Lyons' (2005c) intuitive explanation for transaction flow's out-of-sample prediction power is a time lag between dealer *i*'s customer order flow during period *t*, denoted X_{t+1}^{i}, and information about market-wide order flow in *t*, denoted X_{t+1}, which dealer *i* observes with a one-period delay. Hence, the information set of dealer *i* at the beginning of *t*, denoted Ω_t^i, contains market-wide order flow's history up to *t-1* as well as *i*'s individual order flow history including *t*. X_{t+1}^{i} can be interpreted as a mapping of X_{t+1} in a way that

$$X_{t+1}^{i} = X_{t+1} + \xi_{t+1}^{i} \tag{4.9}$$

with ξ_{t+1}^{i} being an i.i.d. mean zero idiosyncratic shock with constant variance σ_{ξ}^{2}. Market-wide order flow is assumed to be described by an AR(1)-process of the form

$$X_{t+1} = \lambda X_t + \upsilon_{t+1}, \tag{4.10}$$

where $\upsilon_{t+1} \overset{i.i.d.}{\sim} No\left(0, \sigma_{\upsilon}^{2}\right)$, too.

Since all dealers know equation (4.10) and *i*'s information set comprises historical values of both aggregated and individual order flow, any market maker can form an expectation about market-wide order flow after observing his own individual incoming customer flow. Unanticipated order flow can thus be written by substituting expected values for individual and aggregated order flow in equation (4.9) as

$$X_{t+1}^{i} - E_t^i X_{t+1}^{i} = X_{t+1} - E_t^i X_{t+1} + \xi_{t+1}^{i}, \tag{4.11.1}$$

where E_t^i denotes dealer i's expectations conditional on Ω_t^i. As done in a working paper version of their (2005c) study, Evans and Lyons (2004c) show that expectation errors can be re-written[86] by using idiosyncratic error terms only, so that

$$X_{t+1}^i - E_t^i X_{t+1}^i = \upsilon_{t+1} + \lambda\psi\upsilon_t + \xi_{t+1}^i, \tag{4.11.2}$$

where $\psi \equiv \sigma_\xi^2 / \left(\sigma_\upsilon^2 + \sigma_\xi^2\right)$. Because of the MA(1)-component of equation (4.11.2), namely $\upsilon_{t+1} - \lambda\psi\upsilon_t$, informational innovations for dealer i in t are correlated with past innovations in market-wide transaction flow, i.e. υ_t.

As Evans and Lyons (2005c) emphasise, these aspects do not necessarily imply that ε_{t+1}^m is correlated with υ_t. Due to the Bayes-Nash equilibrium structure of the model, Evans and Lyons (2005c) assume that market makers indeed use idiosyncratic information, though not for their own pricing, since they would be subject to arbitrage if they quote different prices than their competitors, but for submitting orders at another dealer's quote.[87] Hence, market makers do not change quotes in the way suggested by equation (4.11.2), because it contains idiosyncratic signals. Instead, dealers change quotes at the start of period $t+1$, when they get information about market-wide order flow in t, i.e. X_t, so that υ_t becomes common knowledge.

In Evans and Lyons' (2005c) stylised model, changes in fundamentals are driven by an AR(1) process as well as by both a common knowledge component, namely y_t, that is observed at the beginning of period t, and innovations in aggregate order flow, i.e. υ_t, market makers learn about with a one-period delay. Formally, this is

$$\Delta f_t = \phi\Delta f_{t-1} + y_t + \delta\upsilon_t. \tag{4.12}$$

[86] See Appendix A.4.2 for details.

[87] This feature provides a potential source of information for the market maker who is approached by that dealer trading on idiosyncratic information. Hence, interdealer order flow might be useful to forecast exchange rate movements – a fact, that will be of particular interest in chapter 4.3.2.

Evolution of aggregated order flow is already known from equation (4.10). It is now "re-written" to hold good for period t, so this is

$$X_t = \lambda X_{t-1} + \upsilon_t . \tag{4.13}$$

As done in Appendix A.4.3, it is straightforward to show that under these conditions, it is only $\delta\upsilon_t$ that is responsible for deviations between actual and expected values of driving fundamentals. By taking these information into consideration, one can formulate a forecasting equation[88] of the form

$$\Delta s_{t+1} = \frac{1-b}{b}(s_t - E_t^m f_t) + \frac{1}{1-b\phi} y_{t+1} + \frac{[1+\phi(1-b)]\delta}{1-b\phi}(X_t - \lambda X_{t-1}) . \tag{4.14}$$

Equation (4.14) shows how subsequent exchange rate changes are affected by lagged order flow, even if the discount factor b approaches one.[89] This is because the difference between recent and previous period's order flow in equation (4.14) is at least multiplied by $\delta/(1-\phi)$ as b becomes unity. In this case, both the market makers' expectations concerning fundamentals and exchange rates in period t are no longer determining spot exchange rates. Common news, incorporated in y_{t+1}, still drive quotations, but they cannot be forecasted and thus are not to be included in an empirically testable equation.

Evans and Lyons (2005c) suggest two empirical models to investigate lagged order flow's forecasting power. The first one, termed *Micro I*, is based on aggregated order flow of all groups of end-users. Hence, Micro I is given by

$$\Delta s_{t+1} = a_o + aX_t^{AGG} + \varepsilon_{t+1} , \tag{4.15}$$

where X_t^{AGG} denotes aggregated order flow across all types of counterparts. The second empirical forecasting equation, termed *Micro II*, uses disaggregated flows from the three customer segments known from earlier analyses in this work, i.e. financial customers, commercial customers, and internal customers. Hence, the Micro II specification is

---

[88] See Appendix A.4.4.

[89] In Evans and Lyons (2005b) the authors find that 1/3 of order flow's forecasting power for spot exchange rates is due to its ability to forecast future flows.

$$\Delta s_{t+1} = a_o + \sum_{j=1}^{3} a X_{j,t}^{DIS} + \varepsilon_{t+1} \tag{4.16}$$

with $X_{j,t}^{DIS}$ being disaggregated order flow from segment *j*. As in Evans and Lyons (2005c), both of the empirical forecasting equations do not include interest rate differentials to account for $s_t - E_t^m f_t$ in equation (4.14), because these models shall be purely micro-based and thus be robust against a discount factor near unity. Notice that it is always *lagged* order flow up to period *t* that is used to explain exchange rate changes in *t+1*.

Before proceeding with some details on empirical investigations, the macro model that is used as one out of two benchmarks[90] for the above-mentioned micro-based equations is introduced here. Macro models, e.g. the money-income model or the Taylor-rule model, are usually based on a present-value equation like the one shown in equation (4.4). However, since there is no space left for forecasting exchange rate changes on deviations of s_t from its expected fundamentals $(E_t f_t)$ when *b* is close to one, Evans and Lyons (2005c) use a common feature of many macro models in their macro-based forecasting equation, namely uncovered interest parity[91] (UIP). Since UIP argues that expected exchange rate movements during the next period are driven by recent international interest rate differentials and a risk-premium in case of imperfect substitutability of foreign and domestic assets, denoted ρ_t, the ex post variant of the macro model benchmark is given by

$$\Delta s_{t+1} = i_t - i_t^* + \rho_t + \varepsilon_{t+1}, \tag{4.17}$$

where i_t is the domestic interest rate, i_t^* denotes the interest rate level abroad and ε_{t+1} is a normally distributed, mean-zero error term. This translates into the following regression

$$\Delta s_{t+1} = a_0 + a\left(i_t - i_t^*\right) + \varepsilon_{t+1}. \tag{4.18}$$

[90] The second benchmark is a naive random walk model that forecasts the exchange rate in period *t* to be the exchange rate in period *t+1*.

[91] See chapter 1 for details.

Calculations indicate that the risk-premium ρ_t is time-variant here, so all results shown in section 4.3.3 refer to the so-called *Fama-model*, meaning that the risk-premium is indicated to be a function of the interest rate differential of the form $\rho_t = \eta_0 + \eta(i_i - i_t^*)$, so $a_0 = \eta_0$ and $a = 1 - \eta$.

4.3.2 Comparing models' relative forecasting performances

As done in Evans and Lyons (2005c), all models are compared over three different forecasting horizons and by using two different measurement statistics. Forecasting horizons are one day (overnight), one week (five trading days), and two weeks (ten trading days). Due to the fact that every single sample at hand is relatively short and does not provide an appropriate number of non-overlapping observations on horizons longer than ten trading days, we refrain from expanding forecasting horizons up to twenty trading days as done in Evans and Lyons (2005c). Interest rates used for calculating equation (4.18) are euro deposit rates with maturities that match forecast horizons. As in chapter 3, all regressions are calculated over the two known sub-samples from October 1, 2002, until September 30, 2003, and from October 1, 2004, until September 30, 2005.

The first out of two tests employed here is based on the models' MSE-ratios relative to a naive random walk forecast as done in Mark (1995) and Faust et al. (2003). This approach was introduced by Diebold and Mariano (1995) and tests whether a model's MSE-ratio to a random walk is significantly different from unity. How this test is employed is described in subsequent paragraphs.

Consider the first and the last day of the test-period[92] are denoted $t = 1$ and T, respectively. The first step is to calculate regressions given by equations (4.15), (4.16), and (4.18) with respective data up to t. Based on resulting coefficients, order flow and interest rate data observed in t are used to calculate a one-step ahead forecast for the (log-nominal) spot exchange rate. This proce-

[92] Notice that the test-period is not equal to the sample-period, because one needs some of the sample's observations to calculate the coefficients of the forecast model. Hence, test-periods start some days later than samples do. In addition, test-periods end a few days later than sample-periods do accordingly, since forecasts calculated with order flow or interest rate data up to T can be aimed up to T+h.

dure is repeated until T, so one gets T one-step ahead forecasts for the log-spot rate. Hence, it is possible to calculate a mean square error (MSE) for every model j over a forecast horizon h[93] by

$$MSE_j = \frac{1}{T-1}\sum_{i=1}^{T}\left(s_{j,t+h}^{e} - s_{t+h}\right)^2, \tag{4.18}$$

where $s_{j,t+h}^{e}$ denotes expectation in t about the log-spot rate in $t+h$, s_{t+h} is the actually realised log-spot rate in $t+h$, and T is corresponding to the total number of observations. The next step is to calculate model j's MSE-ratio to a random walk.

The essence of Diebold and Mariano's (1995) test is to check whether model j's MSE-ratio is significantly different from one.[94] The advantageous features of this approach, e.g. its usability for a variety of accuracy measures and their distributions, made it to be one of the most promising approaches in the field after the pessimistic conclusions on formal forecast accuracy tests mentioned, among others, in Dhrymes et al. (1972), Howrey et al. (1974), and Clark and McCracken (2001). Earlier test, e.g. the one introduced by Christiano (1989), primarily suffer from non-normal asymptotic distributions when analysing nested models. To deploy the Diebold and Mariano (1995) test, the first step is to calculate a sample mean-square error differential by

$$\bar{d}_j = \frac{1}{T}\sum_{i=1}^{T}\left(e_{j,i}^2 - e_{RW,i}^2\right), \tag{4.19}$$

where $e_{j,i}^2$ is squared prediction error of model j at the i-th observation, $e_{RW,i}^2$ denotes the random walk's respective squared prediction error, and T is again the total number of forecasts.

---

[93] Notice that h in this study is one working day, five working days, and ten working days, respectively. However, since all models are re-calculated every single trading day to get the latest coefficient values, every prediction is a one-step-ahead forecast, regardless of the actual magnitude of h. "#-step-ahead" hence refers to the number (#) of forecasts, which are based on constant coefficients. Here, # is one. # is hence not linked to the actual length of the forecasting horizon.

[94] A quite similar test was introduced by Vuong (1989).

Under the Null of equal forecast accuracy, $\bar{d}_j$ is zero. By construction, $\bar{d}_j$ should have a normal distribution, so it should be possible to test the Null by constructing the ratio $\bar{d}_j/\sqrt{\mathrm{var}(\bar{d}_j)}$ and using a standard normal distribution. However, potential serial correlation within the $\{d_{j,t}\}$ series makes calculating $\mathrm{var}(\bar{d}_j)$ specifically challenging. As mentioned in Mark (1995), out-of-sample forecasting induces serial correlation in the estimation error, so it is necessary to use the approach suggested by Diebold and Mariano (1995) to approximate

$$\mathrm{var}(\bar{d}_j)=[\gamma_0+2\gamma_1+...+2\gamma_l](n-1)^{-1} \tag{4.20}$$

with γ_i being the i-th autocovariance of the $\{d_{j,t}\}$ sequence. The Diebold and Mariano (DM)-statistic is hence given by

$$DM=\frac{\bar{d}_j}{\sqrt{[\gamma_0+2\gamma_1+...+2\gamma_l](n-1)^{-1}}}. \tag{4.21}$$

As done in Mark (1995), the truncation lag, l, is calculated by using the data-dependent formula provided by Andrews (1991) and employing an univariate AR(1) process to the elements of the spectral-density matrix. The truncation lag is then given by

$$l=1.1447[\hat{a}(1)]T^{1/3}, \tag{4.22.1}$$

where

$$\hat{a}(1)=4\left[\frac{\hat{\rho}}{(1-\hat{\rho})(1+\hat{\rho})}\right]^2 \tag{4.22.2}$$

and $\hat{\rho}$ is the estimated first-order autocorrelation coefficient of the squared-error differential series.

Unfortunately, Diebold and Mariano's (1995) test is not guaranteed to be positive semi-definite, since negative autocovariances could lead to a non-positive approximation of $\text{var}(\bar{d}_j)$. Following Diebold and Mariano (1995), the Null of equal forecast accuracy is rejected whenever $\text{var}(\bar{d}_j)$ is negative.

As suggested by Harvey et al. (1998), DM-statistics are not only compared to a standard normal distribution, but also to Student's t-statistic with *n-1* degrees of freedom. Since the bulk of tests performed here is based on less than 200 observations, it is appropriate to do so.[95] As mentioned in footnote 93, all predictions here are only one-step-ahead forecasts, so there is no need for further adjustment of equation (4.21) in order to make the approach capable for multi-step predictions.

The second test employed here is the *projection statistic* introduced by Evans and Lyons (2005c). There, $\Delta^h s_{t+h|t}$ denotes *h*-period (out-of-sample) forecast of the change in the (log) spot exchange rate computed by a model that is estimated with data up to *t*.[96] After constructing all forecasts over the forecasting period, predictions are regressed on realised changes in (log) spot exchange rates, denoted Δs_{t+h},

$$\Delta^h s_{t+h|t} = \beta_0 + \beta \Delta s_{t+h} + \varepsilon_{t+h}, \tag{4.23}$$

where ε_{t+h} is a white-noise disturbance term.

Forecasting performance of the model in question against a driftless random walk can be examined by simply testing for statistical significance of β. Obviously, to generate meaningful forecasts, β should possess a positive sign. This is because if the non-random walk model had no predictive power for actual future changes of the exchange rate or if the latter was following a random walk, it is only ε_{t+h} that is responsible for $\Delta^h s_{t+h|t}$ deviating from zero. Note that if the exchange rate indeed follows a random walk, ε_{t+h} cannot be correlated with Δs_{t+h}, since the respective model is calculated with data up to

[95] For more than 200 observations, a t-distribution converges to a standard normal distribution.

[96] Hence, all estimates of any non-random walk model are based on a growing number of observations.

t. As in Evans and Lyons (2005c), β is computed by using Newey and West (1987) estimators to deal with serial correlation in ε_{t+h}.

As mentioned above, interbank order flow here is usually included into the analyses, even though banks are generally skipped in other studies, since transaction flow between banks is often seen to be no proprietary source of information. In this chapter, all micro-based models are computed with and without interbank order flow. Excluding interbank transactions from the data could imply that end-users' structure at the bank at hand is a representative sample of the market-wide end-user universe. Alternatively, it may imply that interbank flow is primarily liquidity driven. On the other hand, interbank order flow might convey information due to the initiating bank's informational advantage resulting from its own respective end-user order flow. By calculating models with and without interbank transactions, it is possible to analyse interbank flows' forecasting power directly and to reassess Sager and Taylor's (2006) conclusion that interdealer order flow should not be very informative for predicting future exchange rate movements. At least, due to the remarkable fraction of interbank transactions in the entire data set, taking these transactions into account should improve data quality.

In the next section, there are three non-random walk models (Fama, Micro I, Micro II) to assess, two of which are micro-based and the third being a standard macro-model based upon uncovered interest parity. Micro models differ in the way they use order flow data (aggregated flows versus disaggregated flows). All non-random models are assessed against a driftless random walk in two ways, namely by conducting Diebold and Mariano (1995) tests and by computing Evans and Lyons' (2005c) projection statistic.

4.3.3 Empirical results

Empirical results shown in table 4.4 and table 4.5 do not share the optimistic view on order flow's forecasting power revealed in Evans and Lyons (2005c). Only a few of the forecasting equations presented here are actually able to outperform a random walk – and even if this is the case, it is achieved by Evans and Lyons' (2005c) projection statistic only and never confirmed by MSE-ratios and respective p-values calculated via the Diebold and Mariano

(1995) procedure. This result holds good for every forecasting horizon under investigation and both of the sub-samples at hand. It is worth mentioning that in line with findings presented in Evans and Lyons (2005c), results based on projection statistics are, in general, more optimistic than MSE-ratios and respective p-values. If one focuses on projection statistic betas for 2002 / 2003 period only, Micro II turns out to be most promising, at least in the medium-run and primarily if interbank order flow is included in the data set. In 2004 / 2005, Micro II remains to be the predominant specification, but now, skipping interdealer flow seems to be advantageous. While the former finding hence is in contrast to Sager and Taylor's (2006) view to interdealer order flow's forecasting power, the second confirms their argumentation.

Results, however, deserve a more detailed investigation. In line with Meese and Rogoff (1983a) and Cheung et al. (2005), there are no strong indications of high-frequent forecasting power of the Fama model in 2002 / 2003. MSE-ratios are, if at all statistically significant, well above one, implying that the model underperforms a simple random walk substantially. In addition, β is positive and statistically significant at a five trading-days horizon only – and this at just ten percent level of significance.

Results on the Fama model at a five days forecasting horizon do not imply that earlier studies on macro models' forecasting abilities are proved wrong. This is because findings are generally weak, as results on β are not confirmed by MSE-ratios significantly below unity. The most promising finding for the Fama model here is that the MSE-ratio is not significantly above one when Evans and Lyons' (2005c) projection statistic indicated positive forecasting power of the macro approach. Furthermore, there is a potential explanation for the macro model's "look-alike" forecasting ability. As figure 4.1 depicts, EUR / USD spot exchange rates follow a distinct upward sloping trend during 2002 / 2003. In addition, interest differentials in overnight euro and U.S. dollar deposit rates are somewhat downward sloping. Consequently, the trend is likely to be the driving force behind this finding and thus, superior forecasting power of the macro model relative to a random walk is due to the sample period under investigation here.

Table 4.5: *Forecast comparison of two micro-based and one macro model*
255 trading days between October 1, 2002 and September 30, 2003

	Forecast horizon *h* (trading days)		
Model	1	5	10
Fama			
MSE-ratio	1.0522*	1.0170	1.4310*
(p value)	(0.0582)	(0.4247)	(0.0901)
β	-0.0191	0.0633	-0.0947
(p value)	(0.1317)	(0.0932)	(0.1279)
Micro I (cum interbank order flow)			
MSE-ratio	1.3563	1.2952	1.1500
(p value)	(0.1401)	(0.1210)	(0.3085)
β	0.0343	0.0624	0.1599
(p value)	(0.1534)	(0.2531)	(0.0032)
Micro I (ex interbank order flow)			
MSE-ratio	1.1110*	1.1207	1.0843
(p value)	(0.0853)	(0.1539)	(0.3156)
β	-0.0030	0.0051	0.1242
(p value)	(0.8256)	(0.8755)	(0.0204)
Micro II (cum interbank order flow)			
MSE-ratio	1.2269*	0.9855	0.9196
(p value)	(0.0559)	(0.4800)	(0.3936)
β	0.0040	0.1267	0.5640
(p value)	(0.9039)	(0.0192)	(<0.0001)
Micro II (ex interbank order flow)			
MSE-ratio	1.1682**	1.0133	0.8130
(p value)	(0.0465)	(0.4522)	(0.2514)
β	-0.0087	0.1016	0.5291
(p value)	(0.8128)	(0.0312)	(<0.0001)

Notes: MSE-ratio is ratio of mean squared prediction error of a non-random walk model to a driftless random walk. P values shown in parentheses below MSE-ratios are based on standard normal distribution. * (**, ***) denotes significance on a 10% (5%, 1%) level based on Student's t-statistic. All p values for MSE-ratio tests are computed with Andrews' (1991) AR(1) rule for truncation lag selection. † denotes cases, where the Null of equal forecast accuracy in the DM (1995) test is rejected because of a non-positive spectral density matrix. β is the coefficient of Evans and Lyons' (2005c) projection statistic. P values below β are for the Null that $\beta = 0$. P values are computed via OLS estimation with Newey-West correction.

In contrast to Evans and Lyons (2005c), none of the micro-based models is consistently proved to outperform a random walk during the 2002 / 2003 subsample. The Micro II model (ex interbank order flow) is the only specification that shows at least slight indications of forecasting power, at least when the focus is on projection statistics only. At a ten trading days forecasting horizon, β indicates a massive forecasting ability of the micro-based model. Although MSE-ratios are below unity, they are not statistically significant, rising doubts against order flow's forecasting power.

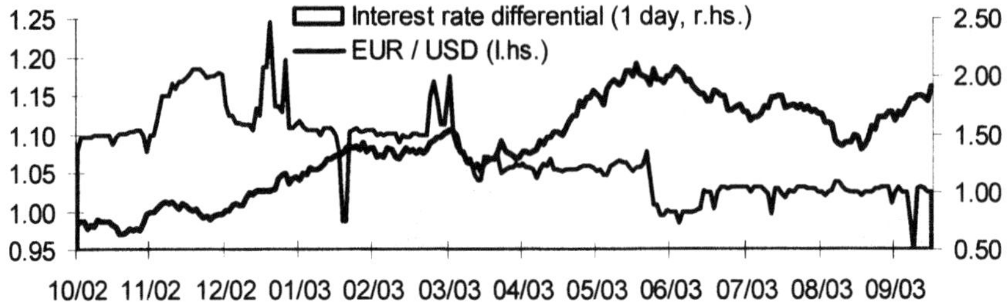

Figure 4.1
USD per EUR spot exchange rate and interest rate differential (overnight deposit rates) between October 1, 2002 and September 30, 2003.

However, as in Evans and Lyons (2005c), MSE-ratios are improving as *h* increases. In addition, using disaggregated order flow seems to be superior to using aggregated flows among all types of market participants. Given earlier findings on correlations between incoming order flow of different groups of customers and the exchange rate presented in chapter 4.1, this finding could have been expected, since different signs on financial and commercial customers' order flow are likely to "cancel out" each other when order flow is aggregated.[97]

Results for 2004 / 2005 presented in table 4.6 generally confirm above-shown findings. There are only slight indications in favour of the Fama model's forecasting power. Evans and Lyons' (2005c) projection statistics show significant prediction power of the macro model at a five days horizon only, but this is neither confirmed nor contradicted by p values for MSE-ratios. However, as depicted in figure 4.2, findings are, again, likely to be driven by trends in the respective time series during the sample period. While euro-interest rates remained stable over time, U.S. rates increased, resulting in an interest rate

[97] Data are cleaned for a few "unusually large" forecasting errors during the last quarter of 2002. Including these errors worsens test-statistics, but do not lead to significant results for them.

differential that becomes more and more negative and forces the euro to depreciate against USD.

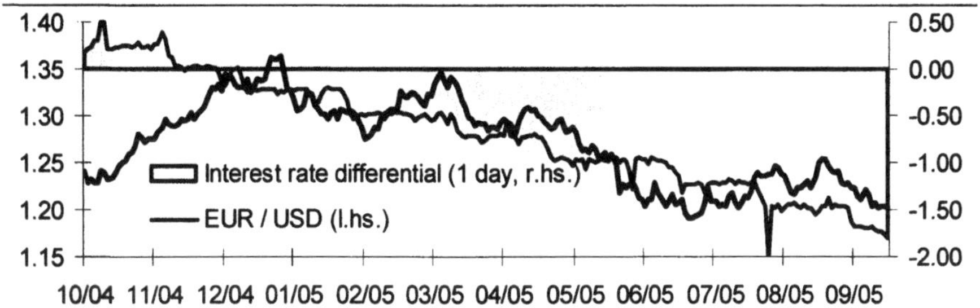

Figure 4.2
USD per EUR spot exchange rate and interest rate differential (overnight deposit rates) between October 1, 2004 and September 30, 2005.

As in table 4.5, projection statistics are consistently more in favour of the models' forecasting power than p values on MSE-ratios. Whenever MSE-ratios are significantly different from unity, they are above one. Nevertheless, tests do not contradict each other as one of them is statistically significant only when the second test is not significant at all. The only contradiction is in Micro I (ex interbank) at the ten trading days forecasting horizon, but significance of the MSE-ratio there is only due to a negative spectral density matrix within the Diebold and Mariano (1995) test.

In contrast to results for 2002 / 2003, there is no distinct evolution of MSE-ratios as *h* increases within the 2004 / 2005 subsample. Nevertheless, projection statistics indicate at least slight improvements of the micro models' forecasting power in the medium run. In addition, using disaggregated order flow, as done in the Micro II specification, seems to be superior to using aggregated flows in Micro I, though overall results are not as clear as they are for the 2002 / 2003 sub-sample.

In addition, there is no terminal judgement on interbank order flow's forecasting power. Results for Micro II indicate that skipping interdealer flow from the dataset is advantegeous, while results for Micro I are rather mixed. However, since results on both specifications are generally weak and forecasting evidence provided by projection statistics is never confirmed by MSE-ratios, one can hardly come to a conclusion concerning Sager and Taylor's (2006) argumentation on interbank flow's forecasting power.

Table 4.6: *Forecast comparison of two micro-based and one macro model*
250 trading days between October 1, 2004 and September 30, 2005

	Forecast horizon *h* (trading days)		
Model	1	5	10
Fama			
MSE-ratio	1.0507*	0.9636	0.9249
(p value)	(0.0951)	(0.3745)	(0.3228)
β	0.0187	0.1502	0.2832
(p value)	(0.3812)	(0.0056)	(0.0005)
Micro I (cum interbank order flow)			
MSE-ratio	1.0092	1.0519	1.0337
(p value)	(0.1635)	(0.4960)	(0.3336)
β	0.0052	0.0929	0.1831
(p value)	(0.0939)	(0.0708)	(0.0232)
Micro I (ex interbank order flow)			
MSE-ratio	0.9987	1.0926***	1.0018†
(p value)	(0.4641)	(0.0054)	(---)
β	0.0181	0.1383	0.1462
(p value)	(0.0393)	(0.0377)	(0.0620)
Micro II (cum interbank order flow)			
MSE-ratio	1.0767	1.1282***	0.9968
(p value)	(0.1251)	(<0.0001)	(0.4801)
β	0.0086	0.1117	0.3175
(p value)	(0.2821)	(0.1237)	(0.0200)
Micro II (ex interbank order flow)			
MSE-ratio	1.3371	1.1100**	0.9914
(p value)	(0.1492)	(0.0170)	(0.4641)
β	0.0188	0.1208	0.3297
(p value)	(0.0029)	(0.1012)	(0.0276)

Notes: MSE-ratio is ratio of mean squared prediction error for a non-random walk model to a driftless random walk. P values shown in parentheses below MSE-ratios are based on standard normal distribution. * (**, ***) denotes significance on a 10% (5%, 1%) level based on Student's t-statistic. All p values for MSE-ratio tests are computed with Andrews' (1991) AR(1) rule for truncation lag selection. † denotes cases, where the Null of equal forecast accuracy in the DM (1995) test is rejected because of a non-positive spectral density matrix. β is the coefficient of Evans and Lyons' (2005c) projection statistic. P values below β are for the Null that $\beta = 0$. P values are computed via OLS estimation with Newey-West correction.

Given weak results for micro-based models shown above, it is hard to see why market makers should subsidise order flow for informational reasons. Based on results presented in tables 4.5 and 4.6, it is not possible to explicitly conclude which one of the two approaches (micro- or macro-based) is actually superior. Nevertheless, answering this question is important, because there would only be an incentive to subsidise informed order flow, if the micro model's predictive power is higher than that of the macro-approach. Hence, it is straightforward to compare MSE's of the micro models and the Fama-specification by using the Diebold and Mariano (1995) statistics whenever both models indicate positive prediction power. Consequently, the Fama model is compared to the Micro II specification in the 2002 / 2003 sample, while it is cross-checked to Micro I during the 2004 / 2005 period. Both comparisons are calculated for the five trading days horizon only.

In 2002 / 2003, the MSE-ratio between the Micro II specification and the Fama model is 1.0733 for data including interdealer flow and 1.0817 for data without interbank transactions, respectively. Both ratios indicate superior forecasting power of the macro model at a first glance, but none of the MSE-ratios is significantly different from unity.[98] Comparison results for Micro I and the Fama model during the 2004 / 2005 sub-sample are very similar. MSE-ratio now is 0.9771, if interdealer flow is included, and 1.0217, if not. However, ratios are once more not significantly different from one.[99] This, obviously, is further bad news for the strategic dealing hypothesis, because there is no need to subsidise informed order flow when its predictive power is not significantly superior relative to a macro model. Subsidising order flow would thus cause additional costs that cannot be justified by economic reasons, so there is no empirical support for the strategic dealing hypothesis in the data.

Why should incoming order flow at the bank at hand be less valuable for exchange rate forecasting than order flow that emerged at the dealer investigated in Evans and Lyons (2005c)? A possible answer to this question is that Evans and Lyons (2005c) analyse order flow data, which originated at Citi-

[98] For the specification including interbank order flow, the p value based on Diebold and Mariano (1995) statistic is 0.2236, while it is 0.2090 for Micro II without interbank order flow.

[99] P value for the specification with interdealer flow is 0.4168, while p value for analysis without interbank transaction flow is 0.4207.

bank, one of the world's largest currency dealers. Citibank maintains business relationships with lots of huge, important and well-informed investors, so it is likely that order flow at Citibank conveys more information about future exchange rate returns than it does at this rather average-sized bank investigated here.

Apart from that, could there be any justification for the strategic dealing hypothesis despite of its lack of significant superiority compared to a macro-based model? Of course, results presented here are covering a period of only one year. However, there are no indications that micro-based forecasting approaches can do consistently and significantly better than a random walk, while the Fama model can not. Only results based on projection statistics indicate that micro-models can do better than a random walk. There are two potential rationale for subsidising order flow in such an environment. First, traders might care about a model's MSE ratio relative to a random walk only and do not take those rather complex significance tests into consideration. Second, inferences are drawn from Evans and Lyons' (2005c) pojection statistic. Prefering micro-based models over the Fama model would be rational under this assumption, though there are indications for positive forecasting power based on macro forecasts at a five days horizon. This becomes clear when one takes another look at figures 4.1 and 4.2. Both of these propose a common trend to be the main driving factor behind interest rate differentials and the evolution of the exchange rate. However, as figure 4.1 depicts, the euro appreciates against the U.S. dollar despite that euro area's interest rate advantage vis-à-vis the United States is shrinking in 2002 / 2003. This, indeed, is contrary to predictions of standard macro models of exchange rate determination. In 2004 / 2005, the European single currency depreciates as the United States improve their interest rate advantage vis-à-vis the euro area. This time, causality is in line with standard macro convictions. The point here is that correlation between interest rate differentials and exchange rates is negative in 2002 / 2003 and positive in 2004 / 2005. This finding indicates an unstable relationship between these two variables over time, so it is very likely that the rather unexpected findings regarding the macro model's forecasting ability based on projection statistics are due to a sample problem. Nevertheless, there are still no convincing indications in favour of the strategic dealing hypothesis in the data at hand.

Given generally weak results presented above, it is not for sure that *any* order flow at a single bank provides useful information to improve dealers' forecasting ability, regardless of whether interdealer flow is included to or skipped from the data set. Based on Evans and Lyons' (2005c) projection statistic, results are basically mixed and seem to depend on the sample-period under investigation. Hence, it is not possible to terminally conclude on Sager and Taylor's (2006) view on interdealer flow's prediction power.

4.4 Is speculation profitable in FX markets?

A different angle to information content of order flow and validity of strategic dealing is to investigate profitability of speculative trading. By assuming that market makers are aware of order flow's potential information content and that they hence back their speculative trading decisions with information extracted from observed incoming customer flows, analysing profitability of speculative trading takes the investigation of the strategic dealing hypothesis to a natural next level. As stated above, results on Evans and Lyons' (2005c) projection statistics shown in section 3 of chapter 4 indicate slight empirical evidence in favour of strategic dealing at a first glance. However, the fact that there is potential forecasting power of order flow does not necessarily evidence that dealers are actually aware of that information and adjust their pricing strategy in order to subsidise informed order flow. The strategic dealing hypothesis is hence supported if and only if there are indications that speculative trading contributes systematically to the dealer's profits.

In other words, the strategic dealing hypothesis suggests that market makers quote narrower spreads to potentially well-informed customers to maximise probability that the respective customer will trade with them. In this way, market makers try to participate in their customers' superior information position and profit from these information while doing their own speculative trading. After previous sections of this work have shown that there is information in incoming order flow that is potentially exploitable, if at all, on a rather medium-term forecasting horizon, sections below aim at investigating whether or not speculative FX trading actually is profitable at the bank at hand during the respective sub-samples.

As mentioned above, it is not unusual that dealers keep open positions over night, though these positions' magnitudes are rather small. Because results so far have shown that order flow potentially improves forecasting power on a medium-term horizon up to ten trading days, an event study is conducted to analyse the evolution of the exchange rate during ten trading before and ten trading days after a speculative position is established by the market maker, and to investigate, whether or not eventually generated profits are significant.

The remainder of this section is as follows. Chapter 4.4.1 describes different approaches to identify revenues from speculative trading and clarifies some basic theoretical and empirical aspects. After that, empirical results are presented in chapter 4.4.2. Section 4.4.3 provides an interim conclusion.

4.4.1 Basic aspects of analysing profits from speculative trading in FX markets

Identifying profits due to speculative trading is not as simple as it might seem to be. As mentioned in Mende and Menkhoff (2005), there is still a lack of useful profit figures and hence, there are only a few studies that take a closer look at banks' speculative trading, at least at frequencies higher than one week. At an intraday frequency, works by Lyons (1998) and Yao (1998) primarily suffer from the short periods, their data sets span, so, to our knowledge, it is only the contribution by Mende and Menkhoff (2005) that provides reliable results and useful insights so far.

The focus of the subsequent investigations is on lower frequency than in Lyons (1998), Yao (1998), and Mende and Menkhoff (2005), but on higher frequency than in Fieleke (1981), Wei and Kim (1997), and Klitgaard and Weir (2004). Here, any single speculative position is analysed by conducting an event-study, lasting from ten trading days before the position was established until ten trading days afterwards.[100] The procedure thus does not take intraday speculation into account (that is of particular importance under the inventory-manipulating proposal of Lyons (1995), which is relaxed here), but

[100] Observing exchange rate evolution during some periods prior to the event itself is common standard in event-studies. Here, doing so helps to identify potentially trend-driven trading strategies.

analyses horizons that earlier tests have shown to be, if at all, the most promising ones for order flow-driven speculative trading in this study.

Besides the event-study approach conducted here, there are primarily two further techniques to analyse profits due to speculation. The first one is based on an exchange rate / volatility-link. As argued in Lyons (1998), speculation's profitability may be positively correlated with exchange rate volatility, since volatile periods are usually seen to provide better trading opportunities for informed and able traders.[101] Hence, one can analyse whether or not exchange rate volatility is determining speculative trading.

Both the event-study approach and the exchange rate / volatility-link suffer from difficulties in identifying speculative trades, even with high-frequency data at the researcher's disposal. This is because there is no way to detect the market maker's motivation to originate an outgoing transaction. As a consequence of this, the second alternative approach to an event study regards speculative profits as the residual beyond non-speculative trading, e.g. resulting from an investigation based on the models by Madhavan and Smidt (1991) or Huang and Stoll (1997), introduced in chapter 3. However, neither this one nor the volatility-based approach will be conducted here, because this chapter is solely longing for further evidence on the strategic-dealing hypothesis, which these two procedures cannot provide. Despite of all difficulties mentioned earlier, the following section deals with the event-study approach only.

There are several ways to cope with the aforementioned identification problem of speculative positions. Lyons (1998) was the first to introduce two approaches to overcome this problem. In his first suggestion, bid-ask spreads of incoming orders are decomposed, in accordance to a dealer's opinion, into revenues from laying off inventory shocks and revenues from interbank trading. Speculation, defined as the residual of these two sources of profit, then explains less than ten percent of total revenues – a result that is very likely to be mainly driven by the defining criteria. In his second approach, Lyons

[101] Mende and Menkhoff (2005) do not find a significant contribution of volatility to profits from speculative trading. Ammer and Brunner (1997) report indirect evidence that banks earn considerable profits from trading with volatility-related products, e.g. options contracts.

(1998) uses non-dealt quotes to identify his dealer's share of inventory that is due to speculative positioning. By conducting Granger-causality tests, he analyses whether these speculative positions forecast future price changes.

In this study, we use five criteria that have to be satisfied to identify a speculative transaction. These criteria are basically proposed by Yao (1998) as an alternative to Lyons' (1998) approaches, which cannot identify the quantity of speculative trading. Following Yao (1998), a speculative transaction has to be *outgoing*, i.e. it must be initiated by the market maker himself. Secondly, market makers are believed to take speculative positions via the *interdealer market*. Consequently, no trades with non-bank end-users are considered here. Third, trades have to be *accumulating*, i.e. the bank has to purchase (sell) euro against U.S. dollars when the bank's euro inventory is positive (negative).[102] In all other cases, the trader's intuition is more likely to be driven by inventory-management considerations than by speculation. Fourth, transactions have to be of *significant amount*. Here, all trades that satisfy the former conditions, but are smaller than EUR one million, are skipped from the data. Lastly, the data is cleaned for all those trades that were obviously traded to *serve later huge incoming customer orders*. Within the 2002 / 2003 sub-sample, 210 transactions satisfy these five criteria, 86 of which are speculative EUR-purchases and 124 of which are speculative EUR-sales. In 2004 / 2005, a total of 426 transactions are speculative. 151 transactions are purchasing euro, while 275 trades sell the European single currency.

During subsequent analyses, all speculative positions are divided into speculative sales and speculative purchases of euro against U.S. dollars. Within any of these two groups and for every single one among the twenty trading days around the opening of a speculative position, a mean indexed performance is calculated relative to the respective spot exchange rate, the position was opened at. The indexed performance j trading days before (-) and after (+) the position was established at in t, denoted $P_{t+/-j}^{index}$, is calculated by

[102] To calculate the bank's inventory position, inventory is set to zero at the beginning of each trading day as proposed by Lyons (1995).

$$P_{t+/-j}^{index} = \frac{S_{t+/-j}^{M}}{S_t}, \tag{4.24}$$

where S_t denotes the spot exchange rate, the speculative position was opened at, and $S_{t+/-j}^{M}$ is the interdealer spot rate at the end of the j'th trading day before or after t, as collected from Reuters. Average indexed performance for any j is then tested to be significantly different from one by conducting a t-test.

4.4.2 Empirical evidence

The first step in analysing profitability of a bank's speculative trading is to investigate whether or not the bank earned positive revenues from FX trading. Following Mende and Menkhoff (2005), daily trading revenues are calculated by multiplying daily bid-ask spread by the amount of EUR traded each day. Indexing trading days by t then gives

$$\text{Revenues} = \sum_{t=1}^{T}\left(\frac{\text{Sales}_t^{USD}}{\text{Sales}_t^{EUR}} - \frac{\text{Purch.}_t^{USD}}{\text{Purch.}_t^{EUR}}\right) \cdot Min\left[\text{Sales}_t^{EUR}, \text{Purch.}_t^{EUR}\right], \tag{4.25}$$

where Sales_t^{EUR} $\left(\text{Purch.}_t^{EUR}\right)$ is daily amount of euro sold (bought) during day t, while Sales_t^{USD} $\left(\text{Purch.}_t^{USD}\right)$ is the respective equivalent in U.S. dollars. $\text{Sales}_t^{USD}/\text{Sales}_t^{EUR}$ $\left(\text{Purch.}_t^{USD}/\text{Purch.}_t^{EUR}\right)$ hence yields an average ask price (bid price) for the European single currency with base currency euro throughout trading day t. Consequently, the difference shown within the parenthesis of equation (4.25) is a daily bid-ask spread. To come to daily revenues, this spread has to be multiplied by traded volume ($Min[\text{Sales}_t^{EUR}$, $\text{Purch.}_t^{EUR}]$) of the respective trading day and summed up for all t in order to come to an overall revenue figure.

Under the assumption of a desired net zero inventory position at the end of each trading day, daily revenues in EUR / USD trading between October 1st, 2002, and September 30th, 2003, sum up to a total of EUR 1,090,140.39. This is slightly more than reported in Mende and Menkhoff (2005). However, since the period analysed here is much longer than the one investigated by them, daily average revenues seem to be rather small.[103] Nevertheless, the dealer does generate positive revenues from trading. In 2004 / 2005, revenues are EUR 3,002,360.26.[104]

Surprisingly, daily revenues show almost no correlation with overall daily trading volume. Correlation coefficient for these two variables is 0.08 in 2002 / 2003, and –0.06 for 2004 / 2005. Another interesting question is whether or not a trader is able to generate positive net profits from trading. Unfortunately, there is no exact means of identifying costs of trading accurately. Mende and Menkhoff (2005) hence suggest to assume transaction costs to be EUR 100 per trade, regardless of the transaction's actual features (volume, traded via EBS or by phone, type of counterpart, etc.). This figure is, in general, confirmed by our dealer in an interview.

Taking transaction costs into consideration, (net) profits for 2002 / 2003 become negative by EUR 115,059.61. This is somewhat surprising, since, with the exception of Yao (1998), all other studies mentioned above find positive profits from trading. Furthermore, it is rather unlikely that losses in the bank's own speculative trading overcompensate earnings from financial intermediation. Hence, there should be further explanations for this finding here.

Potential rationale for negative profits in 2002 / 2003 are manifaceted. Firstly, as usual, the foreign exchange department at the bank is not just acting in spot currency trading. Swap, futures, outright-forward and option transactions do contribute to the overall profit of the department, too. Furthermore, the dealer investigated here trades other currency pairs in addition to EUR / USD. In these other markets, margins tend to be higher, so it is very likely that potential (net) losses in EUR / USD are compensated by profits in other currency pairs. Secondly, there might be close business relations between the bank, our dealer is working with, and some of its corporate customers, who are involved in international business. In this case, trading foreign exchange with

[103] The period in Mende and Menkhoff (2005) covers 87 days, while the data set investigated here consists of an entire year. However, euro / dollar trading took place on only 192 days during that year.

[104] This figure is cleaned from trading revenues on October 28, 2004, when daily revenues were negative by more than EUR five millions.

these customers could be some kind of non-profit service add-on, while the bank earns positive net margins from these clients in other business relations, e.g. corporate- or structured finance. Thus, minor losses resulting from FX trading might by accepted in order to improve the overall business relation with these customers and generate profits in other fields that can, in turn, cross-subsidise the FX trading department. This can be seen as a special case of the strategic dealing-hypothesis to dealer behaviour. Thirdly, transaction costs may not be constant. Hence, profit figures could be systematically biased, when the bulk of transactions can be executed at lower costs, since they are traded, for example, via EBS. Lastly, trading figures may be biased because of the dealer's portfolio-based inventory management approach mentioned in chapter 2. Hence, euro inventories could have been sold or bought against other currencies instead of USD, so trading volumes in equation (4.25) might not explicitly fit to each other.

In 2004 / 2005, revenues are large enough to generate positive profits of EUR 774,260,26.[105] However, positive profits are not a necessary condition for the purposes investigated here. Even if proximate profit figures are negative, it does not necessarily indicate that speculation is not profitable. Profitable speculation might contribute to a negative overall profit in a way that it reduces losses, but is not able to overcompensate them. In addition, by lowering assumed transaction costs to EUR 80 per trade (that dealers would certainly not disagree with, too), profit figures for 2002 / 2003 become, at least very slightly, positive. Hence, the question whether or not speculation is actually profitable in FX trading still remains.

Figure 4.3 depicts the evolution of the average indexed spot exchange rate ($t_0 = 1$) ten trading days before and ten trading days after the dealer has engaged a speculative position. If the dealer has no forecasting power, values for trading days following t_0 should not be significantly different from unity.

[105] Interestingly, findings presented in chapter 3 indicate that order processing costs were lower in 2004 / 2005 than they were in 2002 / 2003. If one abstracts from the fact that revenues (and profits) in 2004 / 2005 are positive only because of an unusual trading day was skipped from the data, or if one accepts that the respective trading day indeed was not representative, differing profit figures of the two sub-samples might indicate that the bank diagnosed its lack of efficiency in FX trading and gained efficiency within two years.

Respective test statistics are to be found in table 4.7. Interestingly, with the exception of the first day after a speculative position, there is no statistically significant (5% level of significance) change in spot exchange rates following a speculative transaction. This finding holds good for both directions of transactions. However, the change of the spot exchange rate one day after the speculative position was established is always in favour of the market maker investigated here. On a daily basis, there is hence some evidence for the market maker's forecasting power. However, it is unlikely that this ability is driven by observed order flow, since order flow should convey, if at all, rather medium-term information, as stated in earlier sections of this study.

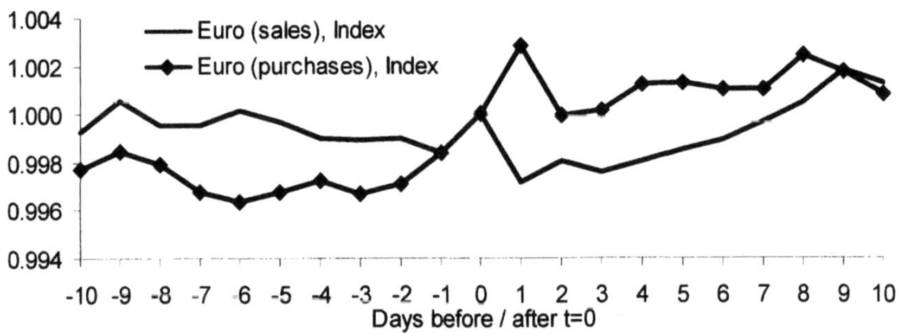

Figure 4.3
Evolution of the average indexed spot exchange rate (t_0=1) ten trading days before and ten trading days after an accumulating, outgoing interbank (speculative) EUR-transaction with volume of more than EUR one million between October 1, 2002, and September 30, 2003.

At least for speculative euro purchases, there seems to be slight evidence that the market maker is trading in accordance to trend-based, chart-technical strategies. This is because average indexed spot exchange rates are significantly (5%) lower up to three days before the speculative transaction happens, and are increasing with *t*. If this was indeed the case, the market maker could be termed, in accordance to Friedman (1953, p. 174 et seqq.), as some kind of *destabilising speculator*. This, in turn, may provide a further explanation for negative profits in 2002 / 2003. Nevertheless, this technical analysis-like trading behaviour is in line with Taylor and Allen (1992) and their finding of a prominent role of technical analysis for currency dealers.

Table 4.7: *Average indexed spot exchange rates around a speculative transaction 255 trading days between October 1, 2002, and September 30, 2003*

	Purchases		Sales	
Days around t_0	Mean	(p value)	Mean	(p value)
-10	0.997710	(0.3987)	0.999292	(0.7161)
-9	0.998495	(0.5326)	1.000539	(0.7674)
-8	0.997895	(0.3804)	0.999541	(0.7928)
-7	0.996751	(0.1044)	0.999519	(0.7687)
-6	0.996373	(0.0648)	1.000116	(0.9404)
-5	0.996803	(0.0518)	0.999665	(0.7903)
-4	0.997219	(0.0634)	0.999013	(0.3753)
-3	0.996692	(0.0107)	0.998949	(0.2491)
-2	0.997090	(0.0118)	0.998984	(0.2485)
-1	0.998380	(0.0106)	0.998394	(0.0316)
1	1.002860	(0.0001)	0.997160	(0.0085)
2	0.999942	(0.9583)	0.998026	(0.1214)
3	1.000174	(0.8939)	0.997568	(0.0990)
4	1.001259	(0.3847)	0.998040	(0.2180)
5	1.001328	(0.4634)	0.998512	(0.3637)
6	1.001018	(0.6172)	0.998930	(0.5711)
7	1.001010	(0.6231)	0.999695	(0.8771)
8	1.002417	(0.2805)	1.000491	(0.8105)
9	1.001789	(0.4238)	1.001820	(0.3635)
10	1.000827	(0.7232)	1.001290	(0.5413)

Notes: Mean is average of indexed spot exchange rates (t_0=1) at the respective day around the opening of a speculative position across all relevant transactions (divided into purchases and sales). Figures are based on a total of 210 transactions, (86 purchases, 124 sales). Speculative trades are identified in accordance to Yao (1998). Purchase (Sale) means purchase (sale) of EUR against USD. P values are generated by Student's t-statistic, testing the Null that the mean for the respective day is equal to one.

However, there might be a much more intuitive reason for this finding. As shown in figure 4.1, the euro steadily appreciated against the U.S. dollar over a long period in 2002 / 2003, resulting in a distinct upward trend. In such an environment, an increasing value of the euro on days before a speculative transaction is more likely than a series of euro-bearish days. This conclusion is supported by results for speculative euro-sales, since there is no indication of trend-following driven trading behaviour of the market maker in this case.

Results for 2004 / 2005 basically confirm the finding that the spot exchange rate does not systematically evolve in the market maker's favoured direction after he had engaged a speculative position. However, changes of average indexed spot exchange rates are, by far, more significant than in 2002 / 2003. Looking at speculative euro purchases, there is an almost distinct downward sloping trend before and even after the transaction. With the exception of trading day number seven after the position was established, all average indexed exchange rate changes are statistically significant and unfavourable for the market maker.

Although the dealer acts like one of Friedman's (1953, p. 162 et seq.) *stabilising speculators* when purchasing euro for speculative purposes, he should generate significant losses due to speculation. At a first glance, it seems that the trader at hand violates a well known financial market perception to *never catch a falling knife*. However, keeping in mind that there is a distinct downward sloping trend in spot EUR / USD exchange rates in the first half of 2005 (see figure 4.2), findings here should be, again, heavily influenced by this trend. Nevertheless, there is absolutely no indication that this market maker is able to exploit medium-term information conveyed in his observed incoming order flow to generate positive profits from speculative trading.

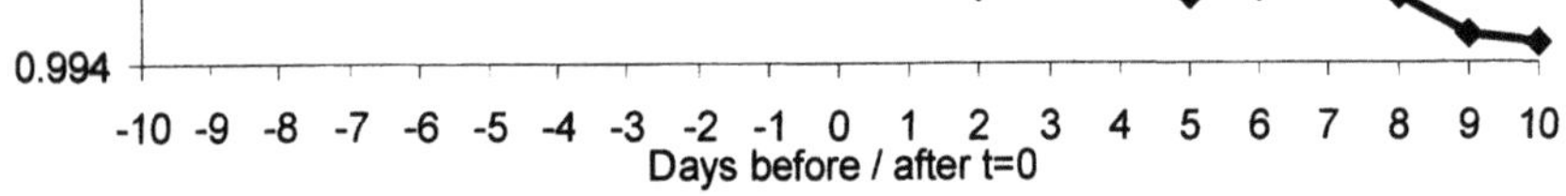

Figure 4.4
Evolution of the average indexed spot exchange rate (t_0=1) ten trading days before and ten trading days after an accumulating, outgoing interbank (speculative) EUR-transaction with volume of more than EUR one million between October 1, 2004, and September 30, 2005.

A closer look at 2004 / 2005 speculative EUR-sales reveals a similar picture. Even though there is, as mentioned above, a distinct downward sloping trend in EUR / USD spot exchange rates over a long period within the sample, there are almost no significant exchange rate movements following an engagement of a speculative EUR-sale. As shown in table 4.8, there are significant exchange rate returns at the first day after a speculative sale, but they are in wrong direction. The only indication for the market maker's systematic profit-earning is on trading days number nine and ten after a speculative sale, whereas day number nine is only significant at a ten percent level. However, this finding is not really appropriate to conclude that the market maker at hand is really successful in speculation.

Table 4.8: *Average indexed spot exchange rates around a speculative transaction 250 trading days between October 1, 2004, and September 30, 2005*

	Purchases		Sales	
Days around t_0	Mean	(p value)	Mean	(p value)
-10	1.008792	(<0.0001)	1.002199	(0.0422)
-9	1.007291	(<0.0001)	1.008330	(0.4189)
-8	1.006787	(<0.0001)	1.001180	(0.2161)
-7	1.006579	(<0.0001)	1.000955	(0.2407)
-6	1.006986	(<0.0001)	1.000631	(0.3881)
-5	1.006879	(<0.0001)	1.000239	(0.7356)
-4	1.006314	(<0.0001)	1.000096	(0.8784)
-3	1.005089	(<0.0001)	1.000164	(0.7614)
-2	1.003472	(<0.0001)	0.999910	(0.8357)
-1	1.001989	(<0.0001)	0.999999	(0.9983)
1	0.998714	(0.0348)	1.001024	(0.0119)
2	0.997799	(0.0093)	1.000749	(0.1804)
3	0.998445	(0.0967)	1.000110	(0.8747)
4	0.997980	(0.0561)	0.999598	(0.6179)
5	0.997380	(0.0211)	0.999213	(0.3444)
6	0.997846	(0.0852)	1.000017	(0.9857)
7	0.997905	(0.1008)	0.999546	(0.6529)
8	0.997347	(0.0539)	0.998806	(0.2647)
9	0.995340	(0.0012)	0.997934	(0.0599)
10	0.994937	(0.0007)	0.997578	(0.0246)

Notes: Mean is average of indexed spot exchange rates (t_0=1) at the respective day around the opening of a speculative position across all relevant transactions (divided into purchases and sales). Figures are based on a total of 426 transactions, (151 purchases, 275 sales). Speculative trades are identified in accordance to Yao (1998). Purchase (Sale) means purchase (sale) of EUR against USD. P values are generated by Student's t-statistic, testing the Null that the mean for the respective day is equal to one.

4.4.3 Concluding remarks on profitability of speculative trading

Although most of the studies analysing profitability of foreign exchange trading (Ammer and Brunner, 1998, Lyons, 1998, Mende and Menkhoff, 2005, among others) reveal that banks indeed are able to generate positive revenues and profits, none of them concludes that speculation is significantly contributing to this. The bulk of earnings generated in FX trading departments is thus due to intermediation services, i.e. the bid-ask spread.

Results presented above confirm these findings, though revenues and profits are only significant after slight manipulations. However, there are several explanations for this outcome. Interestingly, there is almost no correlation at all between daily figures on trading volume and daily revenues earned in EUR / USD trading. This is surprising at a first glance, since it doubts the argumentation that revenues (and profits) are primarily earned for providing intermediation services. Nevertheless, the above-mentioned explanations for negative revenue-figures are all adaptive to this additional puzzle, too.

The basic question of this section, i.e. whether or not the market maker is successful in speculating, is negated by the data. Even on a forecasting horizon that is most likely to be favourable for micro-based exchange rate forecasting during the respective sample periods, there is no indication that the dealer here successfully exploits private information for speculative purposes.

4.5 Is information governing market makers' pricing behaviour – some interim remarks

In previous sections of this chapter, various tests were conducted to investigate mainly two questions. First, is there information in incoming order flow and second, if so, is it exploited by the market maker for his own speculative trading? Both of these questions can be answered very clearly.

Information content of incoming order flow is repeatedly evidenced in this work. However, in contrast to many very optimistic contributions to the literature, which are convinced that order flow is the high powered source of information easily exploitable for short-run exchange rate speculation, results presented here indicate that information aggregation in FX markets happens much slower. By analysing a VECM's speed-of-adjustment-coefficients and conducting tests on micro-based forecasting models, results presented here indicate that order flow can hardly help predicting spot exchange rate movements. If at all, micro-based forecasting techniques seem to be most promising at horizons between one and two weeks. Hence, there is strong evidence for the model of Evans and Lyons (2004b, 2005c) and its complex information aggregation process in FX markets.

To avoid any misunderstanding here, it is worthwhile mentioning that the fact that past order flow is possibly slightly useful in forecasting future exchange rate changes does not contradict the market efficiency-hypothesis, at least in its semi-strong form.[106] This is because end-user order flow is clearly private information for the respective market maker. The hypothesis of FX market's efficiency of strong form, though, should be rejected.

While evidenced information content in order flow supports Osler et al's (2006) strategic dealing hypothesis at a first glance, there is no indication that the dealer considered here actually exploits this information for speculative purposes. Hence, it is straightforward to conclude that it is not information that governs the dealer's pricing behaviour. This is primarily due to a lack of strong forecasting power of order flow in this case, but seems to be at least partly caused by the fact that the dealer is just not aware of the potential opportunities, order flow provides to him. As a consequence of this, one may conclude that this dealer is not rational, since he does not use all available information to back his own speculative trading positions, but this is actually not the case. Given promising results in Sosvilla-Rivero and Garcia (2005), there is no need for this market maker to subsidise order flow in order to gather additional rather weak information from order flow. All these facts tend to reject the strategic dealing hypothesis in the case at hand.

[106] The hypothesis on *information-efficient markets* was introduced by Eugene Fama (1965, 1970). A market is said to be information efficient of semi-strong form, when recent prices incorporate all publicly available information. Hence, in a semi-efficient market, it is not possible to successfully speculate on basis of past prices (e.g. technical trend-analysis) and public information (e.g. macro-economic announcements), but it is possible to profit from private information.

To conclude, strategic dealing behaviour is very unlikely to be the driving force for the dealer's price setting strategy. Our dealer confirmed in an interview that information, for him, is not the major aspect that governs his pricing behaviour. Even without an explicit knowledge of the market power hypothesis, he mentioned that market power considerations should be responsible for the bulk of a dealer's pricing strategy. Information, in turn, certainly is an important source for a market participant's bargaining power. However, information plays a different role then, but this is going to be discussed in greater detail in chapter 5.

Appendix to chapter 4

A.4.1 Derivation of equation (4.6)

Consider equation (4.5) from the text that provides a present value perspective on exchange rates determination. Formally, it is

$$s_t = (1-b)\sum_{i=0}^{\infty} b^i E_t^m f_{t+i}\,, \tag{A.4.1}$$

where s_t is the log-nominal spot exchange rate, b denotes a constant discount factor, E_t^m is the marker maker's expectation operator in period t, and f_t denotes exchange rate's driving fundamentals. If equation (A.4.1) holds good for period t, one can consequently write for $t+1$

$$s_{t+1} = (1-b)\sum_{i=0}^{\infty} b^i E_{t+1}^m f_{t+1+i}\,. \tag{A.4.2}$$

Since s_{t+1} and $E_{t+1}^m f_{t+1+i}$ are not known in t, one has to re-write (A.4.2) in expectations made in t, so it is

$$E_t^m s_{t+1} = (1-b)\sum_{i=0}^{\infty} b^i E_t^m f_{t+1+i}\,. \tag{A.4.3}$$

Dividing equation (A.4.3) by b and substituting recent values for the driving fundamentals then yields

$$E_t^m s_{t+1} = (1-b)/b\sum_{i=1}^{\infty} b^i E_t^m f_{t+i}$$

$$E_t^m s_{t+1} = \frac{1-b}{b}\left[\sum_{i=0}^{\infty} b^i E_t^m f_{t+i} - f_t\right]. \tag{A.4.4}$$

By dividing equation (A.4.1) by (*1-b*), it is known that $s_t/(1-b) = \sum_{i=0}^{\infty} b^i E_t^m f_{t+i}$, so this can be substituted into equation (A.4.4) to get

$$E_t^m s_{t+1} = \frac{1-b}{b}\left[\frac{s_t}{1-b} - f_t\right]. \tag{A.4.5}$$

Expanding the bracket and substituting s_t to get first differences yields

$$E_t^m s_{t+1} = \frac{1}{b}s_t - \frac{1-b}{b}f_t$$

$$E_t^m \Delta s_{t+1} = \frac{1}{b}s_t - \frac{1-b}{b}f_t - \frac{b}{b}s_t$$

$$E_t^m \Delta s_{t+1} = \frac{1-b}{b}s_t - \frac{1-b}{b}f_t \tag{A.4.6}$$

that can be solved for s_t to get to the desired representation

$$s_t = f_t + \frac{b}{1-b}E_t^m \Delta s_{t+1}. \tag{A.4.7}$$

Under the assumption that f_t is not known at t, equation (A.4.7) has to be written as

$$s_t = E_t^m f_t + \frac{b}{1-b}E_t^m \Delta s_{t+1}. \tag{A.4.8}$$

A.4.2 Derivation of equation (4.11.2)

The following derivation is mainly taken from Evans and Lyons (2004c).

To derive equation (4.11.2) from the text, the dynamics of aggregated order flow are written in state space form[107]

$$\begin{aligned} Y_{t+1} &= AY_t + V_{t+1} \\ Z_t &= Y_t + W_t \end{aligned}, \tag{A.4.9}$$

[107] For details on state space modelling and the Kalman filter, see, among others, Kálmán (1960), Koopman et al. (1999), Durbin and Koopman (2001), Julier and Uhlmann (2004a, 2004b), Welch and Bishop (2006), and Koopman and Commandeur (2007).

where $Y'_t \equiv [X_t \; X_{t-1}]$, $Z'_t \equiv [X_t^i \; X_{t-1}]$, $V'_{t+1} \equiv [\upsilon_{t+1} \; 0]$, $W'_t \equiv [\xi_t^i \; 0]$ and $A \equiv \begin{bmatrix} \lambda & 0 \\ 1 & 0 \end{bmatrix}$.

Applying the kalman filtering algorithm to this system gives

$$Y_{t+1} - E[Y_{t+1} \mid \{Z_{t-j}\}_{j\geq 0}] = A(I-K)(Y_t - E[Y_t \mid \{Z_{t-j-1}\}_{j\geq 0}]) + V_{t+1} - AKW_t, \tag{A.4.10}$$

where K is the kalman gain matrix that is the steady state solution to

$$\begin{aligned} S_{t+1} &= A(I-K_t)S_tA' + Var(V_{t+1}) \\ K_t &= S_t(S_t + Var(W_t))^{-1} \end{aligned} . \tag{A.4.11}$$

Now, it is possible to show that

$$K_t = \begin{bmatrix} 1-\psi & \lambda\psi \\ 0 & 1 \end{bmatrix}, \tag{A.4.12}$$

where $\psi \equiv \sigma_\xi^2 / (\sigma_\upsilon^2 + \sigma_\xi^2)$ with σ_ξ^2 and σ_υ^2 being the variance of ξ_t^i and υ_t, respectively. Because $X_{t+1} - E_t^i X_{t+1}$ is equal to the first element in $Y_{t+1} - E[Y_{t+1} \mid \{Z_{t-j}\}_{j\geq 0}]$, substituting for K in equation (A.4.10) yields

$$\begin{aligned} X_{t+1} - E_t^i X_{t+1} &= \lambda\psi\left(X_t^i - E_{t-1}^i X_t^i\right) - \lambda^2\left(X_{t-1} - E_{t-1}^i X_{t-1}\right) + \upsilon_{t+1} - \lambda\psi\xi_i^t \\ X_{t+1} - E_t^i X_{t+1} &= \lambda\psi\left(X_t - E_{t-1}^i X_t\right) - \lambda^2\psi\left(X_{t-1} - E_{t-1}^i X_{t-1}\right) + \upsilon_{t+1} \end{aligned}$$

$$X_{t+1} - E_t^i X_{t+1} = \lambda\psi\upsilon_t + \upsilon_{t+1}. \tag{A.4.13}$$

In the text, equation (4.11.1) defines

$$X_{t+1}^i - E_t^i X_{t+1}^i = X_{t+1} - E_t^i X_{t+1} + \xi_{t+1}^i, \tag{A.4.14}$$

so substituting equation (A.4.13) into (A.4.14) yields the expression of equation (4.11.2) in the text, i.e.

$$X_{t+1}^i - E_t^i X_{t+1}^i = \lambda\psi\upsilon_t + \upsilon_{t+1} + \xi_{t+1}^i. \tag{A.4.15}$$

A.4.3 What is governing deviations between expected and actual values of f_t?

To derive forecasting equation (4.14),[108] it is necessary to prepare the formal setting. First of all, it is assumed that all market participants have full information about the state of the economy during period *t-1* at the start of period *t*. Hence, market makers' expectations in *t* concerning f_{t-1} are equal to f_{t-1}, i.e. $E_t^m f_{t-1} = f_{t-1}$. To see what is governing a market maker's expectation error concerning f_t, one has to derive an expectation about the current state of the economy. Equation (4.12) from the text defines the recent change in fundamentals to be driven by an AR(1) process that is augmented by two mean zero variables, one of them, y_t, being common knowledge news at the beginning of *t*, and the other, υ_t, representing innovations in aggregated order flow, that are private information, but become common knowledge with a one-period delay. Formally, this is

$$\Delta f_t = \phi \Delta f_{t-1} + y_t + \delta \upsilon_t . \qquad \text{(A.4.15)}$$

Remember, $\delta \upsilon_t$ is an independent, mean zero term than can only be observed with an one-period delay, so equation (A.4.15) can be re-written by using expectation operators as

$$E_t^m f_t - f_{t-1} = \phi(f_{t-1} - f_{t-2}) + y_t$$
$$E_t^m f_t = \phi f_{t-1} + f_{t-1} - \phi f_{t-2} + y_t$$

$$E_t^m f_t = (\phi + 1) f_{t-1} - \phi f_{t-2} + y_t . \qquad \text{(A.4.16)}$$

Using the same procedure without expectation operators gives the actual value for f_t

$$f_t = (\phi + 1) f_{t-1} - \phi f_{t-2} + y_t + \delta \upsilon_t , \qquad \text{(A.4.17)}$$

so substracting equation (A.4.16) from (A.4.17) yields

$$f_t - E_t^m f_t = \delta \upsilon_t . \qquad \text{(A.4.18)}$$

---

108 See Appendix 4.4.

Now, there are all information available to proceed with deriving the actual forecasting equation in the next section.

A.4.4 Deriving forecasting equation (4.14)

Consider the present value equation shown in equation (4.5)

$$s_t = (1-b)\sum_{i=0}^{\infty} b^i E_t^m f_{i+t} \, . \tag{A.4.19}$$

Expanding the sum yields

$$s_t = (1-b)\left(E_t^m f_t + bE_t^m f_{t+1} + b^2 E_t^m f_{t+2} + \ldots + b^{\infty} E_t^m f_{t+\infty}\right). \tag{A.4.20}$$

The crucial artifice here is to recognise that $f_{t+1} = f_t + \Delta f_{t+1}$, $f_{t+2} = f_{t+1} + \Delta f_{t+2} = f_t + \Delta f_{t+1} + \Delta f_{t+2}$, $f_{t+3} = f_{t+2} + \Delta f_{t+3} = f_t + \Delta f_{t+1} + \Delta f_{t+2} + \Delta f_{t+3}$, and so on. Hence, equation (A.4.20) contains a series of f_t's and a series of the changes of the fundamentals in every future period. Hence, equation (A.4.20) can be re-written as

$$s_t = (1-b)\begin{bmatrix} E_t^m f_t + bE_t^m f_t + b^2 E_t^m f_t + \ldots + b^{\infty} E_t^m f_t + \\ b\Delta E_t^m f_{t+1} + b^2(\Delta E_t^m f_{t+1} + \Delta E_t^m f_{t+2}) + b^3(\Delta E_t^m f_{t+1} + \Delta E_t^m f_{t+2} + \\ \Delta E_t^m f_{t+3}) + \ldots \end{bmatrix}$$

$$s_t = (1-b)\begin{bmatrix} E_t^m f_t \sum_{i=0}^{\infty} b^i + \\ b\Delta E_m^t f_{t+1} + b^2(\Delta E_t^m f_{t+1} + \Delta E_t^m f_{t+2}) + b^3(\Delta E_t^m f_{t+1} + \Delta E_t^m f_{t+2} + \\ \Delta E_t^m f_{t+3}) + \ldots \end{bmatrix}$$

$$s_t = (1-b)\begin{bmatrix} 1/(1-b)E_t^m f_t + \\ b\Delta E_t^m f_{t+1} + b^2(\Delta E_t^m f_{t+1} + \Delta E_t^m f_{t+2}) + b^3(\Delta E_t^m f_{t+1} + \Delta E_t^m f_{t+2} + \\ \Delta E_t^m f_{t+3}) + \ldots \end{bmatrix}$$

$$s_t = E_t^m f_t + (1-b)\left(b\Delta E_t^m f_{t+1} + b^2(\Delta E_t^m f_{t+1} + \Delta E_t^m f_{t+2}) + b^3(\ldots) + \ldots\right). \tag{A.4.21}$$

The next step is to solve the parenthesis in equation (A.4.21). From equation (4.12) it is known that $\Delta f_t = \phi\Delta f_{t-1} + y_t + \delta\upsilon_t$, so re-writing this to hold good for future changes in fundamentals yields

$$\Delta E_t^m f_{t+1} = \phi\Delta E_t^m f_t . \tag{A.4.22}$$

Because of equation (A.4.22), any future change in fundamentals can be written in terms of recent change in *f*, e.g. $\Delta E_t^m f_{t+2} = \phi\Delta E_t^m f_{t+1} = \phi^2 E_t^m f_t$, $\Delta E_t^m f_{t+3} = \phi\Delta E_t^m f_{t+2} = \phi^3 E_t^m f_t$, and so on. Consequently, because of $\sum_{i=j}^{\infty} b^i = b^j/(1-b)$, substituting (A.4.22) into (A.4.21) gives

$$s_t = E_t^m f_t + (1-b)\left(b\phi\Delta E_t^m f_t + b^2(\phi\Delta E_t^m f_t + \phi^2\Delta E_t^m f_t) + b^3(\ldots) + \ldots\right)$$
$$s_t = E_t^m f_t + (1+b)\left(\phi\Delta E_t^m f_t \textstyle\sum_{i=1}^{\infty} b^i + \phi^2\Delta E_t^m f_t \sum_{i=2}^{\infty} b^i + \phi^3\Delta E_t^m f_t \sum_{i=3}^{\infty} b^i + \ldots\right)$$

$$s_t = E_t^m f_t + (1+b)\left(\phi\Delta E_t^m f_t \frac{b}{1-b} + \phi^2\Delta E_t^m f_t \frac{b^2}{1-b} + \phi^3\Delta E_t^m f_t \frac{b^3}{1-b} + \ldots\right). \tag{A.4.23}$$

This can be merged to

$$s_t = E_t^m f_t + (1+b)\left(\Delta E_t^m f_t \frac{1}{1-b}\sum_{i=1}^{\infty} \phi^i b^i\right),$$

so expanding the parenthesis yields

$$s_t = E_t^m f_t + (1+b)\left(\Delta E_t^m f_t \times \frac{1}{(1+b)} \times \frac{\phi b}{(1-\phi b)}\right)$$

$$s_t = E_t^m f_t + \frac{\phi b}{1-\phi b}\Delta E_t^m f_t . \tag{A.4.24}$$

By definition, $\Delta E_t^m f_t = E_t^m f_t - E_t^m f_{t-1}$, so equation (A.4.24) can be written as

$$s_t = E_t^m f_t + \frac{\phi b}{1-\phi b} E_t^m f_t - \frac{\phi b}{1-\phi b} E_t^m f_{t-1} . \tag{A.4.25}$$

Due to the assumed informational setting of the model, $E_t^m f_{t-1} = f_{t-1}$. In addition, Appendix 4.3 shows that $f_t - E_t^m f_t = \delta \upsilon_t$, so $E_t^m f_t = f_t - \delta \upsilon_t$. Substituting these information into equation (A.4.25) and augmenting it where appropriate gives

$$s_t = f_t - \delta \upsilon_t + \frac{\phi b}{1-\phi b}(f_t - \delta \upsilon_t) - \frac{\phi b}{1-\phi b} f_{t-1}$$

$$s_t = f_t + \frac{\phi b}{1-\phi b} f_t - \delta \upsilon_t - \frac{\delta \phi b}{1-\phi b} \upsilon_t - \frac{\phi b}{1-\phi b} f_{t-1}$$

$$s_t = \left[1 + \frac{\phi b}{1-\phi b}\right] f_t - \left[\delta + \frac{\delta \phi b}{1-\phi b}\right] \upsilon_t - \frac{\phi b}{1-\phi b} f_{t-1}$$

$$s_t = \left[\frac{1-\phi b}{1-\phi b} + \frac{\phi b}{1-\phi b}\right] f_t - \left[\frac{\delta(1-\phi b)}{1-\phi b} + \frac{\delta \phi b}{1-\phi b}\right] \upsilon_t - \frac{\phi b}{1-\phi b} f_{t-1}$$

$$s_t = \frac{1}{1-\phi b} f_t - \frac{\delta}{1-\phi b} \upsilon_t - \frac{\phi b}{1-\phi b} f_{t-1}. \tag{A.4.26}$$

Now, let $\varepsilon_{t+1}^m = s_{t+1} - E_t^m s_{t+1}$. Because of equation (A.4.26), one can write

$$\varepsilon_{t+1}^m = \frac{1}{1-\phi b} f_{t+1} - \frac{\delta}{1-\phi b} \upsilon_{t+1} - \frac{\phi b}{1-\phi b} f_t - E_t^m s_{t+1}. \tag{A.4.27}$$

The market maker's expectation about the spot exchange rate in *t+1* is given in accordance to equation (A.4.26) and with respect to the features of υ_t by

$$E_t^m s_{t+1} = \frac{1}{1-\phi b} E_t^m f_{t+1} - \frac{\phi b}{1-\phi b} E_t^m f_t. \tag{A.4.28}$$

This is also to be substituted into equation (A.4.27) to get

$$\varepsilon_{t+1}^m = \frac{1}{1-\phi b} f_{t+1} - \frac{\delta}{1-\phi b} \upsilon_{t+1} - \frac{\phi b}{1-\phi b} f_t - \frac{1}{1-\phi b} E_t^m f_{t+1} - \frac{\phi b}{1-\phi b} E_t^m f_t$$

$$\varepsilon_{t+1}^m = \frac{1}{1-\phi b}\left(f_{t+1} - E_t^m f_{t+1}\right) - \frac{\phi b}{1-\phi b}\left(f_t - E_t^m f_t\right) - \frac{\delta}{1-\phi b} \upsilon_{t+1}. \tag{A.4.29}$$

As shown above, $f_t - E_t^m f_t = \delta \upsilon_t$, so equation (A.4.29) can be written as

$$\varepsilon_{t+1}^{m} = \frac{1}{1-\phi b}\left(f_{t+1} - E_t^m f_{t+1}\right) - \frac{\delta\phi b}{1-\phi b}\upsilon_t - \frac{\delta}{1-\phi b}\upsilon_{t+1}. \tag{A.4.30}$$

Solving the remaining parenthesis demands a little more effort. First of all, recall that $f_{t+1} = f_t + \Delta f_{t+1}$, and $\Delta f_{t+1} = \phi\Delta f_t + y_{t+1} + \delta\upsilon_{t+1}$. In addition, $E_t^m f_t = f_t - \delta\upsilon_t$, and $E_t^m \Delta f_{t+1} = \phi E_t^m \Delta f_t$. With these information, one can write

$$\varepsilon_{t+1}^{m} = \frac{1}{1-\phi b}\left[f_t + \Delta f_{t+1} - \left(E_t^m f_t + E_t^m \Delta f_{t+1}\right)\right] - \frac{\delta\phi b}{1-\phi b}\upsilon_t - \frac{\delta}{1-\phi b}\upsilon_{t+1}$$

$$\varepsilon_{t+1}^{m} = \frac{1}{1-\phi b}\left[f_t + \phi\Delta f_t + y_{t+1} + \delta\upsilon_{t+1} - \left(f_t - \delta\upsilon_t + \phi E_t^m \Delta f_t\right)\right] - \frac{\delta\phi b}{1-\phi b}\upsilon_t \ldots$$

$$\ldots - \frac{\delta}{1-\phi b}\upsilon_{t+1}$$

$$\varepsilon_{t+1}^{m} = \frac{1}{1-\phi b}\left[\phi\left(\Delta f_t - E_t^m \Delta f_t\right) + y_{t+1} + \delta\upsilon_{t+1} + \delta\upsilon_t\right] - \frac{\delta\phi b}{1-\phi b}\upsilon_t - \frac{\delta}{1-\phi b}\upsilon_{t+1}$$

$$\varepsilon_{t+1}^{m} = \frac{1}{1-\phi b}\left[\phi\delta\upsilon_t + y_{t+1} + \delta\upsilon_{t+1} + \delta\upsilon_t\right] - \frac{\delta\phi b}{1-\phi b}\upsilon_t - \frac{\delta}{1-\phi b}\upsilon_{t+1}$$

$$\varepsilon_{t+1}^{m} = \frac{1}{1-\phi b}\left[(1+\phi)\delta\upsilon_t + y_{t+1} + \delta\upsilon_{t+1}\right] - \frac{\delta\phi b}{1-\phi b}\upsilon_t - \frac{\delta}{1-\phi b}\upsilon_{t+1}$$

$$\varepsilon_{t+1}^{m} = \frac{1}{1-\phi b}y_{t+1} + \frac{1+\phi}{1-\phi b}\delta\upsilon_t - \frac{\delta\phi b}{1-\phi b}\upsilon_t + \frac{\delta}{1-\phi b}\upsilon_{t+1} - \frac{\delta}{1-\phi b}\upsilon_{t+1}$$

$$\varepsilon_{t+1}^{m} = \frac{1}{1-\phi b}y_{t+1} + \frac{(1+\phi)\delta - \delta\phi b}{1-\phi b}\upsilon_t$$

$$\varepsilon_{t+1}^{m} = \frac{1}{1-\phi b}y_{t+1} + \frac{(1+\phi-\phi b)\delta}{1-\phi b}\upsilon_t$$

$$\varepsilon_{t+1}^{m} = \frac{1}{1-\phi b}y_{t+1} + \frac{[1+\phi(1-b)]\delta}{1-\phi b}\upsilon_t. \tag{A.4.31}$$

As shown in equation (4.7) in the text, a change in the spot exchange rate is governed by $\Delta s_{t+1} = [(1-b)/b](s_t - E_t^m f_t) + \varepsilon_{t+1}^m$, so substituting equation (A.4.31) into this yields

$$\Delta s_{t+1} = \frac{1-b}{b}(s_t - E_t^m f_t) + \frac{1}{1-\phi b}y_{t+1} + \frac{[1+\phi(1-b)]\delta}{1-\phi b}\upsilon_t. \tag{A.4.32}$$

Furthermore, according to equation (4.13), aggregated order flow is given by $X_t = \lambda X_{t-1} + \upsilon_t$, so $\upsilon_t = X_t - \lambda X_{t-1}$ and substituting this into equation (A.4.32) finally gives the forecasting equation shown in the text

$$\Delta s_{t+1} = \frac{1-b}{b}(s_t - E_t^m f_t) + \frac{1}{1-\phi b} y_{t+1} + \frac{[1+\phi(1-b)]\delta}{1-\phi b}(X_t - \lambda X_{t-1}). \qquad \text{(A.4.33)}$$

5. Market power and FX pricing behaviour

After concluding that the strategic dealing hypothesis is not evidenced in the data, market power is the remaining alternative in explaining our dealer's pricing strategy. Nevertheless, market power, too, is related to informational aspects. Considerations, however, differ by the actual type of information, these two hypotheses are arguing with. While strategic dealing links information to hints about future exchange rate changes, the market power hypothesis interprets information to be related to customers' knowledge of recent market conditions and competing price quotes. Hence, the market maker's motivation to quote the way he does is rather intrinsic, if strategic dealing was true, while it is some kind of extrinsic in case the market power hypothesis holds good.

Since financial customers have professional information systems at their disposal and communicate intensively with a variety of market makers, Osler et al. (2006) see them to be the best informed market participants across the entire marketplace. According to them, financial counterparts should be even better informed than market makers themselves. A relatively weak bargaining position vis-à-vis financial customers is hence a possible explanation for the pricing behaviour of the market maker investigated here. Of course, this rationale is not altered by the fact that interbank trading is included into financial customers' transactions, since other banks are better informed than commercial counterparts, too.

Commercial customers, consequently, are seen to be in a relatively weak bargaining position. This view, however, is true for commercial customers on average. Obviously, large, probably multi-national corporations employ highly professional and well informed treasury departments, which trade with various market makers and should hence bear relatively strong bargaining power, too. In addition, volume they trade is enormous sometimes. However, since the data set differentiates between financial customers, commercial customers, internal customers, and interbank trading only, there is no chance to further distinguish between specific members within the group of commercial counterparts.

For internal customers, it is not information that is determining these counterparts' bargaining power in the first place. Here, the bank's FX trading department might exercise some kind of monopolistic power due to the institutional setting of the bank. Internal customers might be hampered in trading foreign currency with another market maker by the bank's executive committee, so the bank's own market maker could be a virtual monopolist in providing FX trading services.

The question whether market power is affecting dealer behaviour in a relatively opaque market, as well as the extend to which it may contribute to a dealer's earnings in a specific trade, is difficult for mainly two reasons. First, there is no directly observable variable available to measure the degree of market power exploited during a specific transaction. Second, this fact implies that advanced econometric modelling is required here. In empirical studies, so-called *stochastic frontier models* are often used to deal with this problem.

The remainder of chapter 5 is as follows. Section 1 briefly overviews the small number of contributions to the literature on market power and asset pricing and gives information on how the data at hand is prepared for investigations. Section 2 then introduces theoretical background on the stochastic frontier model analysed in Green et al. (2007). Chapter 5.3 presents empirical evidence thereafter. As usual, the chapter's last section draws an interim conclusion.

5.1 Some basic remarks

Market power is a longstanding subject for theorists, empiricists, practitioners, regulators, and policy makers. Obviously, in a highly decentralised and hence relatively opaque market like foreign exchange, transparency and market power, the latter resulting from a lack of the former, is an even severe issue. Hence, the bulk of studies investigates markets, which are mainly OTC-markets.[109] For example, Chakravarty and Sarkar (1999) study, among others, government bond markets, Hong and Warga (2000), and Schultz (2001) in-

[109] See section 1.1.

vestigate corporate bond trading.[110] Green et al. (2007) focus on the U.S. municipal bond market. Though these markets are large and important, they are smaller in absolute volume than the EUR / USD market. Apart from volume, market structures are relatively similar. Usually, trades are not transacted via a central marketplace, but happen decentralised *over the counter*. Hence, all these markets are relatively opaque, at least with respect to a single dealer's knowledge about market-wide end-user order flow. An opaque market always bears an opportunity to dealers to exercise market power, because a customer's costs for comparison shopping may be too high to find the market maker who quotes her the "best" price for her purposes at the respective time. However, due to a lack of data availability, absolute number of studies in the field is generally low.

Although subsequent analysis is close to the paper by Green et al. (2007), there is a remarkable difference between the EUR / USD market investigated here, bond markets in general, and the municipal bond market they study in particular. Bonds, regardless of the issuing institution, are usually significantly liquid during the first three months after issuance only. During this time, investors purchase these papers and usually hold them until maturity, provided that the bond does not default, of course. During recent years, this tendency to *buy-and-hold* should have become even more distinctive, since investors are able and willing to use credit derivatives, e.g. credit default swaps (CDS), to manage their credit exposure instead of actually trading the bond.

An additional difference between bond and currency markets is the allotment of traded assets. Though overall volume in bond markets is large, volume in single bonds is relatively small. Hence, it is not too complicated to identify markups, a dealer earns with a specific trade. In currency markets, in contrast, trading happens permanently and repeatedly with an enormous volume in a single underlying asset. Consequently, calculating a dealer's markups is a little more difficult and necessitates an eminent procedure to prepare the data. Before introducing the model, subsequent paragraphs first explain how the data is actually manipulated for subsequent investigations.

---

[110] None of these studies explicitly focuses on market power considerations. They rather analyse bid-ask spreads with respect to specific features of the trade that, in turn, can be indirectly related to market power, e.g. trade size.

Similar to section 4.4, one might easily underestimate complexity of data manipulation, so preparation of the data for subsequent investigations demands a detailed description. Note that results presented here are for 2002 / 2003 period only. However, since findings for the two sub-samples at hand are widely comparable in previous chapters of this work, focussing on only one of them will not be much of a shortcoming and skipping the 2004 / 2005 subsample here is not likely to make the work suffering from missing new fundamental insights.

The data is prepared as follows. Firstly, as usual, inventories are set equal to zero at the beginning of each trading day. Afterwards, USD inventories are calculated after every single transaction. In addition to pure inventory figures, the (volume-weighted) average spot exchange rate is calculated to find the mean price, the recent position was established at. To do so, it is necessary to distinguish between accumulating orders, which further increase recent inventory positions (i.e. an incoming sell-order for USD that increases market maker's recent USD long position), and transactions that bring down dealers inventories. Only the latter results in direct earnings for the market maker, whereas the former affects profitability in some kind of indirect way, because it determines the average spot rate, at which the dealer establishes his inventory position. Note that a single order can be of both kinds of transactions mentioned here at the same time. To see that, consider a market maker, who carries a recent USD long position of one million and is approached by a customer, who wants to buy USD two millions. Obviously, this transaction reduces dealer's USD inventory to zero first and causes a USD short position of one million afterwards.

Both of the former kinds of transactions are subject to market power. In accumulating trades, market power affects the average price at which a dealer establishes his recent position. The better a dealer's bargaining position, the better is the price he establishes his inventory at. Hence, a strong bargaining position in accumulating transactions results in a higher profit from selling the inventory position afterwards at any given price. This, however, is the rather indirect way by which trading affects profitability as mentioned above. In subsequent analyses, focus is more on market power the dealer exploits during transactions, which reduce his recent inventory. To continue with the example mentioned above, suppose the market maker has had established his long position of USD one million at an average spot exchange rate of, e.g. USD 1.24 per EUR. If the dealer is in a strong bargaining position vis-à-vis the customer, he is approached by to buy USD two millions, he will be able to prevail a lower euro spot rate, i.e. a higher price for U.S. dollars, say $1.2350 per €. Consequently, the market maker will earn USD (1,000,000.00/1.235 – 1,000,000.00/1.24 =) 3,254.99 by this transaction and sets up a short position in USD at $1.2350 per euro. If the market maker is next approached by a customer, who wants to sell him U.S. dollars, it depends on the market maker's relative bargaining position vis-à-vis this respective counterpart, how much the dealer is actually going to earn with that transaction.

To clarify, market power here is not depending on market maker's inventory position. Inventory figures are only necessary to calculate an average exchange rate that serves as a bid price (in case of USD long positions) or an ask price (in case of USD short positions). When the dealer sells (purchases) USD to reduce his long (short) position, the transacted price of this trade provides the respective ask or bid to previous transactions. Hence, market power is in fact again related to spreads, indeed. Dealer's markups earned during the transactions are calculated in percentage terms instead of absolute values.

As usual, it is not the entire percentage return, a dealer earns with a transaction that is of interest here, but excess return of the respective trade. Hence, market-wide interdealer spot rate collected at the time of the trade is used to calculate the fraction of the exchange rate return that was only due to the market maker's costs of trading and market power. Consider market wide spot EUR / USD exchange rate in the example mentioned above is $1.2375 per € at the time, the market maker is approached by the customer. Consequently, the dealer earned half the profit only due to a market-wide price movement in his favour. In turn, only USD 1,627.50 are attributable to trading costs and dealer's bargaining power. During subsequent analyses, it is only this fraction of market maker's overall earnings from inventory-reducing transactions that is in the spotlight of interest.

5.2 Green et al.'s (2007) model of market power and asset pricing

Green et al. (2007) suggest to analyse a stochastic frontier model to investigate market power in the U.S. municipal bond market. Analysing these kinds of models is particularly advantageous for investigating bargaining power. This is because the market maker's transaction costs as well as his market power relative to the respective customer can be modelled within this approach and estimated by using directly observable variables.

Readers who are not acquainted with stochastic frontier models (SFM) will find a short introduction in this book's Annex. In addition, various textbooks like, among others, Greene (2003a) and Kumbhakar and Lovell (2003), provide valuable insights into this technique. SFMs are particularly promising whenever econometricians aim to analyse deviations from an efficient outcome. Areas of application are hence widespread. Aigner et al. (1977) paved the way for stochastic frontier models by estimating production functions. More recent studies like, among others, contributions by Koop et al. (2000), and Kebede (2001) investigate economic growth and technical efficiency in the agricultural sector by this technique. Greene (2003b) applies SFM to analysing health care systems.

In financial economics, stochastic frontier modelling is used to study efficiency in the banking industry by Berger and Mester (1997), Kraft and Tirtiroglu (1998), as well as Altunbas et al. (2001). Contributions dealing with IPO underpricing are by Hunt-McCool et al. (1996) and Koop and Li (2001). Habib and Ljungqvist (2003) analyse agency costs and Miller et al. (2006) use a stochastic frontier approach to study Real Estate Investment Trusts, so-called REITs.

The basic idea of SFM is the conviction that there exists a cost- or production function that guarantees an absolute efficient outcome. This cost function is termed stochastic frontier. It is stochastic, because a normally distributed, zero mean disturbance term, which is usually due to expectation errors, makes the frontier varying even in absence of inefficiency. In addition, there are deviations between the actual outcome and the efficient result, which are due to inefficiency. By definition, every single one of these latter deviations has to be negative, since there cannot be a higher outcome than achieved under absolute efficiency. It is this condition that makes estimating the model particularly demanding.

Consider a market maker is approached by a customer, who wants to sell him currency.[111] The customer will participate in a trade with this market maker if and only if her reservation value υ, representing her opportunities to continue her search for better terms of trade, is less than the market maker's bid-price S^*. In other words, the customer will only participate in a transaction, if her costs for further comparison shopping exceed her utility from transacting. The customer's indirect utility function is thus driven by $S^* - \upsilon$. The market maker, in turn, quotes his bid-price in accordance to the price he can sell currency for in future, denoted S, and costs he anticipates in intermediating the trade. Clearly, the dealer does not know S, so he has to come to an expectation concerning S, denoted $E(S/\Omega)$, where Ω is a set of information variables, denoted J, which are directly observable. It is assumed that Ω is common knowledge to dealers and customers. Anticipated costs of intermediation are $c(\Omega, \theta)$ with θ being a set of parameters to be estimated. Market maker's expected profit from the transaction in question is thus given by $E(S|\Omega)-c(\Omega,\theta)-S^*$ that is representing his indirect utility function. Note that both dealer and customer are assumed to be risk-neutral here.

From indirect utility functions, it is easy to formulate participation constraints, i.e. requirements that have to be met to make both the dealer and the customer participating in this transaction. A trade takes place if and only if the respective transaction provides non-negative (expected) utility to each single one of the two potential participants. Hence, participation constraints can be written as

$$E(S|\Omega)-c(\Omega,\theta)-S^* \quad \geq \quad 0 \tag{5.1}$$

for the market maker, while for the customer, it is

$$S^*-\upsilon \quad \geq \quad 0. \tag{5.2}$$

[111] Subsequent representations are for market maker's purchases of a specific currency. Considerations for market maker's sales have to be reversed accordingly.

As a result, the market maker will only participate in the transaction if $E(S|\Omega)-c(\Omega,\theta)\geq S^*$, whereas the customer is only willing to trade if $S^*\geq\upsilon$, so a transaction will only take place if there are positive expected gains from the trade. Formally, this is

$$E(S|\Omega)-c(\Omega,\theta)-\upsilon \quad \geq \quad 0. \tag{5.3}$$

Green et al. (2007) interpret negotiations happening between the market maker and his customer, i.e. the price-quoting process, as an alternating offer game with possibility of breakdown.[112] This type of game can be solved by using the generalised Nash solution. Hence, equilibrium price S^* maximises the generalised Nash solution, i.e.

$$\max_{S^*}\left(E(S\mid\Omega)-c(\Omega,\theta)-S^*\right)^{\rho}(S^*-\upsilon)^{1-\rho}, \tag{5.4}$$

where $\rho\in[0,1]$ is the market maker's bargaining power relative to that of the customer. ρ is equal to unity if the market maker has all the bargaining power, whereas ρ equals zero if the dealer has no market power at all relative to the respective customer. Note that equation (5.4) is subject to the participation constraints shown in (5.1) and (5.2).

As shown in Appendix A.5.2, the first order condition when gains from trade are positive is given by

$$(1-\rho)\,(E(S|\Omega)-c(\Omega,\theta)-S^*)+\rho\,(\upsilon-S^*)=0 \tag{5.5}$$

that can be solved for S^* to get to the equilibrium price.[113] Consequently, S^* is

$$S^*=\rho\upsilon+(1-\rho)\left(E(S\mid\Omega)-c(\Omega,\theta)\right). \tag{5.6}$$

From equation (5.6) it is easy to see that the equilibrium price is a weighted average of the market maker's expected net profit and the customer's reservation value, where weight is determined by the market maker's relative bargaining power. Whenever the market maker has all market power and ρ is one, he is able to reduce price to a minimum, the customer still participates in

[112] See Appendix A.5.1 for a brief introduction to alternating offer games with risk of breakdown.

[113] See Appendix A.5.3.

trading, i.e. customer's reservation value υ. There, the market maker's expected net profit $(E(S\,|\,\Omega)-c(\Omega,\theta))$ is at its maximum. In contrast, if all bargaining power is with the customer, S^* will reach its maximum at which the dealer is willing to trade at all. Because of equation (5.1), this will be the case when dealer earns zero expected profits, since $S^* = E(S|\Omega) - c(\Omega,\theta)$.

After the initial trade has happened and the market maker has purchased currency, he will sell it for S. The difference between the market maker's expected price S^* and S is assumed to be a mean zero expectation error of form

$$e \equiv S - E(S|\Omega). \tag{5.7}$$

This expectation error will boost or reduce the market maker's markup, he earns with a specific trade. Because of (5.7), one can write $S = E(S|\Omega) + e$, so it is straightforward to calculate dealer's earnings by substracting S^* from both sides of this representation to get

$$S - S^* = E(S|\Omega) + e - S^*. \tag{5.8}$$

Substituting equation (5.6) for S^* finally yields

$$S-S^* = E(S\,|\,\Omega)+e-(\rho\upsilon+(1-\rho)[E(S\,|\,\Omega)-c(\Omega,\theta)])$$
$$S-S^* = E(S\,|\,\Omega)+e-\rho\upsilon-E(S\,|\,\Omega)+c(\Omega,\theta)+\rho E(S\,|\,\Omega)-\rho c(\Omega,\theta)$$
$$S-S^* = e-\rho\upsilon+c(\Omega,\theta)+\rho E(S\,|\,\Omega)-\rho c(\Omega,\theta)$$

$$S - S^* = c(\Omega,\theta) + e + \rho(E(S\,|\,\Omega)-c(\Omega,\theta)-\upsilon). \tag{5.9}$$

As shown in equation (5.3), a trade takes place only if there are positive gains from the transaction. Equation (5.3) is an element of (5.9), so a trade will take place, resulting in an observation of $S-S^*$, if

$$\rho(E(S\,|\,\Omega)-c(\Omega,\theta)-\upsilon)\geq 0. \tag{5.10}$$

As mentioned earlier, the crucial element of a stochastic frontier model is its capability of a symmetric, mean zero error, as well as an one-sided error, representing inefficiency. In equation (5.9), it is $c(\Omega,\theta)$ that represents efficient outcome, since deviations between the price, the market maker purchases currency for, and the price, he sells it for afterwards, are only due to anticipated costs of transaction, i.e. $S - S^* = c(\Omega,\theta)$. This result, however, will only be achieved if the customer has all the bargaining power, so $\rho(E(S|\Omega)-c(\Omega,\theta)-\upsilon)$ is zero. Note that even in this case the dealer might earn markups different to $c(\Omega,\theta)$, but these are only due to his expectation error e that is the stochastic element of the frontier.

That part of equation (5.9) that is represented by equation (5.10) cannot be negative. Hence, this is the one-sided error within the stochastic frontier model. It conveys dealer's bargaining power and customer's reservation value. Green et al. (2007) use relative variance of the expectation error and the one-sided error as a measure of relative importance of market maker's bargaining power.

As mentioned above, the model is calculated in percentage terms and focuses on excess returns only. Consequently, it is not $S-S^*$ that is relevant to the model, but $\left(S_i - S_i^*\right)/S_i^* - R_{market,i}$, where $R_{market,i}$ is the market-wide change of the exchange rate and i is an index to identify dealers. Furthermore, Green et al. (2007) model costs of intermediation relative to equilibrium price. They focus on these relative price movements only, which exceed expected exchange rate changes. To clarify, since Ω is common knowledge, every agent can form an expectation concerning future changes of the (market-wide) spot exchange rate. Hence, observed excess exchange rate movements based on transacted spot rates have to be attributable to expectation errors regarding $R_{market,i}$ or market power. Because $E(R_{market,i}|\Omega_i)$ is assumed to be unbiased, it is market power that governs excess returns. Formally, excess costs are given by $c(\Omega_i,\theta)/S_i^* - E(R_{market,i}\,|\,\Omega_i)$. The model can thus be re-written as

$$\frac{S_i - S_i^*}{S_i^*} - R_{market,i} = \left(\frac{c(\Omega_i,\theta)}{S_i^*} - E(R_{market,i}\,|\,\Omega_i)\right) + \varepsilon_i + \xi_i, \tag{5.11}$$

where ε_i is the symmetric error term, which is assumed to be normally distributed with zero mean and variance σ_i^2. As shown below, variance is assumed to depend on characteristics of the transaction. For now, write in accordance to Green et al. (2007)

$$\varepsilon_i \equiv \frac{e_i}{S_i^*} - \eta_i . \tag{5.12}$$

Furthermore, ξ_i represents the one sided error that is

$$\xi_i \equiv \frac{\rho_i(E(S_i \mid \Omega_i) - c(\Omega_i, \theta) - \upsilon_i)}{S_i^*} . \tag{5.13}$$

Note that $1/S_i^*$ in equation (5.13) normalises the representation of the error term ξ_i, but does not change its one-sided structure, since S_i^* is guaranteed to be positive.

Next, parametric structure is put on customer's reservation value υ_i. As suggested by Green et al. (2007), reservation value's distribution is said to depend on the market maker's expected net profits from selling currency, so

$$E(\upsilon_i \mid \Omega_i) = E(S_i \mid \Omega) - c(\Omega_i, \theta) . \tag{5.14}$$

This is because as market maker's expected, or desired, profits increase, customers' reservation values are increasing, too, meaning that customers have an increasing incentive for further comparison shopping. In other words, costs of comparison shopping decrease as expected dealer profits go up.

Indeed, although (5.14) describes υ_i correctly on average, there are deviations in both directions. Green et al. (2007) define ν_i to be the deviation of υ_i from its normalised mean, so that

$$\nu_i \equiv \frac{E(\upsilon_i \mid \Omega_i) - \upsilon_i}{S_i^*} . \tag{5.15}$$

Rewriting (5.15) with respect to (5.14) yields

$$\nu_i \equiv \frac{E(S_i \mid \Omega_i) - c(\Omega_i, \theta) - \upsilon_i}{S_i^*} , \tag{5.16}$$

so substituting (5.16) into (5.13) gives

$$\xi_i = \rho_i \nu_i . \tag{5.17}$$

Reservation value's distribution, again, depends on characteristics of the specific trade. v_i is parameterised as double exponential with density on each side of the mean being 0.5 times exponential density with parameter λ_i. The distribution of υ_i conditional on $v_i \geq 0$ is exponential with parameter λ_i, too. Consequently, distribution of ξ_i conditional on $\xi_i \geq 0$ is exponential with parameter λ_i / ρ_i. Hence, the distributions' conditional mean and conditional variance are given by

$$E(\xi_i \mid \xi_i \geq 0) = \frac{\rho_i}{\lambda_i} \tag{5.18}$$

and

$$\text{Var}(\xi_i \mid \xi_i \geq 0) = \left(\frac{\rho_i}{\lambda_i}\right)^2, \tag{5.19}$$

respectively.

As mentioned above, distributions of the symmetric and the one-sided error are assumed to depend on characteristics of the trade. Let $C = (C_{i,n})_{i=1,\ldots N}$ denote a set of N explanatory variables, the one-sided error's exponential distribution parameter ρ_i / λ_i is, as done in Green et al. (2007), specified by the following log-linear function

$$\frac{\rho_i}{\lambda_i} = a_0 \prod_{n=1}^{N} e^{a_n C_{i,n}}. \tag{5.20}$$

Whenever $a_0 = 0$, the market maker has no bargaining power at all. In turn, all variables $C_{i,n}$, which are positively related to ρ_i / λ_i, induce increasing market power of the dealer as the variables increase themselves. Hence, whenever $a_0 \neq 0$, there exists an asymmetric error and thus bargaining power for the market maker. Unfortunately, it is not possible to clarify, whether ρ_i / λ_i is driven by the market maker's relative bargaining power, ρ_i, or by variations in the customer's distribution of υ_i, i.e. λ_i.

In addition to equation (5.20), standard deviation of the symmetric error is specified accordingly by

$$\sigma_i = b_0 \prod_{n=1}^{N} e^{b_n c_{i,n}} . \tag{5.21}$$

At least, excess costs of intermediation are modelled as a linear function of explanatory variables J_i conveyed in Ω_i, so this is formally

$$\frac{c(\Omega_i,\theta)}{S_i^*} - E(R_{market,i}) = \theta_0 + \sum_{g=1}^{G} \theta_l J_{i,g} \tag{5.22}$$

with a total of G regressors. Note here that all explanatory variables are de-meaned to ease their interpretation. Consequently, the model that is going to be estimated is given by

$$\frac{S_i - S_i^*}{S_i^*} - R_{market,i} = \theta_o + \sum_{g=1}^{G} \theta_l J_{i,g} + \varepsilon_i + \xi_i . \tag{5.23}$$

Equation (5.23) is calculated by Maximum Likelihood techniques with Berndt-Hall-Hall-Hausmann (BHHH) (1974) optimisation algorithm. As shown in Green et al. (2007), the contribution to the log-likelihood for one observation is given by

$$\ell_i(\theta,\sigma,(\lambda/\rho);u_i,\Omega_i) = \ln\left(\phi\left(\frac{u_i - \Omega_i\theta}{\sigma} - \sigma(\lambda/\rho)\right)\right) + \ln(\lambda/\rho) - (\lambda/\rho)(u_i - \Omega_i\theta) + 0.5\sigma^2(\lambda/\rho)^2 \tag{5.24}$$

with θ being the coefficients of the cost function to be estimated. u_i represents observed excess returns, so $(u_i - \Omega_i\theta)$ is the estimation's residual. ϕ is the standard normal cumulative distribution function. Parameters (λ/ρ) and σ are modelled as shown in equation (5.20) and (5.21), respectively. This all leads to the log-likelihood function for a sample of T observations that is given by

$$\ell_i(\theta,\sigma,(\lambda/\rho);\{u_i,\Omega_i\}_{i=1}^{T}) = \sum_i \ell_i(\theta,\sigma,(\lambda/\rho);u_i,\Omega_i). \tag{5.25}$$

Moment conditions to equation (5.25) are to be found in Green et al. (2007).

5.3 Empirical evidence

The first step in estimating the model shown in equation (5.23) is to choose the set of explanatory variables for the cost function as well as for the defining representations of the two error terms, respectively. The cost function conveys variables for transaction size and for the dealer's recent inventory position, when the trade takes place. There are two variables for transaction size, showing the Cartesian product of the size dummies used in chapter 3 and the respective deal size in euro millions in each case. Dealer's inventory positions are in euro millions. By differentiating between long and short positions in euro inventories, it is possible to account for imperfect substitutability between foreign and domestic assets. Hence, the cost function accounts for standard determinants of dealers' costs, i.e. transaction costs, depending on trade size, and inventory costs.

As shown in equation (5.20) and (5.21), explanatory variables for the symmetric error's variance and the asymmetric error's parameter (λ / ρ) are identical. Since this chapter's aim is to investigate the dealer's market power relative to different customer groups, customer dummies used in chapter 3 are considered here, too. However, instead of using customer dummy variables alone, specifications used here comprise cross products of the respective dummies and the actual size of the transaction in euro millions. Table 5.1 reports estimates. There, results on a restricted model, calculated without taking an asymmetric error into account, are presented, too. By doing so, it is possible to get a deeper understanding of the unrestricted estimates.

Among the various variables used in the specifications, those describing different types of customers in the asymmetric error specification are indeed of major interest. However, in addition to that, constant terms deserve closer attention as well. The cost function's intercept measures, for example, expected costs of an average trade. Accordingly, volatility of the symmetric error in an usual transaction is described by the constant within the respective part of the model. At least, the intercept on the asymmetric error measures expected profit due to market power.

Table 5.1: *Maximum Likelihood estimates of equation (5.23)*
255 trading days between October 1, 2002 and September 30, 2003

	unrestricted model			restricted model		
Variable	Coefficient (z-statistic)	Standard Error	p value	Coefficient (z-statistic)	Standard Error	p value
Cost Function Parameters						
Constant	0.0528***	0.0020	<0.0001	0.1078***	0.0018	<0.0001
	(26.97)			(61.30)		
largeXeur	-0.0071**	0.0036	0.0469	-0.0089***	0.0027	0.0010
	(-1.99)			(-3.30)		
smallXeur	-0.0205***	0.0008	<0.0001	-0.0002***	0.0007	<0.0001
	(-25.23)			(-36.79)		
Eur. Inv. (long)	0.0007	0.0011	0.4795	0.0005	0.0003	0.1796
	(0.71)			(1.34)		
Eur. Inv. (short)	0.0003	0.0010	0.7682	-0.0009	0.0008	0.2688
	(0.29)			(-1.11)		
Symmetric Error Distribution						
Constant	0.0005***	1.36E-5	<0.0001	2.92E-7**	1.23E-7	0.0181
	(33.82)			(2.36)		
finXeur	-0.1113***	0.0114	<0.0001	-0.1439	0.1815	0.4280
	(-9.77)			(-0.79)		
comXeur	-0.0658***	0.0045	<0.0001	0.0036	0.1093	0.9740
	(-14.51)			(0.03)		
intXeur	0.1329***	0.0226	<0.0001	-0.4314***	0.1106	0.0001
	(5.89)			(-3.90)		
Asymmetric Error Distribution						
Constant	1,110.8***	42.22	<0.0001	---	---	---
	(26.31)					
finXeur	0.0060	0.0357	0.8873	---	---	---
	(0.17)					
comXeur	0.0635***	0.0102	<0.0001	---	---	---
	(6.20)					
intXeur	0.4727***	0.0239	<0.0001	---	---	---
	(19.80)					
Log- likelihood		33,521.67			32,447.65	
Avg. log- likelihood		5.88			5.68	

Notes: Cost function coefficients and respective standard errors are multiplied by 100. All time series used for calculations are in euro millions and demeaned by their full-sample mean. In the restricted model, cost function and volatility of the symmetric error are calculated separately by using OLS estimation with Newey-West correction. Log-likelihood and average log-likelihood figures are for the cost function's part of the restricted model. Log-likelihood (average log-likelihood) for the symmetric error's volatility function within the restricted model is 59,578.31 (10.43).

When focussing on the dealer's cost function, findings revealed by table 5.1 are broadly in line with earlier results presented in chapter 3. Within the restricted model, average markup is about twice the average excess return within the unrestricted model. In addition, average markups decrease with size of the transaction, indicated by negative coefficients on dealsize. This result implies that there are economies of scale in executing FX transactions. However, when allowing for market power in the unrestricted model, the coefficient on small deals is larger in absolute values than the coefficient on large transactions. This is surprising, but is basically in line with earlier findings on dealsize presented in chapter 3. Furthermore, recent inventory positions are, once more, statistically irrelevant for the dealer's cost function – regardless of whether the restricted or the unrestricted model is investigated. This result confirms earlier findings of chapter 3, too.

Within the restricted model, average variance is higher than in the unrestricted specification. In addition, interdealer transactions are the only statistically significant determinant of the symmetric error's distribution's variance. When looking at the unrestricted model, financial customers' and commercial customers' cause a decreasing variance of the symmetric error's distribution, but transactions with internal customers causes variance to increase. This indicates that internal customers are quoted prices, which are significantly different from quotations for financial and commercial counterparts.

The most important part of table 5.1 for this chapter's purposes is, however, the asymmetric error's distribution of the unrestricted model. Therein, some similarities to results reported in Green et al. (2007) are present. The asymmetric error's constant term is, for example, by far greater than cost function's intercept, indicating that a huge fraction of an average transaction's excess return is due to dealer's market power. In addition, cost function's constant term decreases enormously when one allows for the asymmetric error. Nevertheless, the asymmetric error's intercept's actual value is quite puzzling, as it is much larger than one would have expected it to be. Unfortunately, there is no convincing explanation for why the market maker's bargaining power contributes by more than 1000 percent to average excess returns. Hence, there might be some omitted variables, which probably cause the constant term's value to be that large. This econometric problem should be responsible for hampered interpretation of the cost function's constant term's decrease when the model allows for an asymmetric error. In contrast to Green et al. (2007), the symmetric error's distribution's intercept term here increases as one takes market power into consideration. Hence, it is not possible to conclude how much of expected costs of trading and conditional variance are attributable to the market maker's bargaining power. This finding, however, should not be overstressed, since the two components within the restricted model are calculated separately from each other by using OLS estimation for each one of them.[114]

This admittedly unsatisfactory result is not in centre of this chapter's interest, however. Rather, spotlight is on parameters of the asymmetric error's distribution, which describe dealer's market power relative to different customer groups. Though minor shortcomings in the comparison of the restricted and the unrestricted model, results for this chapter's central question are specifically promising.

First of all, all coefficients show the expected positive sign, but only those for commercial and internal customers are statistically significant. This indicates that the dealer has virtually no market power at all when he trades with financial customers. Hence, financial customers' information about recent market conditions and their knowledge of different prices quoted by various market makers force the dealer to quote narrow bid-ask spreads in order to transact any trade at all with a financial customer.

Findings are hence in direct contrast to results for the euro money market presented in Hartmann et al. (2001). There, the authors find no evidence for market power at all. In light of results presented here, this is somewhat surprising, since all players in money markets are banks and hence, financial customers in this work's interpretation.

In case of commercial customers, there is an indication of positive bargaining power for the market maker. The respective coefficient is positive and highly significant. Hence, the dealer is able to assert a wider bid-ask spread to commercial customers than to financial counterparts. Absolute magnitude of the

[114] This is because respective Maximum Likelihood estimation did not achieve convergence for the restricted model.

coefficient for commercial customers is, however, rather small, at least with respect to internal counterparts. This evidences that commercial customers are not as well informed about recent market conditions as financial customers are, but that their absolute bargaining power is far from being weak. Commercial customers, especially those who employ professionally equipped treasury departments, do have quite a clear picture regarding various market makers' current quotes. As mentioned earlier, this is not too surprising, since these market participants have advanced information systems at their disposal. Nevertheless, the group of commercial customers comprises relatively small corporations, too. These customers are usually not equipped that well and market makers are in a rather strong bargaining position vis-à-vis this "sub-category" of commercial customers, resulting in a significantly positive, though rather small coefficient for commercial customers in the asymmetric error distribution as a whole.

Market maker's bargaining position is best relative to internal counterparts. The respective coefficient in the asymmetric error distribution is significantly positive and larger in absolute values than for any other group of customers investigated here. This documents that there might be indeed some internal guidelines to force other departments at the bank to trade with the bank's own market maker.

All these findings concerning the asymmetric error's distribution presented here provide strong empirical evidence for predictions of Duffie et al.'s (2005) theoretic bargaining model. Outside options of strategic agents thus have a crucial influence on market participants' bargaining positions and are an important feature in determining the bid-ask spread they get quoted by a market maker. Duffie et al. (2005, 2007) hence provide theoretical background for Osler et al.'s (2006) market power hypothesis of pricing in foreign exchange markets.[115] Results presented herein provide empirical support for this hypothesis. Dealer's pricing strategy described here, i.e. quoting narrowest spreads to financial customers, medium spreads to commercial counterparts, and largest spreads to internal customers, which is basically in line with find-

[115] In fact, Duffie et al. (2005, 2007) study effects of search and bargaining on market-wide liquidity, so their model is of slightly different focus than chapter 5.

ings often observed in other assets, too,[116] is thus very likely to be due to market power.

5.4 Interim conclusion

Empirical results presented in section 5.3 are exceptionally promising, at least with respect to the main question of this section, i.e. market power's influence on dealers' FX pricing behaviour. After previous chapters concluded that it is very unlikely that information is the driving force behind dealers' pricing strategy, results here reveal that market power seems to be the primary channel by which bid-ask spreads are affected in FX markets.

Financial customers thus get narrower bid-ask spreads, because they are in a superior bargaining position due to their good knowledge of recent market conditions. If the market maker investigated here wants to trade any transaction at all with financial customers, he has to quote narrow spreads, or the financial customer will trade with another market maker at a different bank. Financial customers' marginal search costs are thus relatively low, since they have professional information systems at their disposal.

Commercial customers' bargaining position is slightly weaker than that of financial counterparts. Consequently, market makers can exploit significant positive market power vis-à-vis these customers and hence are able to assert wider spread levels. Having said that, overall bargaining position of the market maker here is weaker than one would have probably expected, indicating that there are some professional players in this group of customers who tend to be seen almost as informed about recent market conditions as financial customers. Indeed, the group of commercial customers is very heterogeneous. There are international corporations, running treasury departments which are professionally equipped and well trained, as well as rather small importers and exporters who are suffering from relatively great costs of comparison shopping and thus have to accept almost the first price they get quoted. Hence, the market maker's bargaining power relative to commercial

[116] See, for example, Schultz (2001) for an investigation of the corporate bond market and Harris and Piwowar (2006) for municipal bonds.

customers as a whole is a function of the fraction of huge multi-national corporations within the group of commercial counterparts.

Internal customers, at least, are facing the weakest bargaining position relative to the market maker. This is not necessarily due to a weak informational position of these counterparts, but may be caused by internal guidelines that force these customers to transact with the bank's own dealers instead of looking for the best price they can get elsewhere in the market. Consequently, the dealer can quote this group widest spreads of all.

Reviewing these results, there is strong evidence for the market power hypothesis proposed by Osler et al. (2006). In chapter 3, those customers are quoted wider bid-ask spreads who are shown here to face relatively weak bargaining positions vis-à-vis the market maker. A customer's informational position concerning recent market conditions is one explanation for this, the other is trading guidelines within the bank. The latter reason, however, is applicable in case of internal customers, only.

Appendix to chapter 5

A.5.1 Alternating offer games with risk of breakdown – an overview

Alternating offer games are a variant of bargaining problems. Bargaining theory, mainly determined by the seminal works of Nash (1950a, 1950b), is closely linked to game theory.[117] To understand alternating offer games, it seems helpful to briefly introduce the basics of Nash's (1950b) framework first.

Any bargaining problem is defined by four objects, namely the set of bargainers, called B, the set of agreements, denoted A, the disagreement event, given by D, and a preference ordering $\geq_i$ for each $i \in B$ over the set $A \cup \{D\}$. Consider two bargainers, so $B = \{1,2\}$. Note that each player's preference ordering is with respect to a set of lotteries over possible agreements and is not directly connected with a specific set of agreements themselves. Hence, players' attitudes towards risk play a prominent role in bargaining, since every single player faces uncertainty about her counterpart's behaviour. In addition, every player's preference ordering is given by a unique utility function u_i, which is possibly dominated by another utility function v_i if and only if $v_i = \alpha + \beta u_i$ for real numbers $\alpha > 0$ and β.

There are two models in the field of alternating offer games, the first taking time preferences into account, while the second considers risk of breakdown. It is only the latter that is of interest here. In both models, bargainers negotiate about a feasible bargaining set, denoted S, that consists of all possible utility combinations achieved at some point $a \in A$, i.e. $(u_1(a), u_2(a))$, and the point $d = (u_1(D), u_2(D))$. Additionally, there exists $a \in A$ such that $s_i > d_i$ for $i = 1,2$.

Nash (1950a) prescinds from differences in players' bargaining ability. Nevertheless, he introduces four axioms, which are crucial for his theory. These are

[117] A helpful introduction to bargaining theory is given in Osborne and Rubinstein (1999, p. 9 et sqq.).

- Invariance to Equivalent Utility Representations,
- Symmetry of the Bargaining Problem,
- Independence of Irrelevant Alternatives, and
- Pareto Efficiency.

Pareto efficiency requires that any realised bargaining solution is located along the frontier of *S*. Figure A.5.1 depicts Nash's general solution of the bargaining problem $\langle S, d \rangle$, with $d = (0,0)$.

The bargainers negotiate in multiple rounds, where any offer is counted one round. The players' offers are alternating. Any round of the game has two possible outcomes, namely the offer can be rejected, resulting in another round, or it can be accepted, leading to the game's end. Consequently, the game either does not achieve any agreement and the bargainers negotiate until infinity, or one of the bargainers agrees in round *t*, so the game ends. In this potentially infinite setting, it is possible to achieve Nash's bargaining solution as shown in figure A.5.1.

Taking the risk of breakdown into consideration, it is very unlikely that the game runs until infinity, because there is a probability *p* that the game ends after each round that ended with a rejection of the offer made. When the game breaks down, both players end at the disagreement point.

Consider player 1 [player 2] starts the game and her offer leads to the indifference curve I_1 depicted in figure A.5.1, so pareto efficiency requires that the offer will be $(s_{1,u}, s_{2,l})$. If player 2 agrees to this offer, the game ends and bargainers achieve $(s_{1,u}, s_{2,l})$. Alternatively, if player 2 rejects the offer, she will face risk that player 1 will leave the negotiation with probability *p*. As the number of rounds increases, the bargaining outcome will get closer to the perfect equilibrium of Nash's bargaining solution. Hence, this solution is the likelier the smaller is *p*. In fact, the outcome of an alternating offer game with risk of breakdown will be somewhere along the frontier of *S* between the first offer's utility combination and Nash's perfect equilibrium.

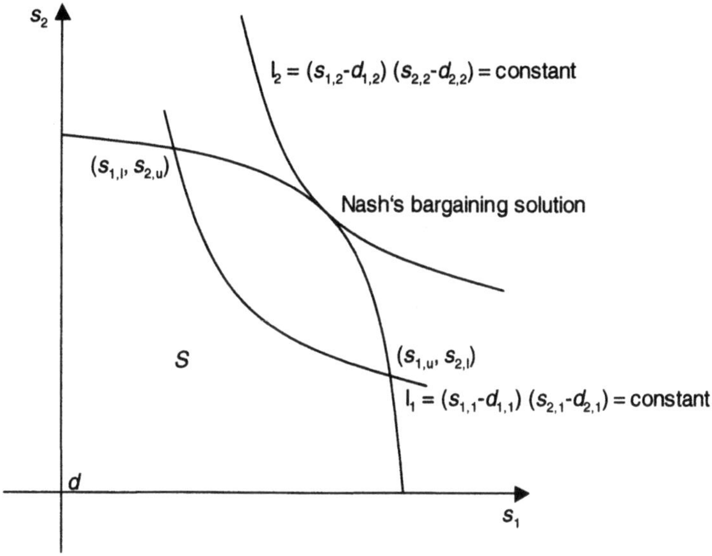

Figure A.5.1
Nash's general solution of the bargaining problem <S,d>. Source: Osborne and Rubinstein (1990, p.16), slightly modified.

A.5.2 Derivation of equation (5.5)

When maximising equation (5.4), one always has to keep in mind the participation constraint shown in equation (5.3). As long as this condition is fulfilled, there are no restriction concerning S^*. Consequently, the utility function (U), which has to be maximised, can be written as

$$U = \left(E(S \mid \Omega) - c(\Omega,\theta) - S^*\right)^{\rho}\left(S^* - \upsilon\right)^{1-\rho}. \qquad \text{(A.2.1)}$$

Differentiating (A.2.1) for S^* yields

$$\begin{aligned} U'_{S^*} = & -\rho\left(E(S \mid \Omega) - c(\Omega,\theta) - S^*\right)^{\rho-1}\left(S^* - \upsilon\right)^{1-\rho} + \\ & (1-\rho)\left(E(S \mid \Omega) - c(\Omega,\theta) - S^*\right)^{\rho}\left(S^* - \upsilon\right)^{-\rho} = 0 \end{aligned} \qquad \text{(A.2.2)}$$

With a little bit of algebra, this can be re-written as

$$-\rho\left(E(S\mid\Omega)-c(\Omega,\theta)-S^*\right)^{\rho-1}\left(S^*-\upsilon\right)^{1-\rho}=\ldots$$

$$\ldots-(1-\rho)\left(E(S\mid\Omega)-c(\Omega,\theta)-S^*\right)^{\rho}\left(S^*-\upsilon\right)^{-\rho}=0$$

$$-\rho\left(E(S\mid\Omega)-c(\Omega,\theta)-S^*\right)^{-1}\left(S^*-\upsilon\right)^{1}=-(1-\rho)$$

$$-\rho\left(S^*-\upsilon\right)=-(1-\rho)\left(E(S\mid\Omega)-c(\Omega,\theta)-S^*\right)$$

$$(1-\rho)\ (E(S|\Omega)-c(\Omega,\theta)-S^*)+\rho(\upsilon-S^*)=0. \qquad \text{(A.2.3)}$$

A.5.3 Derivation of equation (5.6)

Consider equation (5.5) in the text, shown in equation (A.2.3) above. Expanding this representation yields

$$E(S|\Omega)-c(\Omega,\theta)-S^*-\rho E(S|\Omega)+\rho c(\Omega,\theta)+\rho S^*+\rho\upsilon-\rho S^*=0$$

$$E(S|\Omega)-c(\Omega,\theta)-S^*-\rho E(S|\Omega)+\rho c(\Omega,\theta)+\rho\upsilon=0,$$

so solving this for S^* finally gives

$$S^*=E(S|\Omega)-c(\Omega,\theta)-\rho E(S|\Omega)+\rho c(\Omega,\theta)+\rho\upsilon$$

$$S^*=(1-\rho)\ [E(S|\Omega)-c(\Omega,\theta)]+\rho\upsilon. \qquad \text{(A.3.1)}$$

6. Conclusion

After years of intensive research, economists came to the conviction that standard macroeconomic models, in general, are not able to explain exchange rate movements on frequencies higher than one year. According to Lyons (2001, p. 14, 2002a, p. 52), macroeconomic variables can neither explain the absolute level of exchange rates (so-called *determination puzzle*) at this frequency, nor are they able to explain exchange rate volatility (so-called *excess volatility puzzle*). After Flood and Rose (1995, p. 5) concluded that *the most critical determinants of exchange rate volatility are not macroeconomic*, attention has shifted to rather micro-based approaches and investigations of dealer behaviour in FX markets to get a better understanding of short-run exchange rate dynamics. This insight paved the way for the so-called *microstructure approach to exchange rates* that provides particularly promising answers to the above-mentioned puzzles in exchange rate economics.

The work at hand contributes, at least partly, to the *determination puzzle*, as it clarifies the role of incoming customer order flow, or, more precisely, its information content, and market makers' bargaining power during the determination process of tick-by-tick spot exchange rates. However, since we focus on a single market maker only, it is not possible to analyse the actual determination of the exchange rate, because this should happen in accordance to market-wide interdealer order flow. Nevertheless, for market makers, order flow is a means of fortifying their adjustment of expectations regarding a currency's fundamental value. It can thus help economists to understand micro-level learning and information aggregation during the trading process.

Theoretical works on microstructure aspects of asset pricing are widespread. While earlier approaches usually suffer from quite unrealistic assumptions with respect to a dealer's role within the market-wide trading process, models became more realistic during the years. Sequential and simultaneous trade models or general equilibrium approaches today are able to explain specific features of FX markets like *hot potato trading*, i.e. massive inventory management of market makers via the interdealer market, and lagged adjustment of the exchange rate. These models show how dealers' risk aversion, their acting as (rational) speculators, and potential asymmetric information turn out to be crucial determinants of these market properties. However, though hot potato trading and the existence of asymmetric information among market participants are well evidenced in empirical studies, recent works have shown that dealers behave differently than proposed by standard theory, especially when it comes to quoting bid-ask spreads under asymmetric information. Though standard theory suggests to widen bid-ask spreads as probability increases that a specific counterpart has superior information, empirical results broadly evidence that dealers actually narrow spreads in this case.

This work's findings are in line with latest results of empirical studies. Here, the Madhavan and Smidt (1991) model and the Huang and Stoll (1997) model are investigated to analyse how dealers actually set prices when they are approached by different types of counterparts and facing varying order sizes. To do so, two data sets, conveying the full transaction record in EUR / USD of an average-sized German bank, are analysed, each of them spanning a period of an entire year. The first sample covers the period from October 1, 2002, to September 30, 2003, the second conveys all EUR / USD transactions at this bank between October 1, 2004, and September 30, 2005. Although trading activity varies substantially between the two samples, empirical findings are similar. By analysing the two models, up to 46% of volatility in actually *transacted* tick-by-tick EUR / USD exchange rate changes can be explained, especially when taking different deal sizes and groups of customers into account.

As stated earlier, results reveal that dealers often behave in the opposite way to predictions of standard models of asset pricing under asymmetric information. Dealers quote narrower bid-ask spreads to potentially well informed counterparts, while seemingly worse informed customers are quoted wider spreads. Leach and Madhavan (1992, 1993) propose information content of order flow to make dealers subsidising informed order flow by narrowing spreads. Osler et al. (2006) suggest this strategic dealing hypothesis to be one potential explanation for observed dealer behaviour. Hence, a market maker has an incentive to narrow spreads to increase probability that well informed customers trade with him whenever the market maker is able to exploit information conveyed in order flow in his own speculative trading. Alternatively, market power might be the rationale for price-setting in FX markets, meaning that dealers have to quote narrow spreads to well informed counterparts if they want to trade any transaction with them. Thus, both hypotheses are directly linked to information, but while strategic dealing refers to information about future exchange rate changes, market power is linked to customers' information about recent market conditions, i.e. competing quotes by different dealers. In addition to the market maker's price setting behaviour, chapter 3 presents evidence that the dealer at hand seems to offset undesired inventory via (electronic) interdealer trading instead of shading his price, i.e. adjusting his own quotes to attract customers who are willing to trade in accordance to bring the dealer's inventory back to his desired level.

Chapter 4 intensively investigates the strategic dealing hypothesis. Firstly, cointegration analyses reveal that there is indeed a stable equilibrium between cumulative incoming order flow and the level of exchange rates, at least for commercial and financial customers. This finding indicates potential information content of incoming order flow and thus provides first empirical evidence in favour of the strategic dealing hypothesis. In addition, results provide empirical support for the view of Osler (1998) that commercial customers are ultimate liquidity providers in FX markets, since their cointegration coefficient within the analysis is significantly negative. However, when calculating the related vector error correction model, findings on short run adjustment dynamics between cumulative order flow and exchange rates do not support the wide-spread optimism that order flow is the high powered source of information easily exploitable for short-run speculation in FX markets. Figures for information half-life indicate that the adjustment process proceeds rather slowly, supporting the view of Sager and Taylor (2005) that a single market maker's order flow is not an useful predictor of market-wide order flow and is thus unlikely to generate systematic and reliable forecasts for short-run exchange rate speculation. However, results imply support for the complex process of information aggregation across the market place via trading as described by Evans and Lyons (2005b).

Further tests conducted to the question of information content of incoming order flow barely provide any support for order flow's information content concerning future exchange rate returns. By analysing Evans and Lyons' (2005c) model of micro-based exchange rate forecasting, there is almost no evidence that a single bank's incoming order flow conveys predictive power for exchange rate changes; and even if order flow conveys information, it is on a rather medium-term forecasting horizon of up to ten trading days. Order flow based exchange rate forecasts in both samples hardly perform significantly better than a random walk. Results depend significantly on the test procedures used during the analyses and there is no single case where tests consistently indicate superior forecasting power of order flow-based models compared to a driftless random walk prediction. This is certainly not enough evidence to conclude in favour of the strategic dealing hypothesis, not at least because it is quite unusual to keep speculative positions of significant amount open over a couple of days. Lyons' (1995) assumption that dealers aim to hold a net zero position at the end of each trading day is generally confirmed by traders. Nevertheless, minor positions are kept open over night, depending on the market maker's expectation concerning the exchange rate, but these positions are comparatively small in volume.

To come to a broad conclusion about the strategic dealing hypothesis, the assumption that dealers hold a net zero inventory position over night is relaxed and medium-term performances of the market maker's speculative positions are investigated. This is because the dealer might have an incentive to subsidise informed orders for order flow driven medium-term speculative trading, so one can only reject the strategic dealing hypothesis when the dealer does not generate positive profits from speculative trading at respective forecasting horizons. Results reveal that the market maker's speculative positions do not contribute to the dealer's earnings from trading foreign exchange and the dealer's return on these trades fail to become significantly positive in the medium run. Consequently, there is no indication in the data at hand that it is the strategic dealing hypothesis that provides a convincing rationale for the market maker's pricing strategy.

The finding of a lack of forecasting power of order flow does not necessarily indicate a lack of order flow's forecasting power at all. It is quite likely that this result is driven by the fact that the bank at hand is an average-sized player in FX markets and its customer base might hence be not very informative. As shown in the description of the data set in chapter 2, there are almost no "real" financial customers, i.e. institutional investors, who should provide most informative order flow of all. So, while there is no major difference in pricing behaviour and spread-quoting strategies between the dealer at hand and dealers at larger banks, motives for this behaviour might vary. It is not impossible that the dealer at hand does not act in accordance to the strategic dealing hypothesis, while market makers with a larger customer base actually do so.

However, after this negative conclusion on strategic dealing, market power remains a possible channel to affect quotes in FX markets. The better informed a customer is about recent market conditions, i.e. the better her knowledge about competing quotes of different market makers, the better is her bargaining position vis-à-vis a single market maker. Hence, if a market maker wants to trade any transaction with a well-informed counterpart, he has to quote narrow spreads or the customer will trade with another dealer at a different bank. Since financial customers have professional information systems at their disposal and communicate intensively with various market makers at different banks, Osler et al. (2006) propose financial customers to be the best informed counterparts of all. Consequently, market makers might be forced by financial customers' bargaining power to quote narrow spreads to these counterparts. Commercial customers, i.e. importers, exporters, and industry clients, who are, on average, not as professionally equipped as financial counterparts, bear a weaker bargaining position and are thus facing wider bid-ask spreads.

Estimating a stochastic frontier model in accordance to Green et al. (2007) reveals that market power is indeed likely to be the channel by which the dealer's bid-ask spread is primarily affected. Estimates on determinants of an asymmetric disturbance term, representing inefficiency and hence market power in the model, provide evidence that the market maker considered in this work does not have any significant bargaining power relative to financial customers. For commercial customers, the dealer's market power is significantly positive, but smaller in absolute size than one would have probably guessed. This result indicates that the group of commercial counterparts is very heterogeneous, since it consists of professionally equipped treasury departments at large multi-national corporations, which have information about recent market conditions that are almost as good as those of financial customers, as well as of rather small importers and exporters who do not have these information systems at their disposal. On average, the market maker is able to exploit significantly positive market power, but this result does not necessarily hold good for a single commercial counterpart.

The third group of customers investigated here, namely internal customers, i.e. other departments at the market maker's bank involved in foreign exchange, are evidenced to be in the weakest bargaining position vis-à-vis the dealer. There are two potential explanations for this. First, internal customers might not be well informed about recent market conditions and are hence quoted widest spreads. Alternatively, there might be internal guidelines resolved by the bank's management committee that force internal departments to trade foreign exchange with the bank's own market maker instead of looking for the best price elsewhere in the FX market. Such an internal guideline would make the market maker to be a virtual monopolist for FX trading services to internal departments, so he would be able to assert widest spread levels to these customers. Unfortunately, it is not possible to conclude whether or not this result is specific for the bank at hand, because to our knowledge, there is no other study that explicitly deals with internal counterparts.

Recapitulating all these results, there is a clear thread within the data. Dealers quote narrower spreads to potentially better informed customers, because of market power rather than because of order flow's information content exploitable for the dealer's own speculative trading. Hence, the finding that dealers quote bid-ask spreads in the opposite direction of predictions by standard models of asset pricing under asymmetric information can be convincingly explained. In addition, the pricing strategy described here fits to the dealers' own understanding of FX market's functionality.

Although findings here provide further important insights to FX trading and price setting in foreign exchange markets, some questions remain to be unanswered. Given that order flow plays an important role in FX markets, a natural next step is to ask what is driving order flow. Macroeconomic news are likely to be a major determinant of order flow, but macro-news are simply too rare to explain observed flow dynamics entirely, at least in the very short run. Hence, future research should adress the question, whether there are differences in the speed of processing public news and the time elapsing until specific customers groups respond to public announcements. In addition, further research is necessary to investigate potential time-varying information content of FX order flow against macroeconomic announcements, as evidenced in Menkveld et al. (2007) for customer flow in U.S. Treasury Bond futures. This might be of specific interest in light of exchange rates' asymmetric reaction to macro-announcements with bad news having greater impacts than good news, as shown in Andersen et al. (2003).

Moreover, there is need for future research in addressing order flow's reaction to price changes in other currency pairs. Lyons and Moore (2005) show that some currency pairs are never transacted directly, but are always traded via at least one "vehicle-currency". These findings highlight interdependencies across various exchange rates that should have order flow consequences, too. Expanding this view results in investigating FX order flow's reaction to developments in other asset classes and hence in analysing interdependencies across various assets as proposed in Asparouhova and Bossaerts (2005). An actual field of application could be research on currency carry trades, which make the exchange rate being interdependend with expected asset returns in other assets.

At last, Bandi and Russell (2006) divide volatility at stock markets into one part that prevails even in equilibrium and a second fraction, which is due to unobservable microstructure noise. Intraday patterns in equilibrium volatility and / or microstructure noise might result in intraday seasonalities. Microstructure causes for volatility in general and seasonalities in volatility in particular, too, seem to deserve econometricians' future attention in FX markets.

Annex – An introduction to important econometric concepts

(A)1. Generalised Method of Moments

Hansen's (1982) Generalised Method of Moments (GMM) estimators have become one of the most important econometric approaches to estimate a vector of unknown parameters driving an economic system. The technique's popularity is mainly based on its robustness against serial correlation and heteroscedasticity of unknown form. Though econometric literature is still dominated by maximum likelihood estimation, it requires to some extend strong assumptions regarding the parameters' distribution or data generating processes, which GMM does not.

While most contributions to GMM literature are methodically demanding, Pynnonen (2007) provides an useful overview and introduction to the technique's basic principles. The following description draws heavily on his work. In addition, helpful textbook descriptions can be found in Johnston and DiNardo (1997), Matyas (1999), and Greene (2003a), among others. Before proceeding with a description of GMM estimation, it seems to be useful to clarify some basic aspects of econometric estimators in general.

Estimators are generally based on two of the most important features in probability theory, namely the so-called *Central Limit Theory* (CLT) and the (*Weak*) *Law of Large Numbers* (LLN). In its classical version, CLT proposes that a sequence of independent and identically distributed (i.i.d.) random variables with finite means and finite variances tends to be standard-normally distributed as the number of observations increases towards infinity. Formally, this can be written as

$$\frac{(\bar{y}_n - \mu)}{\sigma\sqrt{n}} \xrightarrow{d} z \sim N(0,1), \quad \text{as } n \to \infty, \qquad \text{(Annex 1.1)}$$

where y_i ($i \in [1,n]$) are independent random variables with finite means, $E(y_i) = \mu$, and finite variances, $Var(y_i) = \sigma^2$, and $\bar{y}_n = 1/n\Sigma_{i=1}^{n} y_i$.

LLN, in contrasts, argues that the expected value of a sequence of i.i.d. random variables with identical means converges to the "true" mean of the respective variable. All assumptions remain to be unchanged compared with CLT, so LLN can be formally written as

$$\operatorname{plim} \bar{y}_n = \mu , \qquad \text{(Annex 1.2)}$$

where plim is the limit in probability as $n \to \infty$.

Limit in probability is also known as convergence in probability, being a well known assumption in large sample distribution theory. As mentioned in Greene (2003a, p. 897), *a random variable y_n converges in probability to a constant c if* $\lim_{n\to\infty}$ Prob*(*$|y_n - c| > \varepsilon$*) for any positive* ε. Values for y_n, which are substantially different from *c*, hence become more and more unlikely, as *n* increases.

Estimators, especially so-called *large-sample estimators* like GMM, use CLT and LLN from probability theory to provide estimates of any parameter that governs the distribution of observed random variables. Any estimator should be unbiased, i.e. the expected value of the estimated coefficient should be equal to the parameter in question. The more observations are available, the higher should be probability that the estimated coefficients show this feature, because of LLN. In addition, estimators should be variance minimal. Whenever an estimator shows minimum variance and unbiased coefficients, it is said to be efficient.

To understand GMM, it is necessary to understand the so-called *Classical Method of Moments* first. In classical linear regressions, observations of *y* at time *t* are to be explained by an *m*-vector of explanatory variables, denoted x_t, and an *m*-vector of regression coefficients, denoted β. In addition, there is a stochastic error term, ε_t. Formally, the regression equation is given by

$$y_t = x_t'\beta + \varepsilon_t \qquad \text{(Annex 1.4)}$$

with $x_t = (x_{1t},\dots,x_{mt})'$.

To come to efficient estimates for β, a set of moment conditions has to be met. These conditions refer to the regression's error term, saying that (i) the residual's variance should be constant across all observations, so

$$Var(\varepsilon_t) = \sigma^2 \quad \forall t, \qquad \text{(Annex 1.5)}$$

(ii) its expected value should be zero, i.e. there is no systematic bias in the estimates

$$E[(y_t - x_t'\beta)x_t] = E(\varepsilon_t x_t) = 0 \quad \forall t, \qquad \text{(Annex 1.6)}$$

and (iii) all errors should be serially uncorrelated, i.e.

$$E(\varepsilon_t \varepsilon_u) = 0 \quad \forall t \neq u. \qquad \text{(Annex 1.7)}$$

Consequently, these conditions require that the error term is a white noise process.

Classical Method of Moments aims to identify θ, being the above-mentioned m-vector of parameters β governing the distribution of y, from a sample of T independent random observations by equating the first m population moments $\mu_k(\theta)$ with the corresponding sample moments $\hat{\mu}_k$.[118] Provided that there exists a kth moment of y, it is formally defined as

$$\mu_k(\theta) = E(y^k) \qquad \text{(Annex 1.8)}$$

and sample moments are given by

$$\hat{\mu}_k = \frac{1}{T}\sum_{i=1}^{T} y_i^k, \qquad \text{(Annex 1.9)}$$

so one can solve this system for the components of θ. Due to the fact that moment estimators basically calculate observed variables' means, LLN assures that estimates converge towards their theoretical moments and are thus consistent, as the number of observations is sufficiently large. GMM estimation is just a generalisation of this classical moments procedure. A vital feature of this technique is a set of population moment conditions derived

[118] Pynnonen (2007).

from the econometric model. The approach aims at fitting the model's moment conditions to those observed within the sample in order to minimise deviations between the estimated function and observed realisations of the stochastic process under investigation.

As stated above, x_t is a vector of explanatory variables while θ denotes a vector of unknown parameters. Again, moment conditions play a prominent role within the model. However, they are now usually termed *orthogonality conditions* and refer again to the model's residuals. Most importantly, expected value for the residual term, u_t, given estimated values for θ, denoted $u_t = u(x_t;\theta)$, has to be zero, as it is for the true parameter values, denoted θ_0. Formally this is

$$E(u_t) = E[u(x_t;\theta_0)] = 0. \qquad \text{(Annex 1.10)}$$

It is clear that the error term's expected value under the true parameter values is zero. This fact, indeed, is somewhat of a benchmark result for the estimated parameter vector θ. The disturbance term's mean using θ is

$$g_T(\theta) = \frac{1}{T}\sum_{t=1}^{T} u(x_t;\theta) = \frac{1}{T}\sum_{t=1}^{T} u_t. \qquad \text{(Annex 1.11)}$$

Hence, the best estimate for θ is achieved when $g_T(\theta)$ is as close as possible to zero. Hence, the GMM estimator $\hat{\theta}$ chooses θ to minimise

$$Q(\theta) = g_T(\theta)'Wg_T(\theta), \qquad \text{(Annex 1.12)}$$

where W is a weighting matrix that determines, how each moment condition is weighted during the estimation process to achieve the best estimates.

Introducing the weighting matrix is a crucial difference between Classical Method of Moments and GMM. The idea behind this, though, is quite straightforward. As mentioned before, Classical Method of Moments uses as many moment conditions as there are coefficients to be estimated within the regression, i.e. the number of moment conditions equals the dimension of the parameter vector θ. In GMM, the number of moment conditions can exceed the number of coefficients, resulting in an over-identified system. Skipping a number of moment conditions to ensure that the system is exactly identified would be straightforward, but would result in a disuse of probably important information.[119] Hence, GMM introduces the weighting matrix *W* to solve this over-identification problem. Of course, the weighting of a moment condition should increase with its reliability. Hence, a logical next step is to clarify, how *W* is to be chosen.

Since the error term's expected value is zero, as it is for $g_T(\theta)$ given the true parameter values, a moment condition's reliability can be measured by using the variance covariance matrix, i.e.

$$Cov[g_T(\theta)] = E[g_T(\theta)g_T(\theta)']$$

$$Cov[g_T(\theta)] = \frac{1}{T^2}\sum_{s=1}^{T}\sum_{t=1}^{T}E(u_s u_t'). \qquad \text{(Annex 1.13)}$$

As mentioned in Pynnonen (2007), by taking $j = |t - s|$ and assuming u_t to be stationary, one can write

$$E[u_t u_{t+j}'] = S_j = S_{-j}' \qquad \forall t, \qquad \text{(Annex 1.14)}$$

so equation (Annex 1.13) can be re-written as

$$\sum_{s=1}^{T}\sum_{t=1}^{T}E(u_s u_t') = \sum_{j=-T}^{T}(T - |j|)S_j. \qquad \text{(Annex 1.15)}$$

Alternatively, because of equation (Annex 1.14), one can write

$$\sum_{s=1}^{T}\sum_{t=1}^{T}E(u_s u_t') = TS_0 + \sum_{j=1}^{T}(T - j)(S_j + S_j'). \qquad \text{(Annex 1.16)}$$

By supposing various assumptions mentioned in Hansen (1982, p. 1032 et sqq.), the so-called *long-run covariance matrix of disturbances*, denoted *S*, being a positive definite matrix, can be expressed as

[119] To avoid any misunderstanding, GMM is not limited to over-identified systems, but can be used when the number of moment conditions equals the dimension of θ, too.

$$\lim_{k \to \infty} \sum_{j=-k}^{k} S_j = S. \qquad \text{(Annex 1.17)}$$

Let $\hat{S}_j$ denote an estimate of an autocovariance matrix S_j, based on observations $\hat{u}_t$ on u_t. $\hat{S}_j$ can be achieved by

$$\hat{S}_j = \frac{1}{T} \sum_{t=j+1}^{T} \hat{u}_t \hat{u}'_{t-j}, \qquad \text{(Annex 1.18)}$$

where j runs from zero to l and l denotes the maximum lag length. An estimate of S, denoted $\hat{S}$, can then be achieved by conducting the following weighting equation

$$\hat{S} = \hat{S}_0 + \sum_{j=1}^{l} \omega_j (\hat{S}_j + \hat{S}'_j). \qquad \text{(Annex 1.19)}$$

As shown therein, $\hat{S}$ is given by the sum of estimates on the entire, i.e. non-lagged autocovariance matrix, $\hat{S}_0$, weighted by one, and up to l sums of lagged autocovariance matrices and their respective inverse matrix, weighted by ω_j. Usually, ω_j decreases as j increases. As mentioned in Pynnonen (2007), a common way to choose ω_j is to conduct Bartlett's procedure.

To obtain an estimate of the unknown parameter vector, GMM uses a two-step procedure, that is repeated until the best estimate of the parameter vector θ is achieved. The procedure begins with setting the weighting matrix W equal to the unity matrix and minimising equation (Annex 1.12) by varying θ. Hence, the first estimate for θ, denoted $\hat{\theta}^{(1)}$, is achieved by

$$\hat{\theta}^{(1)} = \arg\min_{\theta} g_T(\theta)' W g_T(\theta). \qquad \text{(Annex 1.20)}$$

Based on this first outcome, disturbances $\hat{u}_t$ are calculated to employ them in estimating the autocovariance matrices $\hat{S}_j$ as described in equation (Annex 1.18). By using equation (Annex 1.19), results for $\hat{S}_j$ provide the basis for the first estimate of the disturbance term's long run covariance matrix, $\hat{S}$. By setting $W = \hat{S}^{-1}$ and deploying it in equation (Annex 1.20), the next round of estimation begins. This procedure is repeated until $\hat{\theta}^{(k+1)} \approx \hat{\theta}^{(k)}$.

Similar to Two Stage Least Squares (TSLS) estimators, GMM uses a set of instrument variables, so-called *predictors*, to avoid the residuals to correlate with these potential additional variables. Formally, let z_t denote a vector of potential predictors and define the residuals u_t in accordance to equation (Annex 1.10) as $y - f(x;\theta)$, the aim is at achieving

$$E[(y - f(x;\theta) \otimes z] = 0, \qquad \text{(Annex 1.21)}$$

where $\otimes$ is the so-called *Kronecker product.*[120] By using instrument variables, GMM provides a suitable way to account for rational expectations.

As mentioned above, the estimation problem is called exactly identified, i.e. it is exactly solvable, whenever the dimension of the parameter vector θ, denoted *m*, being the number of parameters to be estimated, is equal to the number of moment conditions, *r*. Nevertheless, due to the weighting matrix *W*, GMM can cope with over-identification, too. Whenever the number of moment conditions exceeds the number of parameters to be estimated, the model is called over-identified. As mentioned in Pynnonen (2007), over-identification conditions can be tested by using the statistic

$$J = g(\hat{\theta})'Wg(\hat{\theta}_T), \qquad \text{(Annex 1.22)}$$

where TJ has an asymptotical χ^2_{r-m} distribution under the Null H_0: $E[(u_t(\theta)] = 0$. Whenever statistic (Annex 1.22) allows to reject the Null, the model is not supported by the data.

[120] The Kronecker product (Leopold Kronecker, *1823, †1891) *C* of two matrices *A* (*m* x *n*) and *B* (*p* x q), denoted $C = A \otimes B$, is defined as $C = (a_{ij} \cdot B)$, i.e. *C* is an *mp* x *nq* matrix that consists of the products of every element of *A* multiplied by *B*.

(A)2. Cointegration and error correction

Econometric estimators like GMM require stationarity[121] of the time series analysed therein to come to reliable estimates for the parameter vector. In fact, many "real world" economic time series are integrated of order one, written I(1), meaning that not the level of the respective variable is stationary, but its first differences. To analyse non-stationary time series, an econometrician faces two alternatives. Firstly, data can be manipulated by taking first differences, by re-scaling the data or by taking logs. Alternatively, cointegration analysis provides an appropriate way to deal with instationarity.

The term *cointegration* was introduced by Engle and Granger (1987). The basic idea of their work is that there might exist a stable equilibrium between two or more variables that follow an I(d)[122] process, which can be expressed by a linear combination of the respective time series. Formally, in its long-run equilibrium, the system can be written as

$$\beta_1 x_{1t} + \beta_2 x_{2t} + \ldots + \beta_n x_{nt} = 0, \qquad \text{(Annex 2.1)}$$

where β_i $(i \in \{1,\ldots,n\})$ denotes coefficients to be estimated and x_{it} are observations of the respective time series at time *t*.

Whenever the system described in (Annex 2.1) is off kilter, a so-called *equilibrium error* e_t occurs, where $e_t = \beta x_t$.[123] Obviously, there exists a meaningful stable relationship between the variables if and only if e_t follows a stationary process. Hence, in the interpretation of Engle and Granger (1987), there are two criteria that have to be met simultaneously to identify cointegration of or-

[121] Stationarity is a feature of stochastic processes or ordinary differential equations. Weak-sense stationarity, which is usually used in time series analysis, is defined by three features (see Greene, 2003a, p. 611 et sqq.): (i) the time series' expected value is finite and constant among all observations $[E\{x_t\} = m \ \forall \ t \in T]$, (ii) variance is finite $[E\{x_t^2\} = \sigma_t^2 < \infty \ \forall \ t \in T]$, and (iii) observations' covariance depends only on the length of the time span considered, not on its actual position within the sample period $[\mathrm{Cov}(x_s, x_t) = \mathrm{Cov}(x_{s+r}, x_{t+r}) \ \forall \ s, t, r \in T]$. The last feature, called covariance-stationarity, includes variance-stationarity. Note that *T* is an index set of usually integral numbers.

[122] Engle and Granger (1987) define cointegration to exist only between variables that are integrated of the same order *d*.

[123] x_t is a vector consisting of $x_t = (x_{1t}, x_{2t}, \ldots, x_{nt})'$.

der (d, b) between the elements of x_t. First, all variables have to be integrated of the same order d, and second, there must be a so-called *cointegrating vector* $\beta = (\beta_1, \beta_2, \ldots, \beta_n)$ that makes the equilibrium error following a stationary process. If these criteria are met, x_t is integrated of order $(d - b)$ with $b > 0$, written $x_t \sim CI(d, b)$.

It is important to state here that vector β is not unique. As mentioned in Enders (2004, p. 322), multiplying β by any nonzero scalar λ is also a cointegrating vector. It is common practice in cointegration analysis to normalise the cointegration vector by fixing one variable's coefficient at one.

Engle and Granger (1987) do not define a specific causality for cointegration. As long as the above mentioned criteria are met by the economic system in question, variables are said to be cointegrated. It does not matter whether this result is driven by causal or behavioural relationships or whether it is just due to a common stochastic trend underlying the set of time series. The latter is of specific interest in Stock and Watson (1988) and is particularly helpful in understanding the essence of cointegration.

As done in Enders (2004, p. 325 et sqq.), suppose a vector x_t that contains two I(1) variables, denoted y_t and z_t. Each of these two variables is assumed to consist of a random walk process, denoted μ_{it}, representing its stochastic trend, and an irregular and stationary component e_{it}, which is not necessarily a white noise process.[124] Hence, for y_t and z_t write

$$y_t = \mu_{yt} + e_{yt} \qquad \text{(Annex 2.2)}$$

$$z_t = \mu_{zt} + e_{zt}. \qquad \text{(Annex 2.3)}$$

As mentioned above, y_t and z_t are said to be cointegrated, if the linear combination $\beta_1 y_t + \beta_2 z_t$ with $\beta_1 \neq 0, \beta_2 \neq 0$ is stationary. Because of that, one can write with respect to (Annex 2.2) and (Annex 2.3)

$$\beta_1 y_t + \beta_2 z_t = \beta_1(\mu_{yt} + e_{yt}) + \beta_2(\mu_{zt} + e_{zt})$$

$$\beta_1 y_t + \beta_2 z_t = (\beta_1 \mu_{yt} + \beta_2 \mu_{zt}) + (\beta_1 e_{yt} + \beta_2 e_{zt}). \qquad \text{(Annex 2.4)}$$

---

[124] Note that $i \in \{y,z\}$ here.

In (Annex 2.4), $(\beta_1 \mu_{yt} + \beta_2 \mu_{zt})$ represents the non-stationary component of $\beta_1 y_t + \beta_2 z_t$. Thus, variables are integrated of order (1, 1), if

$$\beta_1 \mu_{yt} + \beta_2 \mu_{zt} = 0. \qquad \text{(Annex 2.5)}$$

Provided that μ_{yt} and μ_{zt} are varying over time and β_1 as well as β_2 have to be nonzero, the condition shown in (Annex 2.5) is only fulfilled if

$$\mu_{yt} = -\frac{\beta_2}{\beta_1} \mu_{zt}. \qquad \text{(Annex 2.6)}$$

Consequently, y_t and z_t are cointegrated of order (1, 1), if they have the same stochastic trend up to the scalar $-\beta_2/\beta_1$.

Conducting the Engle and Granger (1987) methodology to test for cointegration between a set of variables is straightforward. In their work, the authors propose a four-step testing procedure that begins with a test of the variables' respective order of integration. Next, an OLS-regression is run and the estimated residuals are tested for a unit root by conducting Augmented Dickey-Fuller (ADF) tests.[125] In step three, an error correction model[126] is estimated to assess whether residuals drawn from the first step regression are helpful in this environment. This is only the case if the variables are CI(1, 1). In the last step, the error correction model is analysed in greater detail by conducting further investigations on speed of adjustment coefficients,[127] impulse / response analysis, and variance decomposition, as proposed by Lütkepohl and Reimers (1992).

Despite of its practical ease, the Engle and Granger (1987) methodology suffers from some significant shortcomings. One of the most severe is the fact that it requires a pre-specified long-run equilibrium equation, where a set of

[125] As highlighted in Greene (2003a, p. 655 et sqq.), critical values provided by usual Dickey-Fuller tables are inappropriate here to test for stationarity of the $\{e_t\}$ sequence. Instead, researchers should rely on tables provided by Engle and Granger (1987), Engle and Yoo (1987), Phillips and Ouliaris (1990), and Davidson and MacKinnon (1993), or, as done in this study, MacKinnon (1991).

[126] Cointegration directly refers to the feature of error correction, an aspect that is clarified below.

[127] See Enders (2004, p. 338).

variables is seen as driving forces of another variable. Consider the above mentioned vector x_t, consisting of the I(1) variables y_t and z_t. To conduct the Engle and Granger (1987) methodology, an econometrician has to specifiy the OLS regression that could be

$$y_t = \beta_{10} + \beta_{11} z_t + e_{1t} \qquad \text{(Annex 2.7)}$$

or, alternatively,

$$z_t = \beta_{20} + \beta_{21} y_t + e_{2t}. \qquad \text{(Annex 2.8)}$$

As mentioned in Enders (2004, p. 347), asymptotic theory implies that both models shown above are equally well suited for testing for cointegration between the $\{y_t\}$ and the $\{z_t\}$ series, since unit root tests conducted on $\{e_{1t}\}$ become equivalent to unit root tests carried out on $\{e_{2t}\}$ as the number of observations grows to infinity. However, with realistic sample sizes at hand, tests on $\{e_{1t}\}$ might indicate cointegration between y_t and z_t, while tests on $\{e_{2t}\}$ might not or vice versa. Indeed, this is very undesirable, because it reduces the methodology's reliability. This shortcoming of Engle and Granger's (1987) approach becomes even more severe when vector x_t consists of more than two variables. For n nonstationary components within x_t, there might be as many as n-1 linearly independent cointegrating vectors. The number of cointegrating vectors is called the cointegration rank of x_t.[128]

In addition to the above-mentioned drawback of the approach, the two-step methodology (calculating a regression model first and then testing its residual sequence for a unit root) proposed by Engle and Granger (1987) suffers from the potential problem that any error during the first step is carried over into the second step. Hence, the advantage of Johansen's (1988, 1991) as well as Stock and Watson's (1988) maximum likelihood approaches is that they (i) do not need a two-step procedure to test for cointegration, (ii) allow the econometrician to test for multiple cointegrating vectors simultaneously, and (iii) provide an opportunity to test for restricted cointegrating vectors and / or speed of adjustment coefficients directly. Consequently, both of these techniques are broadly seen to be superior to Engle and Granger's (1987) ap-

[128] Whenever the cointegration rank of x_t exceeds one, it may not be possible to identify the behavioural relationships from what might be reduced-form relationships. Enders (2004, p. 325 et sqq.).

proach. However, since methods are quite similar[129] and because it is the Johansen (1988, 1991) procedure that is used in this work, subsequent explanations deal with this technique instead of the approach of Stock and Watson (1988).

The advantage of Johansen's (1991) maximum likelihood estimator compared to his approach described in Johansen (1988) is that it allows for a constant term and seasonal dummies. It is especially the constant term that is proved to be crucial for interpreting the model. A straightforward way to understand the Johansen procedure is provided by Enders (2004, p. 348 et sqq., p. 362 et sqq.). As he emphasises, Johansen's (1988, 1991) approach is a multivariate generalisation of Dickey and Fuller's (1981) test for a unit root. Remember, a sequence is said to contain a unit root if its recent value is determined [conditional on (n x n) coefficient matrix A_1] by its lagged values and an innovation, which is stationary. As mentioned above, the approach is based on a vector autoregression model, so its representation for p = 1 is[130]

$$\begin{aligned} y_t &= a_{11}y_{t-1} + a_{12}z_{t-1} + \varepsilon_{yt} \\ z_t &= a_{21}y_{t-1} + a_{22}z_{t-1} + \varepsilon_{zt} \end{aligned} \qquad \text{(Annex 2.9)}$$

with ε_{yt} and ε_{zt} being innovations that might be contemporaneously correlated, but are serially uncorrelated, as well as uncorrelated with elements of x_t. In an application of the Johansen (1988, 1991) procedure, one has to determine the lag structure, p, in advance. As mentioned above, there is only one lag used in (Annex 2.9), but with real-world data including further lags could be appropriate. In the study at hand, the lag structure is determined by conducting Schwartz (SIC) and Hannan-Quinn (HQ) Information Criteria.

For convenience, write (Annex 2.9) in its matrix vector notation

---

[129] Both methods are vector autoregression (VAR) approaches and exploit the relation between the rank of a matrix and its characteristic roots (i.e. eigenvalues) to test for cointegration.

[130] A generalised vector matrix representation of (Annex 2.9) is given by $x_t = A_1x_{t-1} + A_2x_{t-2} + \ldots + A_px_{t-p} + \varepsilon_t$. This form is used in Greene (2003a, p. 656 et sqq.), among others. Of course, in a generalised VAR there can also be at least one d vector w_t of exogenous variables that is multiplied by some coefficient matrix, say ϕ. However, for simplicity, there are no exogenous variables used here.

$$x_t = A_1 x_{t-1} + \varepsilon_t . \qquad \text{(Annex 2.10)}$$

Subtracting x_{t-1} from both sides of (Annex 2.10) then yields

$$\Delta x_t = (A_1 - I)x_{t-1} + \varepsilon_t$$

$$\Delta x_t = \pi x_{t-1} + \varepsilon_t , \qquad \text{(Annex 2.11)}$$

where I is the unity matrix and $\pi \equiv (A_1 - I)$. In (Annex 2.10), x_t has a unit root if A_1 is not significantly different from the unity matrix. In turn, by subtracting the unity matrix in (Annex 2.11), x_t has a unit root and its elements are *not* co-integrated, if π is the zero matrix, i.e. if π consists of all zeros. In this case, the rank of π, denoted rank(π), is zero.[131] As mentioned earlier, one of the advantages of Johansen's (1991) approach compared to his (1988) methodology is that it allows for constant terms that play a specifically important role within the model, since it makes the approach capable of linear time trends. Cointegration is then investigated only in the *detrended* data.[132] Introducing an (n x 1) vector of constants, denoted A_0, into (Annex 2.11) is not too complicated. It can be written as

$$\Delta x_t = A_0 + \pi x_{t-1} + \varepsilon_t . \qquad \text{(Annex 2.11)}$$

If there is cointegration within the detrended data, $\pi x_{t-1} = 0$ and so $\Delta x_t = A_0$ in the long run.

Whenever the time series investigated by cointegration analysis possibly contain both a time trend and an intercept, (Annex 2.11) can be modified to account for this, too. In a first step to do so, any constant term included in A_0 is written as being dependent on the first element of the vector, i.e. $a_{i0} = s_i a_{10}$. Hence, it is possible to include a constant a_{10} in the cointegrating vector itself, so that

131 The rank of a matrix is its maximum number of linearly independent column vectors within a matrix.

132 See Enders (2004, p. 350 et sqq.).

$$
\begin{aligned}
\Delta x_{1t} &= (\pi_{11}x_{1t-1} + \pi_{12}x_{2t-1} + \ldots + \pi_{1n}x_{nt-1} + a_{10}) + \varepsilon_{1t} \\
\Delta x_{2t} &= s_2(\pi_{11}x_{1t-1} + \pi_{12}x_{2t-1} + \ldots + \pi_{1n}x_{nt-1} + a_{10}) + \varepsilon_{2t} \\
&\vdots \\
\Delta x_{nt} &= s_n(\pi_{11}x_{1t-1} + \pi_{12}x_{2t-1} + \ldots + \pi_{1n}x_{nt-1} + a_{10}) + \varepsilon_{nt}
\end{aligned}
\qquad \text{(Annex 2.12)}
$$

In (Annex 2.12), the time trend is terminated, because $\Delta x_{it} = 0$ if $\pi_{11}x_{1t-1} + \pi_{12}x_{2t-1} + \ldots + \pi_{1n}x_{nt-1} + a_{10} = 0$. The second step to achieve a model capable of a time trend and intercept is to modify a_{10} by defining $a_{10} = s_i b_{10} + b_{i1}$. Hence, re-writing (Annex 2.12) yields

$$
\begin{aligned}
\Delta x_{1t} &= (\pi_{11}x_{1t-1} + \pi_{12}x_{2t-1} + \ldots + \pi_{1n}x_{nt-1} + b_{10}) + b_{11} + \varepsilon_{1t} \\
\Delta x_{2t} &= s_2(\pi_{11}x_{1t-1} + \pi_{12}x_{2t-1} + \ldots + \pi_{1n}x_{nt-1} + b_{10}) + b_{21} + \varepsilon_{2t} \\
&\vdots \\
\Delta x_{nt} &= s_n(\pi_{11}x_{1t-1} + \pi_{12}x_{2t-1} + \ldots + \pi_{1n}x_{nt-1} + b_{10}) + b_{n1} + \varepsilon_{nt}
\end{aligned}
\qquad \text{(Annex 2.13)}
$$

The terms b_{10} and b_{i1} are arbitrary and techniques used to identify the respective values differ across software packages.

Recall the higher-order autoregressive process shown in footnote 130. As highlighted in Enders (2004, p. 352), this system can be re-written similar to the Augmented Dickey and Fuller (1981) test as

$$
\Delta x_t = \pi x_{t-1} + \sum_{i=1}^{p-1} \pi_i \Delta x_{t-i} + \varepsilon_t \qquad \text{(Annex 2.14)}
$$

with $\pi = -(I - \Sigma_{i=1}^{p} A_i)$ and $\pi_i = -\sum_{j=i+1}^{p} A_j$.

As mentioned above, the rank of matrix π equals the number of cointegrating vectors. Whenever rank(π) is greater than zero, there are stationary processes within vector x_t. If rank(π) = 1, there is exactly one cointegration relation. But not only does rank(π) inform about the number of cointegrating vectors, it is equal to the number of characteristic roots (or eigenvalues), denoted λ. λ, in turn, is a scalar to square matrix π and vector x_t that satisfies

$$
\pi x_t = \lambda x_t . \qquad \text{(Annex 2.15)}
$$

Whenever there is no cointegration between the elements of x_t, rank(π) and hence λ will be zero. Johansen (1991) provides two test statistics, named Trace test and Maximum Eigenvalue test, to analyse how many eigenvalues of π are significantly different from zero. All tests are conducted by analysing the value of ln(1-λ_i), where *i* denotes the respective λ's position among all the *n* eigenvalues. Because ln(1) = 0, only these characteristic roots are counted, which are not zero. Trace test statistic, being the one that is conducted in the study at hand,[133] is given by

$$\lambda_{trace}(r) = -T \sum_{i=r+1}^{n} \ln\left(1+\hat{\lambda}_i\right), \qquad \text{(Annex 2.16)}$$

where *r* denotes the number of cointegration relations to be tested and $\hat{\lambda}_i$ is the estimated *i*-th eigenvalue in matrix π. The Trace-test investigates whether or not the number of cointegrating vectors is equal or less *r*. The statistic is the larger, the more eigenvalues are significantly different from zero. Critical values to the Trace statistic depend on the exact specification of the model, i.e. whether or not constants, drift terms or deterministic regressors are included.

Before this section comes to an end, it is appropriate to briefly stress the prominence of error correction in cointegration frameworks. As mentioned above, cointegration directly refers to the feature of error correction. This gets clear if one recalls that a cointegration relation is somewhat of an equilibrium between some non-stationary variables. This equilibrium is only meaningful if the sequence of the estimated residuals is stationary and is thus following a mean-reverting process. Whenever an equilibrium error occurs, the cointegrated variables should evolve in a way that this departure from equilibrium is purged or at least reduced during the next period.

This can be clarified by using the vector error correction model (VECM) shown in equation (4.3) from the text, that is

(Annex 2.17)

[133] See, among others, Enders (2004, p. 352 et sqq.) for information on the maximum eigenvalue test.

$$\begin{pmatrix} \Delta S_t \\ \Delta X_{it} \end{pmatrix} = \begin{pmatrix} \alpha^S \\ \alpha^{X_i} \end{pmatrix} (1 \quad \beta_{i0} \quad \beta_{i1} \quad \beta_{i2}) \begin{pmatrix} S_{t-1} \\ 1 \\ trend_{t-1} \\ X_{it-1} \end{pmatrix} + \sum_{j=0}^{J} \Gamma_j \begin{pmatrix} \Delta S_{t-j} \\ \Delta X_{it-j} \end{pmatrix} + \begin{pmatrix} \varepsilon_t^S \\ \varepsilon_t^{X_i} \end{pmatrix}.$$

The equilibrium assumed here is given by

$$S_t - \beta_{i0} - \beta_{i1} trend_t - \beta_{i2} X_{it} = 0, \quad \text{(Annex 2.18)}$$

where S_t is the exchange rate at time t, β_{i0} is a constant, $trend_t$ denotes a linear time trend variable, and X_{it} is incoming order flow from customer type i. VECM analyses how much recent changes of the exchange rate (ΔS_t) and order flow (ΔX_{it}) are affected by last period's departures from this equilibrium. So-called *speed-of-adjustment coefficients* α^S and α^{X_i} then provide information on an (average) equilibrium error's half life. To see how, consider that the magnitude of the equilibrium error ε_t is measured by some index I_t that can be expressed in an error correction representation, i.e.

$$\Delta I_t = b(I_{t-1} - I^*) + e_t, \quad \text{(Annex 2.19)}$$

where e_t is a white-noise error term and I^* represents the equilibrium error's long run expected value, which is usually said to be zero. To calculate information half life, it is necessary to solve (Annex 2.19)'s inhomogeneous (and deterministic) as well as its homogenous part. As a first step, it is easy to show that I_t equals its long-run equilibrium value by assuming that in a stable equilibrium, which is not disturbed by a stochastic element (since e_t is zero in the long run), I_t equals I_{t-1}. To see how, simply write

$$I_t - I_{t-1} = bI_{t-1} - bI^*$$
$$I_t - I_{t-1} - bI_{t-1} = -bI^*$$
$$I_t - (1+b)I_{t-1} = -bI^*$$
$$I_t - (1+b)I_t = -bI^*$$

$$I_t = I^*. \quad \text{(Annex 2.20)}$$

To calculate information half life from speed of adjustment coefficients within a VECM, the homogenous part of the model has to be calculated, too. Hence, set $I^* = 0$ and $I_t^h = Ax^t$, so one can write

$$I_t - (1+b)I_{t-1} = 0$$
$$Ax^t - (1+b)Ax^{t-1} = 0$$
$$Ax^t = (1+b)Ax^{t-1}$$

$$x = 1+b. \qquad \text{(Annex 2.21)}$$

Thus, the homogeneous part's solution $I_t^h = Ax^t$ can be re-written as I_t^h = $A(1+b)^t$. As commonly known, an equation's general solution is the sum of its homogeneous and inhomogeneous part. This is

$$I_t = A(1+b)^t + I^* \qquad \text{(Annex 2.22)}$$

here. Let $t = 0$ denote the beginning of the time series to be investigated, the initial deviation from equilibrium is given by

$$I_0 = A + I^*$$

$$A = I_0 - I^*. \qquad \text{(Annex 2.23)}$$

To calculate information half life, one should ask how many periods (say t's) it will take unless the initial departure from equilibrium is bisected, given the fact that b represents the speed of adjustment or error correction coefficient. Consequently, the system adjusts in response to a potential departure from equilibrium by $(1+b)^t$, so information half life is given by

$$(I_o - I^*)(1+b)^t = 0.5(I_0 - I^*)$$
$$t \cdot \ln[(I_0 - I^*)(1+b)] = \ln[0.5(I_0 - I^*)]$$
$$t = \frac{\ln[0.5(I_0 - I^*)]}{\ln[(I_0 - I^*)(1+b)]}$$

$$t = \frac{\ln(0.5)}{\ln(1+b)}. \qquad \text{(Annex 2.24)}$$

In addition, there are several more tests to be conducted in a VECM framework that provide detailed information on error correction dynamics within the respective economic system. Weak and strong exogeneity are two of those further tests.

Recall the VECM given by (Annex 2.17). By testing for weak-sense exogeneity[134] of the exchange rate S_t, its respective speed of adjustment coefficient α^S is restricted to zero. This test provides an χ^2-statistic-based analysis whether ΔS_t is indeed exogenous. If the test is significant, α^S has to be some function of the economic system, because the imposed restriction can be rejected. Hence, ΔS_t is, at least partly, influenced by departures from equilibrium and thus changes of the exchange rate are not weak-sense exogenous. In fact, testing for weak exogeneity of ΔS_t is just another way to test for significance of α^S. For weak-sense exogeneity of changes in cumulative order flow, tests are conducted respectively.

Tests for strong exogeneity are augmenting weak-sense exogeneity with Granger causality. Its aim is at investigating whether including lagged and recent values of one variable, say X_t, helps predicting future values of another variable, here S_t. Whenever this χ^2-test is significant, the researcher can reject the null hypothesis of strong exogeneity of ΔS_t, so the exchange rate is some function of the analysed economic system.

Both of the aforementioned tests enable researchers to infer which one of the variables within the model performs the adjustment dynamics in case of a departure from equilibrium. In table 4.3, the exchange rate does seem to be exogenous of strong form in case of commercial customers, while cumulative order flow does not. Consequently, it is straightforward to infer that commercial customers' cumulative order flow is determined by the exchange rate rather than vice versa. In most cases presented here, however, findings are not that distinctive and both of the variables involved react to potential departures from equilibrium, indicating that causality in empirical findings is not as clear as it is supposed to be in theory.

---

[134] See Johansen (1995) for details.

(A)3. Stochastic frontier analysis

Stochastic frontier models (SFM) are regressionlike maximum likelihood estimators, which are able to generate error terms with non-normal distributions. Since the seminal work of Knight (1933), an intensive theoretical discussion on non-normal disturbances took place with further important contributions by Debreu (1951) and Farrell (1957) until Aigner et al. (1977) were the first to conduct these techniques in an empirical investigation.

Aigner et al. (1977) use SFM for investigating production functions and inefficiency. By definition, a production function $y = f(x)$ describes a theoretically ideal relationship between input factors, x, and output, y. Since the production function is absolutely efficient, any realised y is equal to or less than $f(x)$. Hence, in a regression model, the disturbance term can only be negative. This feature makes estimating an SFM particularly demanding.

As a consequence of non-positive disturbances, any observed deviation between y and $f(x)$ has to be due to inefficiency. Because of this, SFM are promising for investigating questions concerning market power, since bargaining power is indeed a specific form of inefficiency. A strictly orthodox interpretation of the error term as a purely one-sided, negative disturbance factor would result in a gamma model.[135] In contrast to this, Aigner et al. (1977) propose to interpret any observed error term to be originated in two potential sources, being (i) productive inefficiency, i.e. inefficiency in the common sense, and (ii) idiosyncratic shocks, which are usually distributed normal with mean zero and constant variance σ^2 and can hence bear either sign.

The following two equations show the difference between a strict interpretation of inefficiency in a gamma model

$$y = \alpha + \sum_k \beta_k x_k - u \qquad \text{(Annex 3.1)}$$

with $u \geq 0$, and the SFM as proposed in Aigner et al. (1977)

$$y = \alpha + \sum_k \beta_k x_k - u + \upsilon$$

[135] See Greene (2003a, p. 71, p. 501 et sqq.).

$$y = \alpha + \sum_k \beta_k x_k + \varepsilon , \qquad \text{(Annex 3.2)}$$

where $u \geq 0$, $\upsilon \sim N(0, \sigma_\upsilon^2)$, and $\varepsilon \equiv \upsilon - u$. Due to the idiosyncratic component υ, the efficient frontier itself becomes stochastic, giving the approach its name.

As mentioned in chapter 5, the great advantage of SFM is that all relevant parameters, i.e. the regression coefficients as well as the respective distribution parameters of the one-sided and the normally distributed error term, are estimated simultaneously. The representations that are actually used for estimation purposes are shown in chapter 5 in equation (5.20), (5.21), (5.23), and (5.24), respectively. The two kinds of disturbance terms shown in equation (5.23) are comprised into a single error term and the equation is solved for this disturbance, before it is estimated. As mentioned in chapter 5, the system is estimated by using Berndt-Hall-Hall Hausmann (BHHH) (1974) optimisation algorithm here.

References

Admati, Anat R. and Paul Pfleiderer, 1988, A Theory of Intraday Patterns: Volume and Price Variability, *Review of Financial Studies* **1**, 3 – 40.

Aigner, Dennis J., C.A. Knox Lovell, and Peter Schmidt, 1977, Formulation and Estimation of Stochastic Frontier Production Models, *Journal of Econometrics* **6**, 21 – 37.

Allen, Polly R. and Peter B. Kenen, 1980, *Asset Markets, Exchange Rates, and Economic Integration: A Synthesis*, Cambridge University Press: Cambridge, MA.

Alquist, Ron and Menzie D. Chinn, 2007, Conventional and Unconventional Approaches to Exchange Rate Modeling and Assessment, *International Journal of Finance and Economics,* forthcoming.

Altunbas, Yener, Edward P.M. Gardener, Philip Molyneux, and Barry Moore, 2001, Efficiency in European Banking, *European Economic Review* **45**, 1931 – 1955.

Amihud, Yakov and Haim Mendelson, 1980, Dealership Market: Market Making With Inventory, *Journal of Financial Economics* **8**, 31 – 53.

Ammer, John and Allan D. Brunner, 1997, Are Banks Market Timers or Market Makers? Explaining Foreign Exchange Trading Profits, *Journal of International Financial Markets, Institutions and Money* **7**, 43 – 60.

Andersen, Torben G., Tim Bollerslev, Francis X. Diebold, and Clara Vega, 2003, Micro Effects of Macro Announcements: Real-Time Price Discovery in Foreign Exchange, *American Economic Review* **93**, 38 – 62.

Anderson, Magnus, Lars J. Hansen, and Szabolcs Sebestyén, 2006, Which News Move the Euro Area Bond Market?, *ECB Working Paper Series* No. 631, May.

Andrews, Donald W.K., 1991, Heteroskedasticity and Autocorrelation Consistent Covariance Matrix Estimation, *Econometrica* **59**, 817 – 858.

Asparouhova, Elena, and Peter Bossaerts, 2005, Modelling Price Pressure in Financial Markets, *Working Paper*, University of Utah, October.

Bacchetta, Philippe and Eric van Wincoop, 2003, Can Information Heterogeneity Explain the Exchange Rate Determination Puzzle?, *NBER Working Paper Series* No. 9498, February.

Bain, Keith and Peter Howells, 2003, *Monetary Economics – Policy and its Theoretical Basis*, Palgrave Macmillan: New York.

Balaban, Ercan, 2004, Comparative Forecasting Performance of Symmetric and Asymmetric Conditional Volatility Models of an Exchange Rate, *Economic Letters* **83**, 99-105.

Bandi, Federico M. and Jeffrey R. Russell, 2006, Separating Microstructure Noise from Volatility, *Journal of Financial Economics* **79**, 655 – 692.

Bank for International Settlements, 2005, *Triennial Central Bank Survey – Foreign Exchange and Derivatives Markets Activity in 2004*, BIS, March (available at www.bis.org).

Barner, Martin, Francesco Feri, and Charles R. Plott, 2005, On the Microstructure of Price Determination and Information Aggregation with Sequential and Asymmetric Information Arrival in an Experimental Asset Market, *Annals of Finance* **1**, 73 – 107.

Batten, Jonathan and Warren Hogan, 2005, The Spot AUD/USD Foreign Exchange Market: Evidence from High Frequency Data, *International Review of Financial Analysis* **14**, 61 - 75.

Bauwens, Luc and Pierre Giot, 2000, The Logarithmic ACD Model: An Application to the Bid-Ask Quote Process of Three NYSE Stocks, *Annales d'Économie et de Statistique* **60**, 117 – 149.

Bayes, Thomas, 1763, 1764, An Essay Towards Solving a Problem in the Doctrine of Changes, *Philosophical Transactions* **53**, 376 – 398, reprinted in: *Biometrica* 45 (1958), 296 – 315.

Beltran-Lopez, Helena and Stefan Frey, 2006, Auction Design in Order Book Markets: What Information is Informative?, *Working Paper*, University of Pittsburgh and University of Tübingen, February.

Berger, Allen N. and Loretta J. Mester, 1997, Inside the Black Box: What Explains Differences in the Efficiencies of Financial Institutions, *Journal of Banking and Finance* **21**, 895 – 947.

Berndt, E.K., Brownyn H. Hall, Robert E. Hall, and Jerry A. Hausman, 1974, Estimation and Inference in Nonlinear Structural Models, *Annals of Economic and Social Measurement* **3**, 653 – 665.

Bessembinder, Hendrik, 1994, Bid-Ask Spreads in the Interbank Foreign Exchange Markets, *Journal of Financial Economics* **35**, 317 – 348.

Biais, Bruno, 1993, Price Formation and Equilibrium Liquidity in Fragmented and Centralized Markets, *Journal of Finance* **48**, 157 – 184.

Bjønnes, Geir H. and Dagfinn Rime, 2000, FX Trading ... Live: Dealer Behavior and Trading Systems in Foreign Exchange Markets, *Typescript*, Norwegian School of Management.

Bjønnes, Geir H. and Dagfinn Rime, 2001, Customer Trading and Information in Foreign Exchange Markets, *Working Paper* No. 4, Stockholm Institute of Financial Research.

Bjønnes, Geir H. and Dagfinn Rime, 2003, Dealer Behavior and Trading Systems in Foreign Exchange Markets, *Working Paper* ANO 2003/10, Norges Bank Research Department.

Bjønnes, Geir H., Dagfinn Rime, and Haakon O.Aa. Solheim, 2005, Liquidity Provision in the Overnight Foreign Exchange Market, *Journal of International Money and Finance* **24**, 175 – 196.

Blanchard, Oliver J., 1979, Speculative Bubbles, Crashes, and Rational Expectations, *Economic Letters* **3**, 387 – 389.

Bollerslev, Tim and Ian Domowitz, 1993, Trading Patterns and Prices in the Interbank Foreign Exchange Market, *Journal of Finance* **48**, 1421 – 1444.

Breedon, Francis and Paolo Vitale, 2004, An Empirical Study of Liquidity and Information Effects of Order Flow on Exchange Rates, *ECB Working Paper* No. 424, December.

Burnham, James B., 1991, Current Structure and Recent Developments in the Foreign Exchange Markets, in: Sarkis J. Khoury (ed.), *Recent Developments in International Banking and Finance*, North-Holland: Amsterdam.

Calcagno, Riccardo and Stefano Lovo, 2006, Bid-Ask Price Competition with Asymmetric Information between Market Makers, *Review of Economic Studies* **73**, 329 – 355.

Calvo, Guillermo A., 1999, Contagion in Emerging Markets: When Wall Street is a Carrier, *Mimeo*, University of Maryland.

Campbell, John Y., Andrew W. Lo, and A. Craig McKinlay, 1997, *The Econometrics of Financial Markets*, University Press: Princeton, NJ.

Cao, Huining H., Martin D.D. Evans, and Richard K. Lyons, 2006, Inventory Information, *Journal of Business* **79**, 325 – 364.

Carpenter, Andrew and Jianxin Wang, 2003, Sources of Private Information in FX Trading, *Working Paper*, University of South Wales.

Carrera, Jose M., 1999, Speculative Attacks to Currency Target Zones: A Market Microstructure Approach, *Journal of Empirical Finance* **6**, 555 – 582.

Chakravarty, Sugato and Asani Sarkar, 1999, Liquidity in U.S. Fixed Income Markets: A Comparison of the Bid-Ask Spread in Corporate,

Government and Municipal Bond Markets, *Working Paper*, Federal Reserve Bank of New York.

Chen, Zhaohui, 1997, Speculative Market Structure and the Collapse of an Exchange Rate Mechanism, *Working Paper*, London School of Economics.

Cheung, Yin-Wong and Menzie D. Chinn, 1999, Macroeconomic Implications of the Beliefs and Behavior of Foreign Exchange Traders, *NBER Working Paper* 7417.

Cheung, Yin-Wong and Menzie D. Chinn, 2001, Currency Traders and Exchange Rate Dynamics: A Survey of the US Market, *Journal of International Money and Finance* **20**, 439 – 471.

Cheung, Yin-Wong, Menzie D. Chinn, and Antonio Garcia Pascual, 2005, Empirical Exchange Rate Models of the Nineties: Are Any Fit to Survive?, *Journal of International Money and Finance* **24**, 1150 – 1175.

Cheung, Yin-Wong, Menzi D. Chinn, and Ian W. Marsh, 2004, How do UK-Based Foreign Exchange Dealers Think Their Market Operates? *International Journal of Finance and Economics* **9**, 289 - 306.

Cheung, Yin-Wong and Clement Y.-P. Wong, 1999, Foreign Exchange Traders in Hong Kong, Tokyo, and Singapore: A Survey Study, *Advances in Pacific Basin Financial Markets* **5**, 111 – 134.

Cheung, Yin-Wong and Clement Y.-P. Wong, 2000, A Survey of Market Practitioners' Views on Exchange Rate Dynamics, *Journal of International Economics* **51**, 401 – 423.

Choi, J.Y., Dan Salandro, and Kuldeep Shastri, 1988, On the Estimation of Bid-Ask Spreads: Theory and Evidence, *Journal of Financial and Quantitative Analysis* **23**, 219 – 230.

Chordia, Tarun, Richard Roll, and Avanidhar Subrahmanyam, 2000, Co-Movements in Bid-Ask Spreads and Market Depth, *Financial Analysts Journal* **56**, 23 – 27.

Christiano, Lawrence, 1989, P*: Not the Inflation Forecaster's Holy Grail, *Federal Reserve Bank of Minneapolis Quarterly Review* **13**, 3 – 18.

Christiansen, Charlotte and Angelo Ranaldo, 2005, Realized Bond-Stock Correlation: Macroeconomic Announcement Effects, *Working Paper*, Aarhus School of Business and Swiss National Bank, October.

Clarida, Richard H. and Mark P. Taylor, 1997, The Term Structure of Forward Exchange Premiums and the Forecastability of Spot Exchange Rates: Correcting the Errors, *The Review of Economics and Statistics* **3**, 353 – 362.

Clark, Todd and Michael McCracken, 2001, Evaluating Long-Horizon Forecasts, *Federal Reserve Bank of Kansas City Woking Paper* No. 01-14.

Corsetti, Giancarlo, Amil Dasgupta, Stephen Morris, and Hyun S. Shin, 2004, Does One Soros Make a Difference? The Role of a Large Trader in Currency Crisis, *Review of Economic Studies* **71**, 87 – 113.

Coughenour, Jay and Kuldeep Shastri, 1999, Symposium on Market Microstructure: A Review of the Empirical Evidence, *Financial Review* **34**, 1 – 28.

Dacorogna, Michel M., Ramazan Gençay, Ulrich Müller, Richard B. Olsen, and Olivier V. Pictet, 2001, *An Introduction to High-Frequency Finance*, Academic Press: London.

Da Silva Rosa, Raymond, Nirmel Saverimuttu, and Terry S. Walter, 2005, Do Informed Traders Win? An Analysis of Changes in Corporate Ownership around Substantial Shareholder Notices, *International Review of Finance* **5**, 113 – 147.

Davidson, Russel and James G. MacKinnon, 1993, *Estimation and Inference in Econometrics*, Oxford University Press: New York.

Debreu, Gerard, 1951, The Coefficient of Resource Utilization, *Econometrica* **19**, 273 – 292.

DeGrauwe, Paul and Pablo Rovira Kaltwasser, 2007, Modeling Optimism and Pessimism in the Foreign Exchange Market, *CESifo Working Paper Series* No. 1962, April.

DeGroot, Morris H., 1970, *Optimal Statistical Decisions*, McGraw-Hill: New York, NY.

DeMeyer, Bernard, 2007, Price Dynamics on a Stock Market with Asymmetric Information, *Cowles Foundation Discussion Paper* No. 1604, February.

DeMeyer, Bernard and Hadiza Moussa-Saley, 2003, On the Strategic Origin of Brownian Motion in Finance, *International Journal of Game Theory* **31**, 285 – 319.

Devereux, Michael B. and Charles Engel, 2001, The Optimal Choice of Exchange-Rate Regime: Price-Setting Rules and Internationalized Production, in: Magnus Blomstrom and Linda S. Goldberg (eds.), *Topics in Empirical International Economics: A Festschrift in Honor of Robert Lipsey*, University of Chicago Press: Chicago.

Dhrymes, Phoebus J., E. Philip Howrey, Saul H. Hymans, Jan Kmenta, E.E. Learner, R.E. Quandt, James B. Ramsey, Harold T. Shapiro, and Victor Zarnowitz, 1972, Criteria for Evaluation of Econometric Models, *Annals of Economic and Social Measurement* **1**, 291 – 324.

Dickey, David A. and Wayne A. Fuller, 1981, Likelihood Ratio Statistics for Autoregressive Time Series with a Unit Root, *Econometrica* **49**, 1057 – 1072.

Diebold, Francis X. and Roberto S. Mariano, 1995, Comparing Predictive Accuracy, *Journal of Business and Economic Statistics* **13**, 253 – 263.

Dominguez, Kathryn M.E., 1986, Are Foreign Exchange Forecasts Rational? New Evidence From Survey Data, *Economics Letters* **21**, 277 – 281.

Dominguez, Kathryn M.E., 2003, The Market Microstructure of Central Bank Intervention, *Journal of International Economics* **59**, 25 – 45.

Dominguez, Kathryn M.E. and Freyan Panthaki, 2006, What Defines "News" in the Foreign Exchange Market?, *Journal of International Money and Finance* **25**, 168 – 198.

Dornbusch, Rüdiger, 1976, Expectations and Exchange Rate Dynamics, *Journal of Political Economy* **84**, 1161 – 1176.

Dornbusch, Rüdiger, 1982, Equilibrium and Disequilibrium Exchange Rates, *Zeitschrift für Wirtschafts- und Sozialwissenschaften* **102**, 573 – 799; reprinted in: Rüdiger Dornbusch, 1987, *Dollars, Debts and Deficits*, The MIT Press Classics Series: Cambridge, MA.

Duffie, Darrell, Nicolae Gârleanu, and Lasse H. Pedersen, 2005, Over-the-Counter Markets, *Econometrica* **73**, 1815 – 1847.

Duffie, Darrell, Nicolae Gârleanu, and Lasse H. Pedersen, 2007, Valuation in Over-the-Counter Markets, *Review of Financial Studies* **20**, 1 – 36.

Dunne, Peter G., 2000, A Generalised Bayesian Model of Market Microstructure Behaviour Applied to the Market in Irish Government Securities, *International Review of Financial Analysis* **9**, 369 – 388.

Durbin, James J. and Siem J. Koopman, 2001, *Time Series Analysis by State Space Methods*, Oxford University Press: Oxford.

Easley, David and Maureen O'Hara, 1987, Price, Trade Size and Information in Securities Markets, *Journal of Financial Economics* **19**, 69 – 90.

Easley, David and Maureen O'Hara, 1992, Time and the Process of Security Price Adjustment, *Journal of Finance* **47**, 577 – 605.

Enders, Walter, 2004, Applied Econometric Time Series, 2nd Edition, Wiley Series in Probability and Statistics, John Wiley & Sons: Chichester.

Engel, Charles and Kenneth D. West, 2004, Accounting for Exchange Rate Variability in Present-Value Models When the Discount Factor is Near One, *American Economic Review, Papers and Proceedings* **94**, 119 – 125.

Engel, Charles and Kenneth D. West, 2005, Exchange Rates and Fundamentals, *Journal of Political Economy* **113**, 485 – 517.

Engle, Robert E. and Clive W.J. Granger, 1987, Cointegration and Error-Correction: Representation, Estimation, and Testing, *Econometrica* **55**, 251 – 276.

Engle, Robert E. and Jeffrey R. Russell, 1998, Autoregressive Conditional Duration: A New Model for Irregularly Spaced Transaction Data, *Econometrica* **66**, 1127 – 1162.

Engle, Robert E. and Byung S. Yoo, 1987, Forecasting and Testing in Cointegrated Systems, *Journal of Econometrics* **35**, 143 – 159.

Entorf, Horst and Christian Steiner, 2006, Announcement of Business Cycle Forecasts and the Reaction of the German Stock Market, *Working Paper*, Darmstadt University of Technology, February.

Evans, George W., 1986, A Test for Speculative Bubbles in the Sterling-Dollar Exchange Rate: 1981-84, *American Economic Review* **76**, 621 – 636.

Evans, Martin D.D., 1997, The Microstructure of Foreign Exchange Dynamics, *Typescript*, Georgetown University, November.

Evans, Martin D.D., 2005, Where Are We Now? Real-Time Estimates of the Macro Economy, *International Journal of Central Banking* **1**, 127 – 175.

Evans, Martin D.D. and Richard K. Lyons, 2000, The Price Impact of Currency Trades: Implications for Secret Interventions, *Typescript*, U.C. Berkeley.

Evans, Martin D.D. and Richard K. Lyons, 2001, Why Order Flow Explains Exchange Rates, *Working Paper*, U.C. Berkeley, November.

Evans, Martin D.D. and Richard K. Lyons, 2002a, Order Flow and Exchange Rate Dynamics, *Journal of Political Economy* **110**, 170 – 180.

Evans, Martin D.D. and Richard K. Lyons, 2002b, Are Different-Currency Assets Imperfect Substitutes?, *Working Paper*, U.C. Berkeley.

Evans, Martin D.D. and Richard K. Lyons, 2002c, Time-Varying Liquidity in Foreign Exchange, *Journal of Monetary Economics* **49**, 1025 – 1051.

Evans, Martin D.D. and Richard K. Lyons, 2002d, Informational Integration and FX Trading, *Journal of International Money and Finance* **21**, 807 – 831.

Evans, Martin D.D. and Richard K. Lyons, 2004a, Frequently Asked Questions About the Micro Approach to FX, *Mimeo*, U.C. Berkeley, available at faculty.haas.berkeley.edu/lyons.

Evans, Martin D.D. and Richard K. Lyons, 2004b, A New Micro Model of Exchange Rate Dynamics, *NBER Working Paper* No. 10379.

Evans, Martin D.D. and Richard K. Lyons, 2004c, Meese-Rogoff Redux: Micro-Based Exchange Rate Forecasting, *Working Paper,* Georgetown University and U.C. Berkeley, December.

Evans, Martin D.D. and Richard K. Lyons, 2005a, Do Currency Markets Absorb News Quickly?, *Journal of International Money and Finance* **24**, 197 – 217.

Evans, Martin D.D. and Richard K. Lyons, 2005b, Understanding Order Flow, *NBER Working Paper* No. 11748.

Evans, Martin D.D. and Richard K. Lyons, 2005c, Meese-Rogoff Redux: Micro-Based Exchange Rate Forecasting, *American Economic Review* **95**, 405 – 414.

Evans, Martin D.D. and Richard K. Lyons, 2005d, The Portfolio Balance, Price Impact, and Secret Intervention, in: Paul DeGrauwe (ed.), *Exchange Rate Economics: Where Do We Stand?*, MIT Press: Cambridge.

Evans, Martin D.D. and Richard K. Lyons, 2007a, Exchange Rate Fundamentals and Order Flow, *NBER Working Paper* No. 13151.

Evans, Martin D.D. and Richard K. Lyons, 2007b, How is Macro News Transmitted to Exchange Rates?, *Journal of Financial Economics*, forthcoming.

Fama, Eugene, 1965, The Behavior of Stock Market Prices, *Journal of Business* **38**, 34 – 105.

Fama, Eugene, 1970, Efficient Capital Markets: A Review of Theory and Empirical Work, *Journal of Finance* **25**, 383 – 417.

Fan, Mintao and Richard K. Lyons, 2002, Customer Trades and Extreme Events in Foreign Exchange, in: Paul Mizen (ed.), *Monetary History, Exchange Rates and Financial Markets: Essays in Honour of Charles Goodhart, Volume Two,* Edward Elgar: Cheltenham, UK, 160 – 179.

Farrell, Michael J., 1957, The Measurement of Productive Efficiency, *Journal of the Royal Statistical Society, Series A (General)* **120**, Part 3, 253 – 291.

Faust, Jon, John H. Rogers, and Jonathan H. Wright, 2003, Exchange Rate Forecasting: The Errors We've Really Made, *Journal of International Economics* **60**, 35 – 59.

Fieleke, Norman S., 1981, Foreign-Currency Positioning by U.S. Firms: Some New Evidence, *Review of Economics and Statistics* **63**, 35 – 42.

Flood, Mark D., Ronald Huisman, Kees G. Koedijk, and Richard K. Lyons, 1998, Search Costs: The Neglected Spread Component, *Working Paper*, Maastricht University, January.

Flood, Robert P., 1994, Market Structure and Inefficiency in the Foreign Exchange Market, *Journal of International Money and Finance* **13**, 131 – 158.

Flood, Robert P. and Robert J. Hodrick, 1990, On Testing for Speculative Bubbles, *Journal of Economic Perspectives* **4**, 85 – 101.

Flood, Robert P. and Andrew K. Rose, 1995, Fixing Exchange Rates: A Virtual Quest for Fundamentals, *Journal of Monetary Economics* **36**, 3 – 37.

Flood, Robert P. and Mark P. Taylor, 1996, Exchange Rate Economics: What's Wrong With the Conventional Macro Approach?, in: Jeffrey A. Frankel, Giampaolo Galli, and Alberto Giovannini (eds.), *The Microstructure of Foreign Exchange Markets*, University of Chicago Press: Chicago.

Foster, Douglas and S. Vishwanathan, 1990a, A Theory of the Intraday Variations in Volume, Variances, and Trading Costs in Securities Markets, *Review of Financial Studies* **3**, 593 – 624.

Foster, Douglas and S. Vishwanathan, 1990b, Variations in Volume, Variances and Trading Costs, *Working Paper* 88-108, Duke University, Durham, NC.

Frankel, Jeffrey A. and Kenneth A. Froot, 1987, Using Survey Data to Test Standard Propositions Regarding Exchange Rate Expectations, *American Economic Review* **77**, 133 – 153.

Frankel, Jeffrey A. and Andrew K. Rose, 1995, Empirical Research on Nominal Exchange Rates, in: Gene M. Grossman and Kenneth Rogoff (eds.), *Handbook of International Economics*, Elsevier Science: Amsterdam, 1689 – 1729.

French, Kenneth R. and Richard Roll, 1986, Stock Return Variances: The Arrival of Information and the Reaction of Traders, *Journal of Financial Economics* **17**, 99 – 117.

Frenkel, Jacob A., 1976, A Monetary Approach to the Exchange Rate: Doctrinal Aspects and Empirical Evidence, *Scandinavian Journal of Economics* **78**, 200 - 224.

Frenkel, Jacob A. and Michael L. Mussa, 1985, Asset Markets, Exchange Rates, and the Balance of Payments, in: Ronald W. Jones and Peter B.

Kenen (eds.), *Handbook of International Economics*, Volume 2, North-Holland: Amsterdam.

Friedman, Milton, 1953, *Essays in Positive Economics*, University of Chicago Press: Chicago.

Garman, Mark B., 1976, Market Microstructure, *Journal of Financial Economics* **3**, 257 – 275.

Genotte, Gerard and Hayne Leland, 1990, Market Liquidity, Hedges, and Crashes, *American Economic Review* **80**, 999 – 1021.

George, Thomas J., Gautam Kaul, and M. Nimalendran, 1991, Estimation of the Bid-Ask Spreads and its Components: A New Approach, *Review of Financial Studies* **4**, 623 – 656.

Gil-Bazo, Javier, David Moreno, and Mikel Tapia, 2007, Price Dynamics, Informational Efficiency and Wealth Distribution in Continuous Double-Auction Markets, *Computational Intelligence* **23**, 176 – 196.

Glosten, Lawrence, 1989, Insider Trading, Liquidity, and the Role of the Monopolist Specialist, *Journal of Business* **62**, 211 – 235.

Glosten, Lawrence and Lawrence Harris, 1988, Estimating the Components of the Bid-Ask Spread, *Journal of Financial Economics* **21**, 123 – 142.

Glosten, Lawrence and Paul Milgrom, 1985, Bid, Ask, and Transaction Prices in a Specialist Market With Heterogeneously Informed Agents, *Journal of Financial Economics* **14**, 71 – 100.

Goodhart, Charles A.E., 1988, The Foreign Exchange Market: A Random Walk With A Dragging Anchor, *Economica* **55**, 437 – 460.

Goodhart, Charles A.E. and Lorenzo Figliuoli, 1991, Every Minute Counts in Financial Markets, *Journal of International Money and Finance* **10**, 23 – 52.

Gourieroux, Christian and Joann Jasiak, 2001, *Financial Econometrics: Problems, Models, and Methods*, University Press: Princeton, NJ.

Gourinchas, Pierre-Olivier and Hélène Rey, 2005, International Financial Adjustment, *NBER Working Paper* No. 11155, February.

Green, Richard C., Burton Hollifield, and Norman Schürhoff, 2007, Financial Intermediation and the Costs of Trading in an Opaque Market, *The Review of Financial Studies* **20**, 275 – 314.

Greene, William H., 2003a, *Econometric Analysis*, 5th Edition, Prentice Hall, Pearson Education International: New Jersey.

Greene, William H., 2003b, Distinguishing Between Heterogeneity and Inefficiency: Stochastic Frontier Analysis of the World Health Organization's Panel Data on National Health Care Systems, *Working Paper*, Department of Economics, Stern School of Business, New York University, New York, NY.

Grossman, Sanford J., 1976, On the Efficiency of Competitive Stock Markets Where Traders Have Diverse Information, *Journal of Finance* **31**, 573 – 585.

Grossman, Sanford J., 1988, An Analysis of the Implications for Stock and Futures Price Volatility of Program Trading and Dynamic Hedging Strategies, *Journal of Business* **61**, 275 – 298.

Grossman, Sanford J. and Merton H. Miller, 1988, Liquidity and Market Structure, *Journal of Finance* **43**, 617 – 633.

Guembel, Alexander and Oren Sussman, 2001, Optimal Exchange Rates: A Market-Microstructure Approach, *Working Paper*, Oxford University, July.

Habib, Michel A. and Alexander Ljungqvist, 2003, Firm Value and Managerial Incentives: A Stochastic Frontier Approach, Working Paper, New York University, New York, NY.

Hanousek, Jan and Richard Podpiera, 2003, Informed Trading and the Bid-Ask Spread: Evidence From an Emerging Market, *Journal of Comparative Economics* **31**, 275 – 296.

Hansen, Lars P., 1982, Large Sample Properties of Generalized Method of Moments Estimators, *Econometrica* **50**, 1029 – 1054.

Harris, Lawrence E. and Michael S. Piwowar, 2006, Secondary Trading Costs in the Municipal Bond Market, *Journal of Finance* **61**, 1361 – 1397.

Hartmann, Philipp, 1998, *Currency Competition and Foreign Exchange Markets: The Dollar, the Yen, and the Euro*, Cambridge University Press: Cambridge.

Hartmann, Philipp, Michele Manna, and Andrés Manzanares, 2001, The Microstructure of the Euro Money Market, *ECB Working Paper Series* No. 80, October.

Harvey, David, Stephen Leybourne, and Paul Newbold, 1997, Testing the Equality of Prediction Mean Squared Errors, *International Journal of Forecasting* **13**, 281 – 291

Hasbrouck, Joel, 1988, Trades, Quotes, Inventories, and Information, *Journal of Financial Economics* **22**, 229 – 252.

Hasbrouck, Joel, 1991a, Measuring the Information Content of Stock Trades, *Journal of Finance* **46**, 179 – 207.

Hasbrouck, Joel, 1991b, The Summary Informativeness of Stock Trades: An Econometric Analysis, *Review of Financial Studies* **4**, 571 – 595.

Hasbrouck, Joel, 1993, Assessing the Quality of a Security Market: A New Approach to Transaction Cost Measurement, *Review of Financial Studies* **6**, 191 – 212.

Hau, Harald, 1998, Competitive Entry and Endogenous Risk in the Foreign Exchange Market, *Review of Financial Studies* **11**, 757 – 788.

Hautsch, Nikolaus and Winfried Pohlmeier, 2002, Econometric Analysis of Financial Transaction Data: Pitfalls and Opportunities, *Journal of the German Statistical Society* **86**, 5 – 30.

Heere, E., 1999, Microstructure Theory Applied To the Foreign Exchange Market, *Ph.D. dissertation*, Maastricht University, Faculty of Economics and Business Administration.

Heidle, Hans G. and Xi Li, 2004, Information Leakage and Opportunistic Behavior Before Analyst Recommendations: An Analysis of the Quoting Behavior of Nasdaq Market Makers, *Mimeo*, University of Notre Dame, IN.

Ho, Thomas S.Y. and Richard G. Macris, 1984, Dealer Bid-Ask Quotes and Transaction Prices: An Empirical Study of some AMEX Options, *Journal of Finance* **39**, 23 – 45.

Ho, Thomas S.Y. and Hans R. Stoll, 1983, The Dynamics of Dealer Markets Under Competition, *Journal of Finance* **38**, 1053 – 1074.

Holden, Craig W. and Avanidhar Subrahmanyam, 1992, Long-Lived Private Information and Imperfect Competition, *Journal of Finance* **47**, 247 – 270.

Hong, Gwangheon and Arthur Warga, 2000, An Empirical Study of Bond Market Transactions, *Financial Analysts Journal* **56**, 32 – 46.

Howrey, E. Philip, Lawrence R. Klein, and Michael D. McCarthy, 1974, Notes on Testing the Predictive Performance of Econometric Models, *International Economic Review* **15**, 366 – 383.

Huang, Roger D. and Hans R. Stoll, 1997, The Components of the Bid-Ask Spread: A General Approach, *Review of Financial Studies* **10**, 995 – 1034.

Hunt-McCool, Janet, Samuel C. Kohn, and Bill B. Francis, 1996, Testing for Deliberate Underpricing in the IPO Premarket: A Stochastic Analysis Approach, *Review of Financial Studies* **9**, 1251 – 1269.

Isard, Peter, 1995, *Exchange Rate Economics*, Cambridge University Press: Cambridge, MA.

Ito, Takatoshi and Yuko Hashimoto, 2006, Intraday Seasonality in Activities of the Foreign Exchange Market: Evidence from the Electronic Broking System, *NBER Working Paper* No. W12413, October.

Ito, Takatoshi and Yuko Hashimoto, 2007, Price Impacts of Deals and Predictability of the Exchange Rate Movements, *NBER Working Paper* No. W12682, April.

Ito, Takatoshi, Richard K. Lyons, and Micheal T. Melvin, 1998, Is There Private Information in the FX Market? The Tokyo Experiment, *Journal of Finance* **53**, 1111 – 1130.

Jacklin, C., A. Kleidon, and Paul Pfleiderer, 1992, Underestimation of Portfolio Insurance and the Crash of October 1987, *Review of Financial Studies* **5**, 35 – 63.

Jeanne, Olivier and Andrew K. Rose, 2002, Noise Trading and Exchange Rate Regimes, *The Quarterly Journal of Economics* **117**, 537 – 569.

Johansen, Søren, 1988, Statistical Analysis of Cointegration Vectors, *Journal of Economic Dynamics and Control* **12**, 231 – 254.

Johansen, Søren, 1991, Estimation and Hypothesis Testing of Cointegration Vectors in Gaussian Vector Autoregressive Models, *Econometrica* **59**, 1551 – 1580.

Johansen, Søren, 1995, *Likelihood-based Inference in Cointegrated Vector Autoregressive Models*, Oxford University Press: Oxford.

Johansen, Søren and Katarina Juselius, 1994, Identification of the Long-Run and the Short-Run Structure: An Application to the ISLM Model, *Journal of Econometrics* **63**, 7 – 36.

Johnston, Jack and John DiNardo, 1997, *Econometric Methods*, 4th edition, McGraw-Hill: New York, NY.

Johnston, Ken and Elton Scott, 1997, Exchange Rate Probability Distributions and Fundamental Variables, *Journal of Financial and Strategic Decisions* **10**, 27 – 36.

Julier, Simon J. and Jeffrey K. Uhlmann, 2004a, Unscented Filtering and Nonlinear Estimation, *Proceedings of the IEEE* **92**, 401 – 422.

Julier, Simon J. and Jeffrey K. Uhlmann, 2004b, Correction to "Unscented Filtering and Nonlinear Estimation", *Mimeo*, Department of Computer Science, University of British Columbia, available at: http://www.cs.ubc.ca/~murphyk/Papers/julier04corr.pdf.

Kálmán, Rudolf E., 1960, A New Approach to Linear Filtering and Prediction Problems, *Transactions of the ASME – Journal of Basic Engineering* **82**, 35 – 45.

Kebede, Tewodros A., 2001, Farm Household Technical Efficiency: A Stochastic Frontier Analysis, *Masters Thesis*, Department of Economics and Social Sciences, Agricultural University of Norway.

Keim, Donald B. and Ananth Madhavan, 1998, The Costs of Institutional Equity Trades: An Overview, *Financial Analysts Journal* **54**, 50 – 69.

Killeen, William P., Richard K. Lyons, and Michael J. Moore, 2006, Fixed Versus Flexible: Lessons from EMS Order Flow, *Journal of International Money and Finance* **25**, 551 – 579.

Klitgaard, Thomas and Laura Weir, 2004, Exchange Rate Changes and Net Positions of Speculators in the Futures Market, *Federal Reserve Bank of New York Economic Policy Review* **10**, 17 – 28.

Knight, Frank H., 1933, *The Economic Organisation*, Harper and Row: New York, NY.

Koop, Gary and Kai Li, 2001, The Valuation of IPO and SEO Firms, *Journal of Empirical Finance* **8**, 375 – 401.

Koop, Gary, Janosh Osiewalsko, and Mark F.J. Steel, 2000, A Stochastic Frontier Analysis of Output Level and Growth in Poland and Western Economies, *Economics of Planning* **33**, 185 – 202.

Koopman, Siem J. and Jacques J.F. Commandeur, 2007, An Introduction to State Space Time Series Analysis, Oxford University Press: Oxford.

Koopman, Siem J., Neil Shephard, and Jürgen A. Doornik, 1999, Statistical Algorithms for Models in State Space using SsfPack 2.2, *Econometrics Journal* **2**, 107 – 160.

Kouri, Pentti J.K., 1976, The Exchange Rate and the Balance of Payments in the Short Run and the Long Run: A Monetary Approach, *Scandinavian Journal of Economics* **78**, 280 – 304.

Kraft, Evan and Dogan Tirtiroglu, 1998, Bank Efficiency in Croatia: A Stochastic Frontier Analysis, *Journal of Comparative Economics* **26**, 282 – 300.

Kumbhakar, Subal C. and C.A. Knox Lovell, 2003, *Stochastic Frontier Analysis*, Cambridge University Press: Cambridge, MA.

Kyle, Albert S., 1985, Continuous Auctions and Insider Trading, *Econometrica* **53**, 1315 – 1335.

Laux, Paul A., 1993, Intraday Price Formation in the Stock Index Futures Market, *Working Paper*, University of Texas, Austin, TX.

Leach, J. Chris and Ananth N. Madhavan, 1992, Intertemporal Price Discovery by Market Makers: Active Versus Passive Learning, *Journal of Financial Intermediation* **2**, 207 – 235.

Leach, J. Chris and Ananth N. Madhavan, 1993, Price Experimentation and Security Market Structure, *Review of Financial Studies* **6**, 375 – 404.

LeBaron, Blake, 2006, Agent-Based Computational Finance, in: Leigh Tesfatsion and Kenneth L. Judd (eds.): *Handbook of Computational Economics, Vol. 2: Agent-Based Computational Economics*, North-Holland: Amsterdam, 1187 – 1232.

LeBaron, Blake and Ryuichi Yamamoto, 2007, Long-Memory in an Order Driven Market, *Physica A* (forthcoming).

Lechner, Sandra and Ingmar Nolte, 2006, Customer Trading in the Foreign Exchange Market: Empirical Evidence From an Internet Trading

Platform, *Working Paper*, Center of Finance and Econometrics, University of Konstanz.

Lo, Ingrid and Stephen G. Sapp, 2005, Price Aggressiveness and Quantity: How are They Determined in a Limit Order Market?, *Working Paper*, The Bank of Canada and University of Western Ontario, November.

Lütkepohl, Helmut and Hans-Eggert Reimers, 1992, Impulse Response Analysis of Cointegrated Systems, *Journal of Economic Dynamics and Control* **16**, 53 – 78.

Lyons, Richard K., 1995, Tests of Microstructural Hypotheses in the Foreign Exchange Market, *Journal of Financial Economics* **39**, 321 – 351.

Lyons, Richard K., 1996, Optimal Transparency in a Dealer Market With an Application to Foreign Exchange, *Journal of Financial Intermediation* **5**, 225 – 254.

Lyons, Richard K., 1997, A Simultaneous Trade Model of the Foreign Exchange Hot Potato, *Journal of International Economics* **42**, 275 – 298.

Lyons, Richard K., 1998, Profits and Position Control: A Week of FX Trading, *Journal of International Money and Finance* **17**, 97 – 115.

Lyons, Richard K., 2001, *The Microstructure Approach to Exchange Rates*, The MIT Press: Cambridge, MA.

Lyons, Richard K., 2002a, Foreign Exchange: Macro Puzzles, Micro Tools, *Federal Reserve Bank of San Francisco Economic Review*, 51 – 69.

Lyons, Richard K., 2002b, The Future of the Foreign Exchange Market, *Working Paper*, U.C. Berkeley.

Lyons, Richard K. and Michael J. Moore, 2005, An Information Approach to International Currencies, *NBER Working Paper Series* No. 11220, March.

MacKinnon, James G., 1991, Critical Values for Cointegration Tests, in: Robert F. Engle and Clive W.J. Granger (eds.), 1993, *Long-Run Economic Relationships: Readings in Cointegration*, Oxford University Press, Oxford, 267 – 276.

MacKinnon, James G., 1996, Numerical Distribution Functions for Unit-Root and Cointegration Tests, *Journal of Applied Econometrics* **11**, 601 – 618.

Madhavan, Ananth N., 1996, Security Prices and Market Transparency, *Journal of Financial Intermediation* **5**, 255 – 283.

Madhavan, Ananth N., 2000, Market Microstructure: A Survey, *Journal of Financial Markets* **3**, 205 – 258.

Madhavan, Ananth N. and Seymour Smidt, 1991, A Bayesian Model of Intraday Specialist Pricing, *Journal of Financial Economics* **30**, 99 – 134.

Manaster, Steven and Steven S. Mann, 1996, Life in the Pits: Competitive Market Making and Inventory Control, *Review of Financial Studies* **9**, 953 – 975.

Mankiw, N. Gregory, 2007, *Macroeconomics*, 6th edition, Palgrave Macmillan: New York, NY.

Mark, Nelson C., 1995, Exchange Rates and Fundamentals: Evidence on Long-Horizon Predictability, *American Economic Review* **85**, 201 – 218.

Markowitz, Harry M., 1952, Portfolio Selection, *Journal of Finance* **7**, 77 – 91.

Markowitz, Harry M., 1959, *Portfolio Selection – Efficient Diversification of Investments*, John Wiley & Sons: New York, NY.

Marsh, Ian W. and Ceire O'Rourke, 2005a, Customer Order Flows in Foreign Exchange Markets: Do They Really Contain Information?, *Working Paper*, Cass Business School, February.

Marsh, Ian W. and Ceire O'Rourke, 2005b, Customer Order Flow and Exchange Rate Movements: Is There Really Information Content?, *Working Paper*, Cass Business School, April.

Matyas, Laszlo (ed.), 1999, *Generalized Method of Moments Estimation*, Themes in Modern Econometrics, Cambridge University Press: Cambridge.

McGroarty, Frank, Owain ap Gwilym, and Stephen Thomas, 2005, Private Information, Excessive Volatility and Intraday Empirical Regularities in the Spot Foreign Exchange Market, *Working Paper*, University of Southampton, February.

Meese, Richard A., 1986, Testing for Bubbles in Exchange Markets, *Journal of Political Economy* **94**, 345 – 373.

Meese, Richard A., 1990, Currency Fluctuations in the Post-Bretton Woods Era, *Journal of Economic Perspectives* **4**, 117 – 134.

Messe, Richard A. and Kenneth Rogoff, 1983a, Empirical Exchange Rate Models of the Seventies: Do They Fit Out-of-Sample?, *Journal of International Economics* **14**, 3 – 24.

Messe, Richard A. and Kenneth Rogoff, 1983b, The Out-of-Sample Failure of Empirical Exchange Rate Models, in: J. Frenkel (ed.), *Exchange Rate and International Macroeconomics*, University of Chicago Press: Chicago, IL.

Mende, Alexander and Lukas Menkhoff, 2005, Profits and Speculation in Intra-Day Foreign Exchange Trading, *Working Paper*, University of Hannover, October.

Menkveld, Albert J., Asani Sarkar, and Michel van der Wel, 2007, The Informativeness of Customer Order Flow Following Macroeconomic Announcements: Evidence From Treasury Futures Markets, *Working Paper*, Vrije Universiteit Amsterdam, March.

Miller, Stephen M., Terrence M. Clauretie, and Thomas M. Springer, 2006, Economies of Scale and Cost Efficiencies: A Panel-Data Stochastic-

Frontier Analysis of Real Estate Investment Trusts, *Manchaster School* **74**, 483 – 499.

Mussa, Michael, 1976, The Exchange Rate, the Balance of Payments, and Monetary and Fiscal Policy under a Regime of Controlled Floating, *Scandinavian Journal of Economics* **78**, 229 – 248.

Nash, John, 1950a, Equilibrium Points in n-Person Games, *Proceedings of the National Academy of Sciences* **36**, 48 – 49.

Nash, John, 1950b, The Bargaining Problem, *Econometrica* **18**, 155 – 162.

Newey, Whitney and Kenneth West, 1987, A Simple Positive, Semi-Definite, Heteroskedastisticy and Autocorrelation Consistent Covariance Matrix, *Econometrica* **55**, 703 – 708.

Obstfeld, Maurice and Kenneth Rogoff, 1996, *Foundations of International Macroeconomics*, MIT Press: Cambridge, MA.

O'Hara, Maureen, 1995, *Market Microstructure Theory*, Blackwell Business: Cambridge, MA.

O'Hara, Maureen and George S. Oldfield, 1986, The Microeconomics of Market Making, *Journal of Financial and Quantitative Analysis* **21**, 361 – 376.

Osborne, Martin J. and Ariel Rubinstein, 1990, *Bargaining and Markets*, Academic Press Inc.: London.

Osler, Carol L., 1998, Short-Term Speculators and the Puzzling Behavior of Exchange Rates, *Journal of International Economics* **43**, 37 – 58.

Osler, Carol L., 2003, Currency Orders and Exchange Rate Dynamics: An Explanation for the Predicitive Success of Technical Analysis, *Journal of Finance* **58**, 1791 – 1819.

Osler, Carol L., 2005, Stop-Loss Orders and Price Cascades in Currency Markets, *Journal of International Money and Finance* **24**, 219 – 241.

Osler, Carol, Alexander Mende, and Lukas Menkhoff, 2006, Price Discovery in Currency Markets, *Brandeis University Working Paper*.

Owens, John P., 2005, A Market Microstructure Model with Random Overlapping Information Asymmetries, *Finance Research Letters* **2**, 59 – 66.

Pasquariellô, Paolo, 2000, The Mictrostructure of Currency Markets: An Empirical Model of Intra-day Return and Bid-Ask Spread Behavior, *Working Paper*, New York University, August.

Payne, Richard, 2003, Informed Trade in Spot Foreign Exchange Markets: An Empirical Investigation, *Journal of International Economics* **61**, 307 – 329.

Peiers, Bettina, 1997, Informed Traders, Intervention, and Price Leadership: A Deeper View of the Microstructure of the Foreign Exchange Market, *Journal of Finance* **52**, 1589 – 1614.

Perraudin, William and Paolo Vitale, 1996, Interdealer Trade and Information Flows in a Decentralized Foreign Exchange Market, in: Jeffrey A. Frankel, Giampaolo Galli, and Alberto Giovannini (eds.), *The Microstructure of Foreign Exchange Markets*, University of Chicago Press: Chicago.

Phillips, Peter C.B. and Sam Ouliaris, 1990, Asymptotic Properties of Residual Based Tests for Cointegration, *Econometrica* **58**, 165 – 193.

Phylaktis, Kate, and Long Chen, 2005, Macroeconomic Announcements and Private Information in the Foreign Exchange Market, *Working Paper*, Cass Business School, February.

Portes, Richard and Hélène Rey, 1998, The Emergence of the Euro as an International Currency, *Economic Policy* **26**, 307 – 343.

Pynnonen, Seppo, 2007, A Short Introduction to the Generalized Method of Moments Estimation, *Mimeo*, University of Vaasa, January.

Rangel, Jose Gonzalo, 2005, Macroeconomic Announcements, Price Discovery, and Order Flow Effects in the Stock Market: Evidence from Incomplete Data and Multiple Financial Markets, *Working Paper*, University of California, San Diego, November.

Reitz, Stefan and Mark P. Taylor, 2006, The Coordination Channel of Foreign Exchange Intervention: A Nonlinear Microstructural Analysis, *Discussion Paper Series 1: Economic Studies*, No. 08/2006, Deutsche Bundesbank.

Reitz, Stefan, Markus A. Schmidt, and Mark P. Taylor, 2007, End-User Order Flow and Exchange Rate Dynamics, *Discussion Paper Series 1: Economic Studies*, No. 05/2007, Deutsche Bundesbank.

Rey, Hélène, 2001, International Trade and Currency Exchange, *Review of Economic Studies* **68**, 443 – 464.

Rime, Dagfinn, 2000, Private or Public Information in Foreign Exchange Markets? An Empirical Analysis, *Memorandum* No. 14/2000, University of Oslo, March

Rime, Dagfinn, 2003, New Electronic Trading Systems in Foreign Exchange Markets, in: Derek C. Jones (ed.), *New Economy Handbook*, Elsevier Science (Academic Press): Burlington, MA.

Rogoff, Kenneth, 1996, The Purchasing Power Parity Puzzle, *Journal of Economic Literature* **34**, 647 – 668.

Roll, Richard, 1984, A Simple Implicit Measure of the Effective Bid-Ask Spread in an Efficient Market, *Journal of Finance* **39**, 1127 – 1139.

Romer, David H., 1993, Rational Asset-Price Movements Without News, *American Economic Review* **83**, 1112 – 1130.

Rubinstein, Mark, 2001, Rational Markets: Yes Or No? The Affirmative Case. *Financial Analysts Journal* **57**, 15 – 29.

Saar, Gideon, 1999, Demand Uncertainty and the Information Content of the Order Flow, *Typescript*, Johnson School, Cornell University, NY.

Sager, Michael J. and Mark P. Taylor, 2005, Order Flow and Exchange Rate Movements, *Working Paper*, University of Warwick.

Sager, Michael J. and Mark P. Taylor, 2006, Under the Microscope: The Structure of the Foreign Exchange Market, *International Journal of Finance and Economics* **11**, 81 – 95.

Said, Said E. and David A. Dickey, 1984, Testing for Unit Roots in Autoregressive-Moving Average Models of Unknown Order, *Biometrika* **71**, 599 – 607.

Sarno, Lucio and Giorgio Valente, 2005, Empirical Exchange Rate Models and Currency Risk: Some Evidence from Density Forecasts, *Journal of International Money and Finance* **24**, 363 – 385.

Schultz, Paul, 2001, Corporate Bond Trading Costs: A Peek Behind the Curtain, *Journal of Finance* **56**, 677 – 698.

Schwartz, Gideon, 1978, Estimating the Dimension of a Model, *Annals of Statistics* **6**, 461 – 464.

Sosvilla Rivero, Simón and Emma Garcia, 2005, Forecasting the Dollar / Euro Exchange Rate: Are International Parities Useful?, *Journal of Forecasting* **24**, 369 – 377.

Spiegel, Matthew, 1998, Stock Price Volatility in a Multiple Security Overlapping Generations Model, *Review of Financial Studies* **11**, 419 – 447.

Stock, James and Mark Watson, 1988, Testing for Common Trends, *Journal of the American Statistical Association* **83**, 1097 – 1107.

Subrahmanyam, Avanidhar, 1991, Risk Aversion, Market Liquidity, and Price Efficiency, *Review of Financial Studies* **4**, 417 – 441.

Taylor, Mark P., 1995, The Economics of Exchange Rates, *Journal of Economic Literature* **83**, 13 – 47.

Taylor, Mark P. and Helen Allen, 1992, The Use of Technical Analysis in the Foreign Exchange Market, *Journal of International Money and Finance* **11**, 304 – 314.

Tobin, James, 1978, A Proposal for International Monetary Reform, *Eastern Economic Journal* **4**, Philadelphia, 153 – 159.

van Tol, Michel R. and Christian C.P. Wolff, 2005, Forecasting the Spot Exchange Rate with the Term Structure of Forward Premia: Multivariate Threshold Cointegration, *CEPR Discussion Paper* No. 4958, March.

von Hayek, Friedrich A., 1945, The Use of Knowledge in Society, *American Economic Review* **35**, 519 – 530.

Viswanathan, S. and James J.D. Wang, 1998, Why is Interdealer-Trading so Pervasive in Financial Markets? *Working Paper*, Duke University.

Vogler, Karl-Hubert, 1997, Risk Allocation and Inter-Dealer Trading, *European Economic Review* **41**, 417 – 441.

Vuong, Quang H., 1989, Likelihood Ratio Tests for Model Selection and Non-Nested Hypotheses, *Econometrica* **57**, 307 – 334.

Wei, Shang-Jin and Junshik Kim, 1997, The Big Players in the Foreign Exchange Market: Do They Trade on Information or Noise?, *NBER Working Paper* No. 6256.

Welch, Greg and Gary Bishop, 2006, An Introduction to the Kalman Filter, *Typescript*, Department of Computer Science, University of North Carolina at Chapel Hill, NC.

Werner, Ingrid M., 1997, A Double Auction Model of Interdealer Trading, Stanford Business School Research Paper No. 1454.

Wolinsky, Asher, 1990, Information Revelation in a Market With Pairwise Meetings, *Econometrica* **58**, 1 – 23.

Wongswan, Jon, 2005, The Response of Global Equity Indexes to U.S. Monetary Policy Announcements, *Working Paper*, Division of

International Finance of the Board of Governors of the Federal Reserve System.

Wright, Jonathan H., 2003, Bayesian Model Averaging and Exchange Rate Forecasts, *Board of Governors of the Federal Reserve System (U.S.) International Finance Discussion Paper* No. 779, Washington.

Yao, Jian M., 1998, Market Making in the Interbank Foreign Exchange Market, Salomon Center Working Paper #S-98-4, New York University, New York, NY.

Zabel, Edward, 1981, Competitive Price Adjustment Without Market Clearing, *Econometrica* **49**, 1201 – 1221.

Studien zu Internationalen Wirtschaftsbeziehungen

Herausgegeben von Prof. Dr. Michael Frenkel

Band 1 Christiane Nickel: Insider und Outsider bei der Osterweiterung der Europäischen Währungsunion. 2002.

Band 2 Georg Stadtmann: Noise-Trader auf Devisenmärkten. Viel Lärm um Nichts? 2002.

Band 3 Wolf-Heimo Grieben: Trade and Technology as Competing Explanations for Rising Inequality. An Endogenous Growth Perspective. 2003.

Band 4 Alexander Mende: Order Flow Analyses and Foreign Exchange Dealing. 2005.

Band 5 Torsten Wezel: Determinants of Foreign Direct Investment in Emerging Markets. An Empirical Study of FDI Flows from Germany and its Banking Sector. 2005.

Band 6 Steffen Kern: The Behaviour of Interest Groups in Trade and Industry Towards Monetary Policy and Central Banks. Theory and Evidence on Germany and the Euro Area. 2006.

Band 7 Holger Michaelis: Kapitalbilanzliberalisierung in der Volksrepublik China und ihre Einbettung in den volkswirtschaftlichen Reformprozess. 2006.

Band 8 Ralf Fendel: Monetary Policy, Interest Rate Rules, and the Term Structure of Interest Rates. Theoretical Considerations and Empirical Implications. 2007.

Band 9 Katja Funke: Balance of Payments Issues in Central and Eastern European Countries' Run-Up to Euro Area Accession. 2007.

Band 10 Isabell Koske: Equilibrium Exchange Rate Models, the Euro and the 2004 Expansion of the EU. 2007.

Band 11 Dennis Stremmel: Protektionsmöglichkeiten in der WTO? Geistige Eigentumsrechte im TRIPs-Abkommen und die Forderung nach Sozial- und Umweltstandards. 2007.

Band 12 Daniela Beckmann: From Early Warning Systems to Asset Managers' Behavior: Evidence for Mature and Emerging Markets. 2008.

Band 13 Markus A. Schmidt: Information or Market Power: What is Governing Dealers' Pricing Behaviour in FX Markets? An Investigation in the Spirit of the Microstructure Approach to Exchange Rates. 2008.

www.peterlang.de

Daniela Beckmann

From Early Warning Systems to Asset Managers' Behavior: Evidence for Mature and Emerging Markets

Frankfurt am Main, Berlin, Bern, Bruxelles, New York, Oxford, Wien, 2008.
181 pp.
Studien zu internationalen Wirtschaftsbeziehungen.
Herausgegeben von Michael Frenkel. Vol. 12
ISBN 978-3-631-56955-9 · pb. € 41.10*

Asset managers have often been considered as key drivers behind financial globalization. As they have been both praised as leaders of global financial integration and blamed as originators of financial crises, any understanding of the international financial markets – and financial crises among them – should be based on a thorough understanding of its core actors, i.e. asset managers. The contribution of this work is thus twofold: In its first part, it addresses evidence from early warning systems and the role of fundamentals in financial crises. With the help of macro-level data for 20 countries and based on a new framework to assess the variety of contributions in this young field of research, different models of early warning systems are reviewed, replicated and critically tested for practical application. The work's second part turns the attention to financial markets from a behavioral perspective. Individual asset managers' views, perception and behavior are analyzed in detail with the help of a unique micro-level data set, generated in an international survey project with 1,165 participating financial market professionals from six countries. In particular, the role of professional asset managers' behavioral biases, risk taking, cultural background, and gender differences are analyzed by both selected country studies and cross-country evidence from mature and emerging markets.

Contents: Early Warning Systems and the Role of Fundamentals · Early Warning Systems: A Survey of New Approaches · Robust Lessons about Practical Early Warning Systems · Financial Markets from a Behavioral Perspective · and more